EMBASSY ROW

EMBASSY ROW *The Life & Times of Diplomatic Washington*

BY

HOPE RIDINGS MILLER

Holt, Rinehart and Winston
NEW YORK   CHICAGO   SAN FRANCISCO

To C. L. M.

Contents

EMBASSY ROW

1

World Within a City

In November 1800, when John and Abigail Adams traveled from Philadelphia to Washington to establish themselves in the new executive mansion, seven foreign countries had opened relations with the United States, but only four—Great Britain, France, the Netherlands and Spain—were represented by ministers, the top diplomats of the time. Portugal and Prussia had chargés d'affaires and Denmark had a consul who functioned until a minister was assigned. The entire foreign corps was comprised of less than twenty individuals. Twelve diplomats attended the first big social affair, the 1801 New Year's reception, in the President's House, but there were no ministers in the group. None had yet taken up residence in the fledgling Federal City.

The British minister Robert Liston, who had been envoy since 1796, when he replaced the first British emissary, George Hammond, had been in Washington a week before President and Mrs. Adams arrived. He disliked the new capital instantly and departed to visit his wife's relatives in the West Indies. Edward Thornton was left behind as chargé d'affaires. He served for the next two years, handling his nation's business in the new country through Secretary of State Thomas Pickering until Anthony Merry took over as minister in 1803.

Spain was the only nation with a minister in Washington during the first six months of the city's existence. He was

Llosa Ojeda, and he spent much of his time in Philadelphia or New York. Denmark was represented by a consul, Pedro Peterson, who worked out of New York until his country sent Peder Blicher Olson as minister during the latter part of 1801 and became the seventh country to establish a permanent mission in the United States. (Denmark is the only one of the original seven that has never broken diplomatic relations with us.)

The French minister, the Marquis François de Moustier, went home by his own request when the capital moved from Philadelphia to Washington; and France had, as its chief representative in the new capital, a chargé d'affaires, André Pichon.

In the next eight decades, the diplomatic corps gradually increased, but from Thomas Jefferson to Grover Cleveland, our government periodically had its troubles with disgruntled foreign envoys who openly loathed serving in Washington, the "hardship post" of diplomacy.

The Netherlands, with representation in this country since 1783, sent R. G. van Polanen to Philadelphia in 1796. He did not move to Washington until the latter part of 1801. He left the following year, complaining about the rigors of living in a frontier country. The Netherlands did not send another minister until 1814.

Sir Charles Bagot, the first British minister after the War of 1812, writing from Washington to a friend in England, complained:

> Talking of summer, a pint of American summer would thaw all Europe in ten minutes. Sir, it is dreadful—it is deleterious—it leads to madness. Ice houses take fire and scream because they cannot beat it. There is no enjoyment here—all I can hope to do is to prevent being unhappy, and that I shall manage by looking forward, or upward, or backward any way but Yankeeward.

Bagot's letter shows that the youthful envoy (at thirty-five the youngest ever sent by Great Britain) had forgotten the advice given him by a veteran diplomat, George Canning, whose counsel Bagot sought when he was appointed minister. Bagot had asked how he should conduct himself in the "Yankee country," which so recently had won its second war with England. Canning observed, "The problem confronting you is not so much what you can do in America, but *how much you can bear.*"

In time, the British government, to make amends for sending envoys to such an uncomfortable capital, gave them "hill allowances," as were provided for British diplomats in India, to enable them to get away from the capital for the three hottest months of the year. Other governments underwrote similar allowances, so from early June to September, most of the foreign missions were manned by lesser staff members while their superiors summered in more pleasant locales.

In addition to the problem of the weather, for the first eighty years in Washington history, the city was regarded abroad as a post unfit for first-grade diplomats on many counts. Housing was inadequate. Restaurants and public entertainment were both scarce and inferior. In general, "civilized" living according to European standards was nonexistent.

The picture began to change in the late 1880s, when Great Britain, France and Prussia, world powers at the time, recognized the growing importance of the United States by indicating that they wished to send ambassadors, direct emissaries from their chiefs of state to the president, rather than ministers, who conferred with the president through the secretary of state, if at all.

The suggestion met with mixed reactions in democratic America. In the minds of many, the exalted title "ambassador" carried unpopular connotations of Old World courts, crowns and coronets. But while Congress muddled over the idea and argued about it volubly, London, Paris and Berlin sent notice that they wished to exchange ambassadors with Washington immediately.

Galvanized into action by the implied threat that if the offer was not accepted, the United States, with only ministers abroad, would be diplomatically inferior to at least three other sovereign countries, Congress in 1893 enacted a law to make the proposal possible.

Shortly thereafter, bewhiskered Sir Julian Pauncefote presented his credentials as the first personal emissary of Queen Victoria to Grover Cleveland. Sir Julian had enjoyed enviable prestige in the United States as an envoy even before that. As British minister since 1889, he resided in one of the two legations owned by foreign governments. In 1870, England had purchased property on Connecticut Avenue at N Street and established a chancery with separate quarters for the envoy's residence.

Prussia, the next year, bought for Minister Friedrich von Alvensleben a house only a few blocks away, on 15th Street. Other countries subsequently acquired properties.

At the turn of the century, most of the diplomatic missions were ensconced within a small area, stretching roughly from Connecticut and N westward to 15th Street and northward on 16th Street. The section had come to be known as Embassy Row.

Today, the vastly larger diplomatic conglomerate still is called Embassy Row, although its establishments are located all over the city's Northwest section—except Georgetown—and its activities extend far beyond the length and breadth of the District of Columbia.

The State Department's latest *Diplomatic List* catalogs ambassadors, ministers and staffs of 116 countries (down from the 118 high just before the 1967 Middle East conflict). The Organization of American States, also headquartered in Washington, has twenty-two ambassadors. In addition, several thousand foreign secretaries, clerks, chauffeurs, maids and butlers are attached to the corps.

Largest of its kind in the world, the colorful contingent represents every sovereign nation under the sun, from A— the Kingdom of Afghanistan—to Z—the African Republic of Zambia.

Faces and inflections in this world-within-a-city change constantly, but aims and methods rarely do. Each diplomat has a job to get done, and the capital's social structure is admirably suited to his purposes. It enables him to get around, get acquainted and get attention where it counts. And if he entertains often and graciously enough, he can make important contacts in short order.

Like Napoleon's army, diplomacy moves on its stomach. The average embassy calendar includes an annual series of dinners for from twenty to sixty select persons, and mass receptions on national holidays and other anniversaries take care of countless other acquaintances, and sometimes draw scores of the uninvited. Even the big and sometimes indiscriminate functions play a role in promoting diplomatic prestige. Hundreds are entertained at one fell swoop, accounts and photographs in the newspapers are generally flattering, and the popularity of the embassy increases accordingly.

The business of entertaining numerous citizens of another country, in an effort to reach those who really matter, calls for a combination of elegance and humility not often understood throughout our country. To appreciate the reasons behind this exceptional blend of pomp and modesty is to understand the basic oddity of diplomacy, the grim background of the soirees that Harry Truman once called the "tragedy under the chandeliers."

Diplomatic entertaining is generally done with all the pomp that the donors can command, and the galas are held to a certain lofty level by cast-iron customs that only the boldest dare defy.

Elaborate parties in keeping with diplomatic tradition are synonymous with Embassy Row, even though the social calendars of several embassies have to be underwritten by governments that must pinch to pay the bill. Actually, more than half of the envoys in Washington today are from poverty-stricken nations. A few emissaries represent countries of the highest level of civilization and culture and, at the same time, governments in such desperation as to make their very survival a question.

Envoys of even the richest nations are plagued by world tensions and the ever-present fear that war may bring swift national reversals. Consequently, it is difficult to find a snob among ambassadors and their ladies in Washington today. To the contrary, diplomats, as a class, have a firm grip on reality. The envoy is bent on keeping his nation's flag flying high with every facility at his command, while his wife negotiates the social end with the soberness of a social worker rather than the manner of a nineteenth-century duchess.

Brocaded walls and marble floors fit into their scheme of things merely as part of the traditional setting for the task at hand.

Fiction writers with little knowledge of Washington sometimes portray it as a razzle-dazzle center of intrigue and duplicity, in which exotic hussies prey on pompous senators and State Department officials, while aging envoys chase cuties in their spare time and devote their working hours to the social whirl.

Diplomats who distinguish themselves make it their business to meet and get along with high-placed Americans whose regard and cooperation is essential to the welfare of their countries. Few envoys today have time for the kind of extracurricular dalliances that engaged some of their amoral forebears. Diplomacy has become an involved, tense and time-consuming business; and because the incessant entertaining on Embassy Row is so patently purposeful, the pursuit of personal pleasure has little to do with its crowded social calendar. Australia's Sir Howard Beale, just before he left Washington in 1964 at the close of a brilliant five-year tour of duty, put it this way:

> Society is an important part of the diplomatic game. Success depends on building confidence for one's country on a person-to-person basis. The logical way to begin—the only graceful way, in fact—is through social contact. We envoys can't haunt the halls of Congress, the State Department, and the White House to get acquainted with the people we need to know. We have to entertain and be entertained, in order to meet them. The real work, the hard work, comes after that. A diplomat's career is like an iceberg. The glittering part shows; the other is below the surface.

Another of Embassy Row's brightest adornments in recent years, General Carlos Romulo, who was Philippine ambassador until 1962, spoke in 446 American cities in a single year, received 30 honorary degrees while he was envoy, was the first non-American to win a Four Freedoms award and wrote several books; but he was also one of the city's most active party givers. "Society is not only helpful to the diplomat, it's also essential, and often pleasant," he said, shortly before he departed to become president of the University of the Philippines. "It's important even when it's tiresome. Besides," he added with a twinkle, "an able diplomat knows how to yawn without even opening his mouth."

The *Diplomatic List* notes 115 national independence days—Germany is the only country with no such day indicated—and most of them are celebrated at big receptions. Other special occasions also inspire lavish parties, as do state and official visits of foreign leaders.

Many embassies depend on their own chefs and domestics staff for the bounteous buffets and gourmet dinners that delight their guests and enhance their own prestige. Others employ caterers to handle their mammoth affairs. Still others take the easy, but more expensive, way out by entertaining in hotel ballrooms.

For catered parties in the envoy's residence, prices range from eight to twelve dollars a person—or higher—for a complete buffet, and from twenty to twenty-four dollars for seated dinner. This does not include drinks.

The cost, however high, is generally a profitable investment. Hospitality pays off on Embassy Row in a big way. It often leads to valuable friendships; it always offers a gracious opportunity for an envoy to spotlight attractions and customs of his homeland.

As many as seventeen varieties of tulips sprout in big bouquets all over the Netherlands Embassy for the annual duo of spring receptions to remind several hundred hand-picked guests that it's tulip time in Holland. The British Embassy garden party celebrating Queen Elizabeth's birthday is, in the words of a long-time British diplomat, "exactly the kind of party we might have back home—even to the striped marquees and the strawberries with Devonshire cream."

The finest wines of France accent gourmet menus at the French Embassy, a great neo-Tudor chateau on Kalorama Road. The mansion is also frequently used for showings from the *haute couture* of Paris. Famous Italian singers are featured in the chandeliered drawing rooms of the Italian Embassy, and Oriental dress gets the spotlight when ladies of the Japanese Embassy appear in exquisite kimonos at events during the annual Cherry Blossom Festival.

In other national capitals, "embassy" generally refers to the diplomatic office building. In Washington, the ambassador's residence is "the embassy." His offices are housed in "the chancery." Embassies with richly adorned interiors symbolize the world within the capital city.

The Italian Embassy is a Renaissance villa with multiple exotic attractions, including a Roman travertine floor, seventeenth-century wood baroque doors, multicolored Murano chandeliers, eighteenth-century Venetian mirrors, and paintings of Italian masters. The white stone Spanish Embassy is the epitome of elegance, with wrought iron doors and grilles, a tiled and pillared patio, priceless tapestries, and objects of art. The Brazilian Embassy, enhanced with marble and Caen stone accents, has a ballroom lavish with gold leaf details on walls and ceilings, and a dining room with extraordinary nineteenth-century wallpaper. The Mexican Embassy is distinguished by Cuevo del Rio's stunning murals portraying the life, history and scenic wonders of the country.

The Danish Embassy is modern, with a pristine marble entrance, teakwood floors, functional furniture, and chandeliers that appear to be masses of inverted sherry glasses. The Turkish Embassy is a palace with a sweeping center staircase and luxurious effects evincing the great cultures of both the East and the West. At least ten other foreign residences are equally magnificent.

Every embassy in the city affords a glimpse of patterns of life and cultures that are fascinating because they are different from our own and from each other. When the social season is in full swing, therefore, hundreds of capital residents are regular travelers on a foreign circuit that provides a good two-thirds of the important parties in Washington—and much of its glamour. In turn, the capital showers attention on envoys and their staffs, inundates them with invitations, caters to them assiduously. Society reporters keep constant tab on their activities and report them in detail.

The individuals on Embassy Row are as varied as the settings in which they operate. There are career diplomats, of course, but there are also lawyers, doctors (and one veterinarian), authors, and one-time bankers, merchants and tribal chiefs. There are revolutionaries, sheiks and other Arabian knights, nobility, capitalists and communists. There are emissaries of sovereign kings and queens and of figureheads who reign but do not govern; of oil-rich emirs, democratic presidents and those who pretend to be. There are four envoys who double as ambassadors to the United States and to the OAS and twenty-three who serve as ambassadors to the United States and also at the United Nations.

"But don't get the idea that the United States and United Nations jobs are similar," said former Burmese Ambassador U on Sein, while he was wearing his two important hats with aplomb. "In Washington, I am a diplomat; in New York, I am a politician."

Visiting Washington some years ago, a pretty young matron from the Middle West attended her first diplomatic reception and came away ecstatic. Within an hour, her hand had been kissed by a Spanish count, a German baron and the courtly dean of the diplomatic corps. She had admired the exquisite sari of a Pakistani begum, the butterfly-sleeved *terno* of a lady from the Philippines and the spectacular *boubou* worn by an African ambassadress. She had glimpsed a bearded Saudi Arabian sheik, a dapper Peruvian diplomat and the smiling Soviet ambassador who, as she later observed to her companion, "looked like anything but a dangerous communist." She had been enchanted with the Danish ambassador's wife; the delighted Countess Knuth-Winterfeldt had talked at length about her teen-age son, who was learning the poultry business on a Virginia farm, where he worked for eighty cents an hour and paid a dollar a day for his room.

On leaving the soiree, the visitor turned for a final survey of the exotic throng and paused for a moment to listen to the overtones of innumerable foreign voices, speaking many languages.

"Why, it's a delightful Tower of Babel—in living color!" she said, blinking her eyes. "And *what* color! Don't tell me," she burbled on, "that parties like this go on all the time in Washington!"

On Embassy Row, they certainly do.

2

The Awesome Protocol

$\mathbf{A}$T A PRIVATE WASHINGTON party for Adlai Stevenson in the spring of 1964, over pre-luncheon cocktails, the hostess quietly asked a favor of her ranking guest, French Ambassador Hervé Alphand. She said she knew that His Excellency was entitled to the luncheon place at her right, but since the party was in honor of Stevenson and he was also United States ambassador to the United Nations, she hoped Alphand would not mind sitting on her left at the table while she had Stevenson on her right.

Politely, but firmly, Alphand refused. Personally, he did not "mind" where he sat, he insisted, but as the ambassador of France, he would either occupy the place of highest honor or leave the party. The hostess hastily had the cards shifted, and when the company went in to luncheon, Alphand found his seat, properly enough, on her right, while Stevenson sat on her left.

The following month, however, when Iceland's Ambassador Thor Thors feted Stevenson at dinner and gave him the honor place—on the right of Mme. Thors, with Alphand on her left—the French ambassador raised no objection. "Who am I to take issue with the vice dean of the diplomatic corps?" he asked, lightly. "Anyway, he gave me no choice."

"In an official foreign residence in Washington, a U.S. ambassador ranks higher than in an American household, and we give him the honor place whenever possible," Thors said later. "I knew my French colleague wouldn't mind, because the honors were divided. Mme. Alphand, as the ranking lady, sat on my right."

Precedence, defined by Webster as "the act, right, privilege, or fact of preceding in time, place, order, rank or importance," is of supreme concern to the diplomat—not because of himself but for the honor it portends to the country he represents. Precedence dictates his place at the table, the sequence in which he and other ranking guests walk into a room and leave it and where he sits with other notables in any gathering.

A British diplomat was very much to the point when he said, "Since the good God made us so that we cannot all get through the same door at once, there must be precedence." Relative rank, therefore, must be reckoned with—or should be—at any event in America at which an envoy, the representative of a sovereign nation, is present. And today, unless United States officials of higher rank are at the table, a foreign ambassador rates the place of honor, to the right of the hostess. If he is not thus seated, the results can be embarrassing.

This was impressed on a Newport dowager, Mrs. Cornelius Vanderbilt, in 1903, when she gave a dinner in honor of Grand Duke Boris and had among her guests the imperial Russian ambassador, Arthur Paul Nicholas, Count Cassini. When Cassini arrived at the table and found his place card at her left—and noted that the grand duke was at her right—he refused to sit down. "In my person I represent the Emperor of all the Russias," he declared, "while the grand duke is only his nephew. I shall not remain unless I am properly seated." Flustered, Mrs. Vanderbilt ordered the place cards changed, and the grand duke meekly dropped into the chair on her left, while the ambassador took the seat on her right.

To the uninitiated, such preoccupation with priority of

position and superiority of rank may seem trivial in the extreme; but in Washington, as in other national capitals, precedence (or, broadly speaking, protocol) is observed by all those who have to do with the official and social machinery of government—as a tribute to the position, not the individual. Calvin Coolidge, who had little patience with trivialities, once said, "Washington protocol honors the office, not the man."

There is nothing forbidding or baffling about protocol. It is merely official social procedure, prescribed by rules that have evolved from years of adaptation to ever-changing conditions. From time to time, American authorities have disagreed on the code, and innumerable squabbles have resulted. Officially, the President of the United States is the final arbiter, if he chooses to be. Otherwise, decisions rest with the Department of State, our custodian of official manners.

Since most authorities are in basic agreement on what has been called a "formula of international politeness," the situation today is simpler and much less dangerous than it was centuries ago when emissaries of crowned heads (themselves rarely in accord as to which ranked the other) sometimes risked life to protect their sovereigns' pretentions abroad.

What, exactly, is *protocol*, this awesome term that irreverent Americans ridicule as "the holy protocol"? Strictly speaking, it is a name given to a variety of written documents and is derived from the Greek *protos*, meaning "first," and *kolla*, meaning "glue." Originally, "the protocol" referred to the first leaf glued to a manuscript as a guide to its contents. A recent chief of protocol, James W. Symington, had his own amusing description as it applied to his office. "In a sticky situation," he said, "the protocol chief is to make sure things don't become unglued."

Technically, *protocol* applies to the minutes (*procès verbaux*) of a congress or conference; and in the broader aspect (*protocole diplomatique* or *protocole de chancellerie*), it is the body of ceremonial rules to be observed in written or personal association between heads of state or their emissaries, with full clarification as to forms and customary courtesies for all international intercourse.

Virtually every administration since the beginning of the United States government has been confronted with problems of protocol, particularly those relating to precedence ("the handmaid of protocol"). When the late Bernard Baruch, commenting on precedence, said, "The people who matter don't mind; the people who mind don't matter," he was not realistic about either historic or contemporary officeholders. Important men expect to be accorded the places to which they are entitled.

In Great Britain, the Crown has the prerogative of conferring rank where it sees fit. The statute of Henry VIII, "for the placing of the Lords," designates the scale of general precedence, beginning with the sovereign and ranking the sovereign's immediate kindred, the principal ministers of the Crown and court and others on down to "esquires" and, finally, "gentlewomen." Since the degree of recognized distinction is not dictated by heredity in the United States, precedence depends solely on official position.

Precedence follows a mass of traditions, some based on twentieth-century common sense and others that are holdovers from the 1815 Treaty of Vienna. Their purpose, to a large extent, is the avoidance of the kind of incidents that caused confusion in the earlier days of our country and, in some cases, had international repercussions.

With calculated disregard for punctilio, President Thomas Jefferson offended Anthony Merry, the first British minister assigned to Washington, setting off a chain of annoyances that almost led to British support of a plot to disrupt the Union. According to a letter the envoy wrote to Josiah Quincy of Boston, a Federalist and an antagonist of Jefferson, Merry was accompanied by "Mr. Madison" to the executive mansion and was "in full official costume, as the etiquette of my place required on such a formal introduction of a Minister from Great Britain to the President of the United States." Instead of receiving the envoy in one of the sitting rooms of the White House, Jefferson met him in a small enclosure near his study and, as Merry's letter continued, wore "slippers down at the heels, and both pantaloons, coat and underclothes indicative of utter slovenliness and indifference to appearance, and in a state of negligence actually studied." Then, adding insult to injury, the President, to quote the emissary further, "took his seat on a sofa and diverted himself by tossing up a slipper and catching it on his toe."

If Merry was affronted at this first meeting with the President, he was livid shortly afterward—and so was his wife —when Jefferson did not escort Mrs. Merry in to dinner at the White House. Instead, the President offered his arm to Dolley Madison and seated her on his right. The discomfited Merrys were left to shift for themselves and ended up by going in with the French chargé d'affaires and his wife and selecting seats from the few that were still vacant. Jefferson's system of *pêle-mêle* (meaning, in effect, "sit wherever you can find a place") was already in force.

Augustus John Foster, then secretary of the British legation was minister to the United States during 1811–1812. In his *Memoirs*, he commented on Jefferson's attitude toward the Merrys and observed that Jefferson must have been "too much of a gentleman not to feel ashamed of what he was doing, and consequently did it awkwardly, as people must do who affect bad manners for a particular object." The object, of course, was premeditated and obvious. The President wanted to show that he had no special respect for the British and also that he subscribed to the principle of Jacobin *égalité* and had the courage to enforce it. The Merrys fumed—the minister vowed he would never again set foot in the White House, and Mrs. Merry openly criti-

cized the President as "a man with no respect for the pro-
prieties"—while Jefferson issued a statement, entitled "Etiquette," which he and his Cabinet drew up to enunciate his
principle of social equality. It read in part:

> When brought together in society, all are perfectly
> equal, whether foreign or domestic, in or out of office.
> No title being admitted here, those of foreigners give
> no precedence. Differences of grade among the diplo-
> matic members give no precedence.

Then, applying directly to members of the president's
official family, the document concluded:

> To maintain the principle of equality, or of *pêle mêle*,
> Cabinet officers in their own homes give no preced-
> ence other than that of gentlemen in the mass giving
> precedence to ladies in the mass.

As Jefferson's secretary of state, James Madison had to
follow the rulings laid down by his chief and approved by
the majority of the Cabinet; therefore, when he and Dolley
gave their next dinner for members of the small diplomatic
corps, *pêle-mêle* prevailed. The Merrys were not there to
deplore it; they had declined the invitation. Other diplomats were annoyed at the confusing procedure, however,
particularly the Spanish Minister and Señora de Yrujo, who
then joined forces with Mrs. Merry in lambasting Jefferson
and the Madisons.

The President was unperturbed. What the Spaniards
thought of his official "Etiquette" bothered him not at all,
and he was just as unconcerned about pleasing the British
at that particular time. He had an election coming up and
was well aware that a large percentage of voters still har-
bored Revolutionary sentiments. Also, he was personally
annoyed at continued British impressment of American
seamen and had shifted James Monroe from Paris to London to protest the practice.

In a letter to Monroe in January 1804, the President

made it clear that his "Etiquette" had been aimed directly at George III's minister in Washington. The letter was as follows:

> Mr. Merry is with us, and we believe him to be personally as desirable a character as could have been sent to us. But he is unluckily associated with one of an opposite at every point. She has already disturbed our harmony extremely. *He* began by claiming the first visit from our national Ministers. He corrected himself on this. But a pretension to take precedence over all others is persevered in. We have told him that the principle of society, as well as of government is with us, is the equality of the individuals composing it; that no man here would come to dinner where he would be marked with inferiority to any other; that we might as well attempt to force our principle of equality at St. James's as he with the principle of precedence here.

Monroe felt the repercussions of British displeasure in London. The American minister and his wife were mercilessly snubbed in social circles, and Jefferson's *pêle-mêle* was constantly ridiculed in their presence; but, in time, the Monroes learned that an attitude of cold dignity toward the British brought a measure of respect.

Meanwhile, in Washington, undiplomatic blasts at Jefferson were heard on Capitol Hill. The Senate retaliated by withdrawing from foreign envoys a privilege they had enjoyed since the beginning of the Republic—that of always being seated on the right of the vice president. By a voice vote the Senate approved Jefferson's "Etiquette" in full.

The Merrys did not capitulate. Mrs. Merry proceeded to point out another propriety to the President through his daughter Martha (Mrs. Thomas Mann Randolph), who was spending the winter in Washington. Mrs. Merry wrote to inquire whether Mrs. Randolph was staying at the White House as the wife of a Virginia gentleman or as the President's daughter. If the latter, Mrs. Merry wrote, she, the wife of the British minister, would call first; if the former, she would wait Mrs. Randolph's first call. Probably with the advice of her father, Mrs. Randolph replied that she was visiting the White House as the wife of a Virginia gentleman and as such expected to receive the first call from the British minister's wife because the President had asked residents of the capital to call upon visitors first.

Mrs. Merry told anyone who would listen that she would never make the initial call on Mrs. Randolph, and she kept her word. But by that time, the animosity between Jefferson and the Merrys had developed into a threat to the United States. The British minister had teamed with Senator Timothy Pickering of Massachusetts and Roger Griswold of Connecticut, powerful Federalist enemies of Jefferson, in trying to set up a separate New England republic. Later, Merry was receptive to overtures from Aaron Burr, who sought support from Britain to bring about a cleavage between the western states and the Union. The Burr-Merry cabal might have developed into a precarious situation had fate not intervened. The British Prime Minister, whom Merry had persuaded to finance Burr, died in May 1806, and the next prime minister, intent on establishing more friendly relations with Jefferson, recalled Merry and sent David Montague Erskine to the United States.

Erskine's wife was the former Frances Cadwalader, daughter of General John Cadwalader of Philadelphia. They were charming young people, with two small children, Frances and Thomas Americus; and they arrived in Washington determined to correct some of the unfavorable impressions left by the Merrys. From the beginning the Erskines were socially successful, with assistance from Jefferson, who was ready to bend a bit on his own. In an early letter to her brother Thomas in Philadelphia, Mrs. Erskine wrote of being the President's guest and added,

"Dinner at the great House went off quite to our satisfaction." One of the reasons, perhaps, was that although *pêle-mêle* was observed in the dining room, Jefferson made a concession to international politesse: he took Mrs. Erskine in to dinner.

As Jefferson's secretary of state, Madison faithfully abided by the President's principles of precedence (or, rather, "no precedence"), but as president himself, Madison tried to observe the expected amenities. He employed as a consultant on such matters Jean Pierre Sioussant and named him Master of Ceremonies. A precursor of our present chief of protocol, Sioussant advised on proper seating arrangements and took great care to see that the President escorted the wife of the ranking guest in to dinner. Sioussant, a young French refugee, was well versed in procedures of European courts and had been employed first in Washington by protocol-conscious Minister Merry. Sioussant left the British legation to work for Jefferson and, with the innocuous title of Doorkeeper of the Executive Mansion, became one of the President's confidants. Jefferson, of course, had no interest in tapping the Frenchman's knowledge of etiquette; but James and Dolley Madison made the most of it.

However, the Madisons' geniality toward the diplomatic corps caused trouble for their immediate successors. Any envoy was welcomed at any time he chose to confer with James Madison. Dolley was at home to all visitors, made innumerable first calls and returned every call.

James Monroe, as president, with the assistance of Secretary of State John Quincy Adams, put a stop to those time-consuming practices. With the conviction that he could command greater respect from European diplomats if he let them know he expected them to operate, in his own words, "upon much the same footing as the American Ministers were placed in European courts, upon a footing of form and ceremony," Monroe instructed Adams to produce and circulate a set of rules to ensure that procedure. Adams' diary refers to Monroe's edict as follows:

> The former Presidents, particularly Jefferson and Madison have admitted to a certain extent social visits from foreign ministers. Mr. Monroe upon principle, has precluded that sort of intercourse and receives them only: 1, at a private audience requested by them; 2, at the drawing room; 3, at diplomatic dinners, once or twice a year.

The formula had authentic basis in international rules that had been codified shortly before. In 1814–1815, after the Napoleonic Wars, the Congress of Vienna drew up "The Protocol," a body of principles to govern the deportment of diplomats and a group of ceremonial rules to govern their social conduct. "The Protocol" eliminated many touchy problems, including the one long posed by ostentatious monarchs who had insisted that their envoys should rank first regardless of length of service. Adopted once and for all was the precept of "first come, first served"—meaning that ambassadors who had served longest in the host country had seniority and, therefore, were to be accorded first place, with others rated accordingly. The same principle was to be followed for ministers. At that time, there were only ministers in Washington. Seventy-five years were to pass before foreign ambassadors were to be received by the United States president.

Monroe's "new order," which eliminated informal White House visits by diplomats, also applied to wives. Elizabeth Monroe had neither the inclination nor the strength to carry on Dolley Madison's incessant routine of receiving and making calls. Envoys were informed that their wives would be welcomed at the executive mansion only by previous arrangement or by invitation and that Mrs. Monroe would make no calls. Mrs. Adams would return visits but make no initial ones.

Great Britain's minister, Sir Charles Bagot, and France's minister, Baron Hyde de Neuville, promptly asked permission for their wives to call on Mrs. Monroe, and Lady Bagot and Baroness Hyde de Neuville were invited to the next Wednesday evening drawing room at the mansion. That matter successfully settled, the British and French envoys moved for revision of a custom that had bothered diplomats for some time. At the annual New Year's reception at the White House, they had been herded in with the throng. Bagot and Hyde de Neuville requested that the corps be received in a group, ahead of the other guests. Monroe, after consulting his Cabinet, agreed to welcome the diplomats at 11:30 in the morning and the remainder of the company at noon.

Nonetheless, the Monroes' social difficulties with the foreign emissaries continued. The President's daughter Eliza (Mrs. George Hay) lived at the White House for a time and carried on her own feud with the envoys' wives. As her mother's assistant hostess, she held that they should call on her first. They refused, and in turn they were not invited to the drawing rooms. Hyde de Neuville attempted to heal the rift between the White House and the foreign corps. He implored Secretary Adams to persuade President and Mrs. Monroe to attend his gala ball to celebrate the evacuation of France by the allied troops of Great Britain, Austria, Prussia and Russia. Following the practice of George Washington and John Adams in not accepting invitations to the houses of foreign envoys, Monroe declined. So did Mrs. Monroe; but the President informed Hyde de Neuville, through Adams, that the White House would be represented by Mrs. Hay—on condition, among several, that her name not be mentioned in any newspaper accounts of the ball. According to Adams' diary, the French minister "was apparently much mortified but suppressed his feelings within the bounds of decency."

Mrs. Hay's unpublicized presence at the ball did not help matters. The envoys' wives still declined to call on her; and she retaliated by seeing that no diplomat was invited to the White House wedding of her sister Maria to Samuel Lawrence Gouverneur in 1820. Mrs. Hay further offended the corps when the ministers inquired as to whether they were expected to send presents and she replied, again according to Adams' informative diary, "that her young sister could not receive and return visits which she herself could not reciprocate and therefore that the foreign Ministers should take no notice of the marriage; which was accordingly communicated to them."

Indignant though they were, the diplomats were also impressed. European envoys, accustomed to regarding leaders of the new nation as an assemblage of impressionable novices who could be shaken by arrogance, suddenly found themselves defeated at their own game. The unrelenting social attitude of the Monroes plus the affirmation of the Monroe Doctrine in 1823 gave rise to a new respect for the United States. Never again would foreign emissaries or their wives dare to feud openly with the White House, although there would be sporadic instances in which diplomats would vie with several official echelons as to precedence.

For many years, foreign ministers ranked immediately after the president. In 1831, Andrew Jackson upset that order because he was indignant that diplomatic wives would not mingle socially with the wife of the Secretary of War, Mrs. John Eaton (Peggy O'Neale). The President demanded the recall of Dutch Minister Bamgeman Huygens, whose wife refused to visit Mrs. Eaton. Then "Old Hickory" decreed that his Cabinet ministers were to have precedence over the envoys.

America was emerging from adolescence, and the nation's

growing pains for some time had been reflected in the pa-
triotic sensitivities of American officeholders, who were becoming as concerned as the diplomats with preserving the
prerogatives of position. From Jackson's administration to
the 1960s the ranking of the United States elective and
appointive hierarchy vis-à-vis the foreign envoys was a matter of frequent, and heated, debate.

As late as 1941, one of the most reliable unofficial guides
to capital etiquette ever written—*Social Washington* by
Anne Squires—discussed at length the long-standing dispute as to whether an ambassador should precede the chief
justice and a minister an associate justice, and observed:

> The Chief Justice precedes everyone at dinner except
> the Vice President. It is not correct, however, to ask
> him with Ambassadors, because there is an irreconcil-
> able difference of opinion as to which should take
> precedence over the other. Associate Justices are
> placed below Ambassadors, but the unsolved problem
> of the Ambassadors and the Chief Justice holds good
> as between Associate Justices and Foreign Ministers.
> . . . Until there is a ruling, it amounts to a faux pas to
> ask the Chief Justice to social functions with an
> Ambassador or the Associate Justices with Ministers.

Andrew Jackson's edict, years before, that the Cabinet
should rank foreign envoys gave rise to controversy as to
the relative power of the Supreme Court and the Senate,
with each body staunchly insisting that it should also be
recognized above the foreign envoys. In his short career as
president, James A. Garfield, with full approval of Vice
President Chester A. Arthur and Secretary of State James
G. Blaine, favored the priority of all United States appointive or elective officials (down to the House of Representatives) over the envoys. Arthur, as president, directed
Blaine to draw up a precedence list, with the vice president, the Supreme Court, the Senate and the Cabinet, in
that order, ahead of the emissaries. Rumblings continued.

Diplomats insisted that their rating be elevated, and, periodically, it was; but a development in 1893 gave them a decided edge on United States officialdom and for a time raised them to rank immediately after that of the president.

The escalation occurred just after the United States, for the first time, received ambassadors (instead of ministers) from the three "great powers"—Great Britain, France and Germany—and Washington, in the international sense, at last became a "capital of the first class."

Fleet-footed Sir Julian Pauncefote as personal representative of the British Crown, managed to present his credentials a day before his French and German rivals and became the first ambassador to the United States and the first dean of the diplomatic corps in Washington. He was making the most of his exalted position when he let it be known that as Queen Victoria's emissary he expected first calls from all United States officials, except the President himself, the implication being that as an ambassador he ranked above the vice president. The impression soon became generally accepted, and Cleveland did not bother to correct it. He was not overly fond of Vice President Adlai Stevenson, anyway, and Stevenson did nothing to protect his own position. Instead, he appeared to approve the priority of the ambassadors by making first calls on all of them. They enjoyed this envied position, second only to the chief executive, until the McKinley administration, when both Vice President Garret A. Hobart and Chief Justice Melville W. Fuller challenged the order of precedence.

As an opener, Hobart insisted that his office entitled him to rank above Pauncefote, since the position of the vice president in the United States was analogous to that of the Prince of Wales in England. Refusing to yield, Ambassador and Lady Pauncefote waited for several weeks for Vice President and Mrs. Hobart to make the first call; then Pauncefote appealed to Secretary of State John Sherman for guidance. Sherman suggested that he consult British Prime Minister Robert Salisbury. Finally, from London, Salisbury advised that the vice president as heir apparent to the highest office in the United States did, indeed, occupy a position comparable to that of the Prince of Wales and ordered Pauncefote to call on Hobart.

The rank of the vice president has never since been challenged, but other precedence issues arose before the McKinley administration ended. At a White House dinner, the British ambassador was given the seat of highest honor when Chief Justice Melville W. Fuller was present. Immediately after dinner, before the coffee was served, Fuller departed in high dudgeon, announcing on the way out that he would never accept another dinner invitation unless assured in advance of his proper place at the table. A month later, all the justices declined invitations to the annual White House dinner for diplomats and the Supreme Court after learning that the envoys and their wives would be received first. The justices, further affronted when they were seated behind the diplomatic corps at a memorial service in the Capitol, informed the State Department that, under the existing system, they would attend no more official gatherings to which envoys were invited.

More concerned with pacifying the Supreme Court than in bolstering the prestige of the emissaries, the State Department at the request of the White House ruled that at future events in the Capitol, diplomats were to be seated in a front row on one side of the chamber, with the justices in a front row on the other side. At the same time, plans for separate White House dinners for the diplomats and the justices were inaugurated.

McKinley's protocol problems were minor, however, compared with those that beset Theodore Roosevelt. United States dignitaries pressed for rank as never before. Speaker of the House Joseph (Uncle Joe) Cannon insisted that, as head of the most powerful body in the nation, he deserved precedence above the justices. The Senate and the Cabinet debated about their relative prerogatives. The Supreme Court claimed priority over the foreign emissaries, and tempers flared when the justices, on arriving at a White House reception, learned that the diplomatic corps had already assembled. Chief Justice Fuller and Associate Justice John Harlan complained so bitterly to the President that he had the envoys shepherded into a separate salon while he received the justices first.

Roosevelt tried his best to settle protocol disputes as they arose, not only to ease his own headaches but to guide future administrations. He was in difficulty, however, from the moment he had an electric carriage call installed to summon coachmen, in the proper precedence order, following White House parties—thus creating problems at both ends of each official function.

Finally, Roosevelt drafted Colonel Theodore A. Bingham, commissioner of public buildings and grounds, to keep a detailed diary of White House functions, so that all the controversies could be recorded and, if possible, solved. Bingham soon came to regard himself as the authority on protocol and added to the confusion by taking issue with the State Department on who preceded whom. On at least one account, Bingham had the backing of the dean of the diplomatic corps, the German Ambassador Theodor von Hölleben. They insisted that at a White House reception the recently arrived chargé d'affaires of France had incorrectly been received ahead of the chargé d'affaires of Switzerland, who had been in Washington longer. The State Department reasoned that France had an embassy, Switzerland only a legation. Secretary of State John Hay approved. "While I bow to this decision," Bingham observed in his record, "I still do not regard it as correct."

During the Hoover administration, the diplomatic corps was indirectly involved in the Gann-Longworth Precedence Battle of the Century and was also the medium through which it was almost settled. When Vice President Charles Curtis, a bachelor, wrote to Secretary of State Henry L. Stimson requesting that Dolly (Mrs. Edward Everett) Gann, Curtis' sister, be accorded rank above the wives of the foreign envoys, he got no action. He appealed to his good friend Sir Esmé Howard, the British ambassador and dean of the diplomatic corps—and was gratified with the result. Sir Esmé immediately announced that Mrs. Gann would properly be "second hostess" at all diplomatic affairs. Then, out of the protocol blue, came a challenge from House Speaker Nicholas Longworth's wife, Alice, who insisted that if the Vice President had a wife she would certainly be "second hostess" at any event but that there was no such thing as a substitute wife—and besides, Dolly had a perfectly good husband of her own. Mrs. Longworth further pointed out that in any case if rank followed power, the wife of the speaker should be second only to the first lady. On that basis, the Longworths defied the diplomatic dean's edict by declining invitations to all parties at which Mrs. Gann was to be the ranking lady.

The diplomats, meanwhile, had gone along with Sir Esmé. Chile's Ambassador Carlos Davila set the example by being the first to escort Mrs. Gann in to dinner and place her at his right, when he gave a banquet for his visiting minister of finance at the Pan American Union. Mrs. Longworth was not present.

One clever envoy, however, made headlines by managing to get Mrs. Gann and Mrs. Longworth to the same affair. He was Sesostris Sidarous Pasha, the Egyptian minister, a man of ample proportions, a personal fortune, and a legation as elaborate as an Oriental palace. He invited forty-eight guests to a formal dinner in January 1931 and declined to divulge any part of his guest list in advance. The fact that he always served the finest imported liquors, while the United States was still plagued by prohibition, may have been at least partially responsible for the fact that no one declined his crescent-embossed invitations. Anyway, the party took on tense interest when both Mrs. Gann and Mrs. Longworth appeared. The company speculated over cocktails on what would happen later. Which lady would the host escort in to dinner? If he chose Dolly, would Alice leave in a huff? Or would the bachelor envoy have Dolly as his hostess, at the opposite end of the table, so Alice could sit on his right?

The more observant guests, however, noticed that there was no seating chart, so they were not too surprised when the doors to the dining room were opened and the host announced, "Kindly sit where you please!" Instead of the conventional arrangement at one long festive board, tables for four had been set up, so seating could be no problem. The Egyptian minister carefully avoided sitting with either Mrs. Gann or Mrs. Longworth.

The feud, avidly fanned by the press, entertained Washington until Franklin Delano Roosevelt's New Deal offered even more controversial topics. But precedence vagaries continued to plague capital hostesses, with the relative rank of ambassadors and the chief justice in dispute for years; and as late as 1947, memory of the Gann-Longworth squabble prompted at least one high official not to insist on the rating to which he was raised by law.

The trend was in strong evidence during the latter part of the FDR administration when the chief justice was officially recognized as ranking just above ambassadors. Under President Truman, the speaker, who had been fifth in precedence, was upgraded by a law that ranked him over the chief justice and placed him two notches above the ambassadors. The Presidential Succession Act of 1947 designated the speaker as heir to the White House in the event of "the removal, resignation, death, or inability of both the President and Vice President" and gave him the third place in line. But for some vague reason, the official list was not revised for several years. Truman did not force the new order, and Speaker Joseph W. Martin himself made no effort to establish it. In his book, *My Fifty Years in Politics*, Martin explained his reticence by recalling the Gann-Longworth squabble and observed, "This conflict over which of the two women had precedence kept Washington in turmoil for years. . . . I did not wish to risk making it appear that every time a Republican obtained one of the high offices in Washington, an unholy war over social precedence followed."

The chief justice, therefore, continued in recognized rank as immediately following the vice-president until John F. Kennedy was elected president. Then, while seated on the inaugural platform with Vice President-elect Lyndon Johnson and House Speaker Sam Rayburn, JFK whispered to the latter, "I'm going to see that you're put where you belong in protocol—second only to the vice president."

In due course, the promise went into effect. The new order, established in 1961, designated the speaker as just after the vice president and ahead of the chief justice and placed ambassadors on the sixth rung, just below former presidents of the United States. The following year, another revision was in the making, which would move envoys even further down the line.

The change had been indicated for some time. President Dwight D. Eisenhower was displeased because emissaries of even the least strategic countries preceded his secretary of state, John Foster Dulles. After the first White House diplomatic dinner at which Dulles was ranked by every envoy present, Eisenhower said, "Foster, I don't like this arrangement at all. Next time we have a diplomatic dinner, we'll either fix it so you can sit close to me, or else don't come to the party at all. I don't want you at the foot of the table." A stickler for protocol, Dulles averted the possibility of either annoying his chief or upsetting the envoys when the next diplomatic dinner was scheduled. Pleading "United Nations business," he declined the invitation and took off to New York a few hours before the party.

Eisenhower had been restive about the rank of his secretary of state; JFK was active in upgrading his. Determined to dispose of the custom that had given foreign envoys precedence over the official in charge of America's foreign policies, Kennedy instructed Chief of Protocol Angier Biddle Duke to revamp the protocol list so Secretary of State Dean Rusk could precede the ambassadors.

Changes in protocol are not made lightly or quickly. This revision took time and, before the new order was announced, the protocol chief laid the groundwork diplomatically. He informed Nicaraguan Ambassador Guillermo Sevilla-Sacasa, dean of the diplomatic corps, who was privileged to precede his colleagues, that all chiefs of mission soon were to rank after the secretary of state in keeping with the custom of many countries that give precedence to their secretaries of foreign affairs over foreign ambassadors. On behalf of the corps, Sevilla-Sacasa approved the change, termed it "logical, indeed." By the time it went into effect, another office—that of the secretary general of the United Nations—had been added above the ambassadors, moving them down to eighth in order of precedence but still well above all members of the Cabinet (except the secretary of state), the Senate and the House of Representatives. The ranking of ministers was no longer a matter of dispute. They had been accorded priority to which they were entitled; but within a comparatively short time, that was to have little bearing on the social picture in Washington. Most legations had been raised to embassies by 1967, with the "ghost governments" of Latvia, Lithuania and Estonia having the only remaining legations noted in the *Diplomatic List* and with Estonia's mission headquartered in New York City.

The government's precedence order is not public property, but lists carefully indicated as "unofficial" are available, and most of them are accurate enough to serve as reliable guides to Washington hostesses.

Arbiter of ceremonial customs approved by the government, the Office of Protocol today is also the working United States liaison between the foreign corps and the White House in handling all questions—and problems—that have to do with protecting the safety and prerogatives of diplomats assigned to Washington, as well as with the reception of official visitors to our country and the ceremonial conduct of United States officialdom toward them. The proliferation of independent nations in the past twenty years, and the consequent increase in the size of the corps plus the steadily increasing number of distinguished guests from abroad, has brought the chief of protocol very much into focus as one of the most important functionaries in America.

An embarrassing incident at a state affair led to the establishment of the Division of Protocol. Calvin Coolidge was president, and the event was the annual diplomatic dinner at the White House. Since the foreign corps then included less than forty missions, the seating, strictly according to seniority, ostensibly posed no problem; it was worked out at the executive mansion without advice from the State Department.

Otto Wiedfeldt, who had once been director of the Krupp munitions works, was Germany's first ambassador to the United States after World War I. When he first arrived in Washington shortly after the Treaty of Versailles, he was coolly received, and he spent years unsuccessfully trying to make friends. However, his humiliation was complete in 1927 when he went in to a Coolidge dinner at the White House and started to take his seat beside an envoy's wife—who promptly insulted him. She was the American-born Baroness de Cartier de Marchienne, wife of the Belgian ambassador, and she loudly refused to sit next to "a Hun whose guns violated the sacred soil of Belgium!" White House aides rescued Wiedfeldt and took him to a seat as far away as possible, while place cards were shifted. The dinner proceeded in an atmosphere of tenseness, and unpleasant repercussions evolved into gossip as to who had been responsible for the unfortunate seating arrangements. A newspaper editorial suggested that the White House henceforth might well follow Woodrow Wilson's prewar pattern by giving two annual diplomatic dinners until animosities subsided.

The incident recalled a similar disturbance precipitated by a baroness during the McKinley administration. Baroness Hengelmüller von Hengervár, wife of the Austrian minister, refused to walk in to a White House dinner with the Mexican minister, Manuel Aspiroz, because as an army officer he had officiated at the execution of Maximilian some thirty years before! Summoning a White House aide, Aspiroz quietly arranged to escort a senator's wife and to find a place at the foot of the table, while the senator took in the ruffled Austrian and sat beside her. The transfer was arranged so gracefully that President and Mrs. McKinley knew nothing about it at the time.

President Coolidge, on the other hand, was painfully aware of the contretemps during his dinner. Determined not to risk criticism for future seating arrangements, Coolidge shifted responsibility to the State Department by naming James Clement Dunn, a Foreign Service officer, as director of ceremonies at the White House and indicating that he was to have all the time and help he needed to handle the job. By 1928, Dunn had a new title: chief of international conferences and protocol. The importance of the position was to grow steadily in the next forty years, with several significant changes in scope and responsibility along the way.

For example, George T. Summerlin, as protocol chief from 1937 to 1946, had to make many decisions about official conduct as foreign notables visited in droves and in some instances took up wartime residence in our country.

Summerlin, known as "Summy" to his many friends, also had to issue edicts on innumerable trivialities; but on one, at least, he balked at advising private citizens. Before the 1939 visit of Great Britain's King George and Queen Elizabeth, distaff Washington bothered about whether to curtsy to Their Majesties, and the question was repeatedly put to Summerlin. "Do as you wish," was his invariable reply, with the addendum, "but, of course, a curtsy is always a courtesy." However, he did advise Mrs. Roosevelt not to curtsy, on the basis of the long-accepted custom that heads of sovereign nations and their wives do not bend the knee to each other; and she followed his instruction.

John Farr Simmons, who was protocol chief from 1950 until after he reached the age of retirement seven years later, saw the diplomatic corps expand from sixty embassies and ten legations to seventy-five embassies and seven legations. He attended between 400 and 500 diplomatic parties a year and traveled some 65,000 miles. Tall, ruddy-cheeked and unfailingly unruffled, Simmons took pains with significant gestures of hospitality as well as the smaller amenities, such as arranging for the nonwine-drinking French Premier, Pierre Mendès-France, to be served a glass of milk at the state dinner Secretary Dulles gave in his honor and ruling out small fezes as part of the decorations planned for a reception honoring President Clelal Bayar of Turkey, after the fez had been abolished in his homeland.

By the time Wiley T. Buchanan, Jr., assumed the office in 1957, the Division of Protocol comprised five sections—visits, ceremonial, courtesies and privileges, accreditation and administrative—and was geared to handle matters ranging from the issuance of DPL license plates to the planning and management of official visits, not only in Washington but throughout the United States. At our government's invitation, guests arrived so frequently that Buchanan often bade good-by to one in New York, while Deputy Chief of Protocol Clement E. Conger welcomed another at National Airport. Buchanan and his staff coped with two especially difficult guests in a single year—1959—when Fidel Castro visited the United States in April and Nikita Khrushchev, in September.

When Angier Biddle Duke was named chief of protocol in 1961, the Division of Protocol became the Office of Protocol, and he assumed the post with the expressed purpose of giving even more depth and substance to protocol duties. President Kennedy made it clear that Duke was to have the personal rank of ambassador and that he was to have leeway in expanding that position. Shortly after the appointment, Secretary Rusk directed him to propose rules to simplify protocol. Standardization of diplomatic procedure was very much indicated. Duke's achievement in that regard and in streamlining official visits were significant on his first tour of duty (1961–1965). But even more noteworthy was the dedication with which he tackled a more difficult task than any that had confronted his predecessors: the problem of dealing with racial rebuffs when newly independent African countries began sending diplomats in sizable numbers to the United States. As vexations in obtaining suitable housing and discourteous treatment for these emissaries mounted and threatened to have damaging effects on our foreign policy, the State Department was brought into the field of civil rights and a deputy chief of protocol for special services was appointed to assist Duke in looking into discriminatory practices and stopping them where possible.

In addition to that onerous task, Duke and his staff looked after the welfare of other personnel in the growing corps of well over a hundred missions, handled from fifteen to twenty state or official visits a year—and many other of prime importance—and took care of innumerable routine duties, including the operation of the president's guest house (Blair House). Mrs. Duke, the former Robin Chandler, with the assistance of Cabinet wives and other friends, redecorated Blair House (called "Robin's nest" by Labor

Secretary Willard Wirtz) and made it a beautiful home-away-from-home for visiting dignitaries.

Appointed ambassador to Spain in January 1965, Duke was succeeded by Lloyd N. Hand, who was followed in March 1966 by James W. Symington. Duke resumed the protocol post in April 1968 and held it until he was sent as ambassador to Denmark. His replacement was Tyler Abell, husband of the White House social secretary and son of George Abell, who had been Assistant Chief of Protocol for some time. In October 1968, Tyler Abell took over as Uncle Sam's number one public relations expert, the official in charge of directing protocol as a kind of extension of corporate courtesy.

3

Charmed Circles

IN THE EARLY 1800s, AFTER
a long and uncomfortable coach-and-four ride over the un-
paved streets from Georgetown to Washington, a distinguished Portuguese diplomat revised Pierre L'Enfant's description of Washington, "the city of magnificent vistas,"
calling it instead, "the city of magnificent distances." José
Francisco Correa da Serra, known in Washington as Father
Serra, had been trained as a priest but was at odds with the
Holy Office when he took refuge in the United States and
chose Washington as his home in exile. A naturalist and an
author, he was soon a crony of Jefferson and a frequent
guest at the executive mansion. He heartily endorsed Jefferson's *pêle-mêle* system and further endeared himself to the
President by pronouncing his dinners, where guests sat
without regard to rank at a round table, as "charmed circles."

In 1816, when Madison was president, Correa da Serra,
having composed his difficulties with the Catholic hierarchy, was appointed Portuguese minister to the United
States, and he continued to be a regular recipient of presidential hospitality until 1820, when he was recalled to head
his country's financial council. At the last party he attended
in the President's house, an elegant drawing room affair held
by James and Elizabeth Monroe, he mentioned "the charmed
circles of Washington" as "all the social gatherings I have
been privileged to attend in this house." He added, "As an

unofficial guest, I found them enjoyable; as a diplomat, I found them invaluable."

More than a century later another Portuguese minister, Dr. João Antonio de Bianchi, a dapper and delightful man with a fine flair for repartee, was popular in official Washington circles and also with the press. In fact, reporters hovered around him at parties to such an extent that he sometimes had difficulty in conversing with anyone else. At a White House diplomatic reception in 1937, while he was chatting with a Cabinet member, he was so constantly interrupted by a persistent society columnist that he finally observed, with a wan smile, "One of my earliest predecessors had another definition of Washington, but I call it *the Capital of unfinished conversations!*" Asked whether he agreed with his predecessor's opinion of White House parties as "charmed circles," he replied, "But, of course. And it is important for us to penetrate them as often as possible. You see, we diplomats are very much like you Americans. We cherish every opportunity to meet your management."

His allusion brought into focus the company-town aspect of official Washington society, largely comprised of employees pressing either personal or national claims for profit, dividends and dues. Employees of other governments are eager to cultivate working friendships with employees who run USA, Inc., and a White House reception, with the president as host and the vice president, Cabinet members and other leaders among the guests, gives them a welcome opportunity "to meet the management" on a social basis.

From then on, the envoy can proceed to nurture the contacts that are important to him. Every high official he sees at the White House is a potential embassy guest—every one, that is, except the president, and the prospect of entertaining even the chief executive has been realized by several ambassadors during official visits of their chiefs in recent years.

With few exceptions, the annual White House reception

for the foreign corps prior to World War II was a kind of international pageant, magnificently costumed and produced on traditional lines. Diplomats in full ceremonial uniforms, loaded with gold braid and resplendent decorations, and their ladies in elaborate evening dress, were received by the President and the First Lady in the Blue Room. Then they were ushered into the Red Room and the State Dining Room, where the vice president, members of the Cabinet and other notables, including a selective number from residential society, waited in white ties and elegant gowns to meet the honor guests. The event carried by far the greatest éclat in the capital and was America's nearest approximation to court society, with sovereign trappings. Once having greeted their guests, the President and First Lady generally retired to their private quarters, while the diplomats lingered in the State Dining Room to sip nonalcoholic punch as they chatted among themselves for perhaps an hour. The affair was all as formalized, as elegantly routine, as might have been expected at similar gatherings in any European capital at the time. Lengthy newspaper accounts carried detailed descriptions of the pageantry and the dazzling attire.

Diplomatic uniforms ceased to be worn to these affairs after World War II, and the steady growth of the foreign corps prompted the White House to restrict invitations to mission chiefs and their wives and a highly select group of United States officials and social notables.

A pronounced shift in White House entertainment was indicated when President and Mrs. Kennedy sent out invitations to their first diplomatic reception honoring ninety-seven chiefs of mission and ten ambassadors to the Organization of American States. The hours were different. Previous receptions had been in the evening. This one began in the late afternoon—the hours were five to seven—and many guests were puzzled about what to wear. Some of the envoys appeared in striped trousers with morning (or "club") coats, as did the President. Mrs. Kennedy wore an afternoon frock, and so did most of the other women; but three wore semitailored dresses and hats. African and Asian ambassadors and their wives in colorful national costumes wore the only obvious reminders that this was a cosmopolitan assemblage.

With Vice President and Mrs. Johnson and Secretary and Mrs. Rusk, the host and hostess shook hands with envoys to the United States and the Organization of American States and then dispersed the receiving line to mingle with the company for almost two hours. Buffets with a wide variety of cocktail-time dainties were set up in the East Room and the State Dining Room, and the general atmosphere of the party was as light and as bubbly as the French champagne. Diplomats who had braved a blizzard to attend the event left in a warm glow of admiration for the youthful new President and First Lady, who had successfully projected the impression that every guest was a White House intimate.

The foreign corps had increased by ten missions when the Kennedys gave their second diplomatic reception in 1962. The hours were from six to eight; the President wore a dark business suit and the hostess, a sleeveless afternoon dress. Many of the 277 guests for the first time saw some of the White House rooms that had been redecorated under Jacqueline Kennedy's aegis.

The atmosphere was slightly more formal at the Kennedys' last diplomatic soiree, in April 1963. There was a bit of traditional pageantry at the beginning, as a ruffle of drums announced the appearance of the President and Mrs. Kennedy, who were preceded down the stairway by a color guard. Following were the military aides in full uniform, the dean of the diplomatic corps and Señora de Sevilla-Sacasa, Secretary and Mrs. Rusk and Chief of Protocol Angier Biddle Duke.

Chiefs of mission and their wives, from 110 countries, went down the line. Then President and Mrs. Kennedy went to the Red Room to welcome the envoys to the OAS and their wives. There, as in the East Room, a photographer snapped pictures of each envoy as the President shook hands with him. (Later Jacqueline Kennedy went over all the prints, selected the best of each ambassador, and sent it to him with a card reading, "With Mrs. Kennedy's compliments.")

During the Johnson administration each of the five diplomatic receptions differed in some respect from the others and from all those in previous administrations. Traditional ceremony was restricted to the initial appearance of the President and the First Lady, descending with their select company to the main floor and then receiving in the Blue Room. A reporter describing the 1965 reception in *The London Observer* called it "a routine party" and observed that "the mode was unchanged." Actually, "the mode" noticeably varied from the party given by the Johnsons in 1964, when the host and Western diplomats wore business suits and their wives, afternoon dresses, while most of the Asians and Africans were costumed as they would have been for official affairs in their homelands. For the 1965 event and for all other such parties in the Johnson administration, the hours were the same—six-thirty to nine for the diplomatic corps and seven to nine for other guests—but the stipulated dress, "black tie," brought out a wide variety of attire: dinner coats and national garb, floor-length evening frocks, Oriental brocades, rich caftans and exquisite saris.

The type of food and drink at White House diplomatic receptions through the years has undergone as much change as the atmosphere and attire. At the first big party in the executive mansion, John and Abigail Adams offered their guests coffee, tea, wine, syllabub and tarts. Most of their nineteenth-century successors also served light refreshments. Punch spiked with wine was generally available until 1877, when Mrs. Rutherford B. Hayes ("Lemonade Lucy") banned liquor at the White House. Guests at the first diplomatic reception in the Hayes administration were sharply critical of the omission, and one described the event as "Altogether brilliant—water flowed like champagne." Drink of any kind was scarce at Calvin Coolidge's gatherings for the foreign corps. Mrs. William Vanderbilt, on the verge of fainting at one affair, asked Henry Hopkinson of the Canadian legation to fetch her a glass of water. After a quarter of an hour, he returned with a paper cup filled from a cooler in the ushers' office. There must have been a number of complaints, for at the next Coolidge reception, a small water cooler was working in the State Dining Room.

A few presidents served notable reception repasts. William Howard Taft treated diplomats to lobster and champagne suppers and enjoyed them with the company. Woodrow Wilson provided an ample buffet with wine. But Herbert and Lou Henry Hoover, who drew on their private fortune to supplement their entertainment allowance and gave memorable diplomatic dinners, offered reception guests only nonalcoholic punch, cookies, bonbons and nuts. Similar refreshments were provided at receptions given by the Franklin Roosevelts, the Trumans and the Eisenhowers.

The Johnsons surpassed all their predecessors in the sumptuous buffets laid out for chiefs of mission and those invited to meet them. Since the numerous state functions for visiting dignitaries had eliminated the traditional White House dinner for the mission chiefs, Johnson-style hospitality took care of the omission by climaxing the annual reception with a full-scale buffet dinner.

The potential usefulness of the event was as noteworthy as the food. New envoys discovered that, at the crowded buffet, they could get acquainted with more VIPs in a single evening than they might otherwise meet in a month. Diplomats accustomed to the unstilted operation of Johnson parties felt free to move about as they pleased and to enjoy themselves in relaxed surroundings, bolstered by two bars, delicious food, and warm hospitality.

Each Johnson reception for the mission chiefs had a surprise element. In 1965, the President disappointed at least
fifty ambassadorial wives and others, with whom he had
danced the previous year. After filling a plate for himself at
the buffet and talking briefly with the dean of the diplomatic corps and a few other envoys, he called Secretary
Rusk aside for a word and then quietly observed to the
reporters trailing him, "I've got to get back to work."

The party went on and on. Mrs. Johnson continued to
move through the crowd, surrounded at every stop. The
throng of guests eddied and flowed down the Great Hall,
through the reception rooms and onto the terrace. Vice
President and Mrs. Humphrey joined the dancers in the
East Room. Secretary Rusk and Soviet Ambassador Dobrynin sat down in the Red Room and began to converse. An
hour later, they were still talking. Most of the other guests
had gone, and Mrs. Johnson had disappeared when the tête-
à-tête finally ended, and Rusk and Dobrynin found their
patient wives at the buffet in the dining room.

Vice President and Mrs. Humphrey had no time to dance
at the last Johnson reception for the mission chiefs, in April
1968. Every envoy wanted to talk to HHH, and many managed to do so, but the Americans present were just as eager
to shake hands with the man they thought might be the
host at the next diplomatic reception. The crowd was the
largest ever assembled by the Johnsons for this hearty annual, and getting around at all in the jammed State Dining
Room was difficult. A frustrated American woman momentarily forgot who the honor guests were. Bumping into a
stranger, she grumbled, "There are entirely too many diplomats here!" Then she added hastily, "You're an American,
aren't you?" The soft answer, "No, I'm not," came from
Mrs. Frank Corner, wife of the New Zealand ambassador,
attending her first White House reception.

The air of informality pervading many White House

parties in recent years would have delighted Thomas Jefferson, the first President to shake hands with guests. But he was far ahead of his time, and his determination to break with stilted tradition distressed not only diplomats but also some of his countrymen, who expected formalized presidential hospitality to compensate for America's lack of throne and diadem. All such hopes were blasted when Jefferson announced that he would hold no weekly levees for select groups but would welcome the public to annual receptions on New Year's Day and July 4.

Joining "the public" at his first New Year's gathering were emissaries of Great Britain, France, Portugal, Denmark and Spain, in full court uniform. They were aghast that he was not formally dressed (he eschewed powdered hair and knee breeches and appeared in pantaloons and a loose fitting jacket without frills), and they were affronted when he greeted them perfunctorily and devoted his time to a delegation of Indian chieftains. Augustus John Foster, of the British Legation, reported: "The President passed to the upper end of the room and appeared wholly taken up with his natives." Foster's account further pointed out that British Minister Merry took umbrage at his host's discourtesy and "declared he would not stay and be treated so; and we went away after remaining five minutes."

Merry stayed away from Jefferson's next New Year's reception. Others in the corps appeared, but at least one wished that he had followed Merry's example; the Spanish minister was vexed that the President paid more attention to "Father Serra," who had no portfolio at the time, than to "the sovereign representatives."

Jefferson continued to pay little attention to the diplomats in residence, but one envoy he could not ignore was Sidi Suliman Mellimelli, who arrived in Washington in 1806 as a special emissary of the Bey of Tunis. The latter, unsuccessful in attempts to extract tribute from American ships searching the Barbary Coast for pirates, dispatched Melli-melli and an entourage of eleven to negotiate the claim. Jefferson later declared, "Those pirates sent their diplomats *collect!*"—meaning they were sent with the obvious expectation that they would be entertained, and underwritten, as invited visitors.

Although he had no intention of complying with the Bey's demand for tribute, the President did his best to treat the "guests" hospitably. He directed Secretary of State Madison to take over Stelle's Hotel to accommodate them, but they were hardly settled before they complained that no concubines had been provided. The omission was promptly corrected. Eleven women procured by a madam known as "Georgia the Greek" were summoned into service for the duration of the visit. It lasted six weeks.

The President had entertained Mellimelli at dinner several times before he appeared at the New Year's Day reception in 1807, and created a sensation. In his gold-embroidered robe, surmounted by twenty yards of silk wound into a turban, the bearded envoy was accompanied by his entourage, also richly arrayed. But the exotic group soon had competition. A band of Osage Indians, in native regalia and with their heads shaved except for a tuft at the crown, arrived and were warmly welcomed by Jefferson. Resident diplomats were overheard mumbling among themselves that the President had virtually ignored them, again, and had devoted himself to "the aborigines" and "the gaudy Tunisian."

Before Mellimelli finally left Washington, he embarrassed Jefferson by presenting him handsome gifts and also asking if he would accept four Arabian stud horses. Jefferson declined the latter, but he could not refuse the gifts already on hand without insulting the Bey of Tunis; so he accepted muskets, jewel-inlaid sabers, silver dressing cases, silken robes, brocades and perfumes and thanked Mellimelli profusely. Later, he had most of the items sold at auction and used the proceeds to defray the enormous cost of the uninvited visit. The remainder went to the National Museum.

The first White House reception ever given specifically to honor diplomats tied in with an even more expensive array of presents, which disturbed one of Jefferson's successors, James Buchanan. Three ambassadors headed a delegation of seventy-two Japanese who arrived in Washington in May 1860 for the announced purpose of obtaining an English copy of the first commercial treaty between Japan and the United States, signed in 1854 when Franklin Pierce was president. The English version had burned in the great fire of Yedo (Tokyo) in 1857.

These emissaries were not sent "collect." The Japanese government took care of the three-months' bill at Willard's Hotel, but the visitors were lavishly entertained at the White House. President Buchanan began with a reception honoring them and the resident diplomatic corps and including the Cabinet, the Congress and wives. Although it was a noon affair, Miss Harriet Lane, the President's niece and official hostess, appeared in a white satin gown with crinoline, and Buchanan wore his famous "Lancaster" cutaway, with emblems of the thirty-one States of the Union embroidered on the black lining. Members of the diplomatic corps, decked in court ceremonial attire, were assembled with the President in the Blue Room when the Japanese arrived. Resplendent in robes of richly embroidered silk and brocaded pillbox hats tied under the chin, the party, proceeding three by three with deliberate steps, approached the President and bowed almost to the floor. The warm handshakes with which he returned their greeting took them by obvious surprise; but with more bows, they departed, while the President received his other guests. Within half an hour, the delegation returned and presented a message from the Tycoon (shogun) of Japan to the host. Then they retired to the Red Room, where they met Miss Lane and the Cabinet wives. According to published account, "They refused to allow any other ladies to be presented to them in the President's house, considering it a want of respect to so high an official."

The following week, Buchanan gave a sumptuous dinner for the visitors and the next day Secretary of State Lewis Cass opened negotiations for the first Japanese mission in the United States. The emissaries returned home early in August, and the legation was opened in Washington in November.

Buchanan, a lame-duck president finishing his term in the executive mansion, had been a target of unrelenting political censure even before he entertained the initial Japanese mission. In fact, a congressional committee had launched a general investigation "of all his actions," and his enemies were keenly vigilant for any excuse to make him more uncomfortable. The Japanese delegation added to Buchanan's woes by bestowing on him a fortune in gifts, in gratitude for his hospitality. Though he had made it a rule never to take presents of any value from friends or supporters, he was fearful that refusal of Japanese generosity might disrupt the newly established diplomatic relations. He graciously accepted saddles embossed with silver and gold, silk kimonos, two swords exemplary of the finest in Oriental craftsmanship, an ornate lacquer cabinet and a tea set inlaid with gold, silver and pearls (valued at $3,000). His detractors had a field day, further enlivened after the Japanese commission returned home and the Tycoon sent Secretary Cass twenty-eight boxes filled with gifts for the Cabinet and an enormous blue porcelain basin for the President. The clamor subsided when Buchanan announced that he had accepted the treasure trove for the White House, not for himself, and that all items would remain there after his departure. Determined to avoid any further criticism, however, he exercised special precautions before he entertained the next distinguished visitor from abroad.

As minister at the Court of St. James's, Buchanan had

been a favorite of Queen Victoria, and when he learned that the Prince of Wales (later Edward VII) was planning a trip to Canada, he wrote to the Queen, asking her on his behalf to extend an invitation to her son to visit the White House. The Prince promptly accepted; and the President, in a series of conferences with Lord Lyons, the British minister, outlined his plans for entertaining the royal visitor and at the same time expressed the earnest hope that no costly presents would be given in return.

The Prince, traveling as "Baron Renfrew," arrived. There was a minimum of fanfare, at his request, but his three-day visit at the White House made glittering history. Buchanan gave two elegant dinners for him. At the first dinner, the diplomatic corps and the Cabinet attended and guests heard for the first time the Marine Band playing "Listen to the Mocking Bird," in honor of His Royal Highness. Members of Congress were invited to the second dinner, which was followed by a reception open to the public. The crowd reached such proportions that Buchanan had to order the White House doors closed. The Prince, at Lord Lyons' suggestion, went to an upstairs window, where he could be seen and cheered as he waved to the throng outside.

The Prince did not shower Buchanan with expensive gifts; but after he returned home, Queen Victoria sent a personal letter, thanking the President for his courtesies to her son, with a small silver box bearing the crest of Her Britannic Majesty and an inscription. Accompanying it was a set of engravings of the royal family for Harriet Lane.

Even Buchanan's staunchest enemies could not quarrel with acceptance of those modest presents. Instead, there were pointed questions as to whether the President might well have tendered a gift of some kind to the Prince. The politesse of a government appropriation for such a courtesy in the future came up for congressional discussion, as it had, intermittently, since 1824, when the Marquis de Lafayette arrived, laden with gifts for the President and the

First Lady. James Monroe drew on his own funds to purchase a writing case for Lafayette, while Elizabeth Monroe searched among her personal possessions for items to send to his wife and children.

Presents for official visiting dignitaries pose no special problems today. The cost is absorbed in the sizable presidential entertainment budget. The State Department ascertains, well in advance, whether the invited notable plans to bestow gifts on the president, the vice president and the secretary of state; and, if so, Uncle Sam prepares to reciprocate with items that are appropriately American in theme and not too costly.

Abraham Lincoln's initial effort to honor the foreign corps brought disappointment. Lines were sharply drawn between the North and the South when he was inaugurated, and several states had seceded. Some foreign governments were sympathetic to the South but all were hesitant in openly siding with either faction. Nonetheless, the Lincolns launched an extensive social schedule. After their first public levee, they scheduled a reception in honor of the diplomatic corps. It was a failure. A contemporary account observed: "The Legations were not out in full force. Nor did they come together in a body, as was their custom. The French Minister, Mercier, was absent. Lord Lyons was coldly dignified. Already the nations were looking at us askance."

Lincoln was distressed, and the First Lady, who had chosen one of the finest gowns in her extensive wardrobe for the occasion, was heartbroken. Secretary of State William H. Seward made some judicious inquiries and learned that the French minister was "indisposed" and that the diplomats, generally, were unaccustomed to receiving "notices of, rather than formal invitations to, official functions in their honor."

So that no such excuse could serve a second time, Lincoln sent out, a month in advance, handsomely engraved invitations to a state dinner for the diplomatic corps on June 4, 1861. All recipients accepted, and the event was a tremendous success. Mrs. Elizabeth Todd Grimsley, the First Lady's sister, wrote that the event "passed off with the usual complimentary toasts, decanters passed, and with this, a new feature to me, was the exchange of civilities in the tendering of elaborate snuff boxes, not only among the diplomats, but all the ladies." The New York *Herald Tribune* referred to the dinner as "most *recherché* and elegant."

Every president from Lincoln to John F. Kennedy honored the diplomatic corps at dinner, and in several administrations the event was an annual affair. Just before the United States entered World War I, Woodrow Wilson gave two diplomatic dinners in a single season, so that envoys of enemy countries would not have to sit at the same table. Harry and Bess Truman feted ambassadors and ministers and their wives at two dinners in 1946, for a different reason: the corps had increased to sixty missions and two such affairs at the traditional U-shaped table were easier to handle than one. All envoys whose names coincided with odd numbers on the State Department's official list were invited to the first; the remainder, to the second.

Two dinners for the envoys were annual fixtures on the calendar during the Eisenhower administration, with guests seated at an E-shaped table to accommodate the still expanding corps, until the President's heart attack put a stop to all White House entertaining for a time. Then, when the official schedule was resumed, diplomats were distressed that dinners for them were not on the list, although all the other traditional events were included. Complaints on Embassy Row echoed to the White House, and the diplomatic dinner, in two parts, went back on the calendar. Each was an elegant white-tie affair, to which additional guests were invited for the musicales that followed.

With the advent of the Kennedy administration, the presidential dinner for the mission chiefs was discontinued, but the void was filled by a formal event, at which Secretary and Mrs. Rusk annually honored envoys and their wives. The State Department's reception suite, a museum of treasured Early American furnishings, was the setting. Ambassadors in full dress, adorned with dazzling decorations, beautifully gowned women, and African envoys and wives in elaborate national attire assembled for cocktails in the John Quincy Adams Room and dined at tables-for-ten in the Benjamin Franklin Room. Each of the galas was a masterpiece of official entertainment with an American theme. The 1968 edition, for example, was a "Salute to Thomas Jefferson," with place cards bearing a picture of the third United States President, a menu such as he—the greatest gourmet who ever lived in the White House—might have offered his guests, and songs by the University of Virginia glee club. Secretary Rusk's wit surfaced in his brief after-dinner speech; an eloquent response from the diplomatic dean, Nicaragua's Ambassador Sevilla-Sacasa, completed the program.

President Johnson's adherence to less formal dress for functions at even the highest level had eliminated white-tie attire at the White House. The State Department dinners, giving diplomats their one opportunity of the year to step out in full dress with decorations, became the last strongholds of traditional elegance.

Rumors along Embassy Row had it that Johnson's aversion to full dress stemmed from a traumatic experience when, as vice president, he appeared at a late-evening reception of the National Gallery of Art in white tie and tails when all the other men had on dinner coats. Intimates denied that this unhappy experience had anything to do with the black-tie edict after he became president. They insisted that, like many other men, he long had abhorred uncomfortable evening attire and abandoned it as soon as he could. After his first black-tie state dinner, he said, "I always despised those monkey suits, and now that I don't have to wear them, I won't." Most of his male guests were delighted to follow his lead, but envoys to whom full dress is, as one European ambassador put it, "virtually a working uniform for evening," deplored the sartorial downgrading that prohibited their displaying sashes, medals and sunbursts, which can be properly worn only with white tie.

Devotees of full dress-with-decorations held out in every way they could. Asked whether the diplomats' dinner for Secretary and Mrs. Rusk in 1964 would be white tie or black tie, Ambassador Sevilla-Sacasa replied, "White tie, of course! It's a formal occasion!" Like many of his colleagues, he was delighted that the State Department dinners for the mission chiefs continued the tradition.

Secretary Rusk found a way to be comfortable in full dress. He simply discarded the winged collar and wore his white tie with a soft shirt. At his 1967 dinner for the diplomats he recalled that Edward VII was responsible for the fashion that had tortured men for so many years. When the British King wearied of the ascot and had it cut from his suits, the remaining neckline was unbecoming. Tailors improved the appearance by raising the collar and, to keep it from cutting the royal neck, turned down the corners. "And we've been stuck with it for fifty years," Rusk said. "I refuse to be stuck with it any longer."

Early in 1965, LBJ suddenly became aware that his relationship with the foreign corps left something to be desired. Not long after the 1964 presidential election, the dean of the diplomatic corps relayed to Rusk some of the complaints from envoys who were troubled by Johnson's apparent lack of regard for them. Sevilla-Sacasa said, in effect, that a lack of communication between the mission chiefs and the President had become a serious problem. They had difficulty in arranging appointments with him, rarely were able to confer with him privately, sometimes were kept

waiting for an hour and then had little chance to talk because he preempted the conversation by airing his own
views. Most of all, they were irked at the rumor that he had
termed the corps "the monkey-suit bunch." Johnson got the
message in due course, and a change in presidential attitude
was forthcoming.

An opportunity presented itself at the time of the State
Department dinner for the diplomats in February 1965,
when acting Secretary of State George Ball was scheduled
to be host while Rusk was vacationing in Florida. Before
the affair, Ball appeared at the White House congressional
reception; but, on arrival, he told the President that he
could not stay long, as he had to be at the State Department
before eight o'clock to receive the mission chiefs at the
white-tie dinner. "But didn't you know that the Johnson
administration wears black tie?" the President asked, with a
twinkle.

"Yes, sir," Ball replied, "but the diplomats prefer white
tie, so they can wear their decorations. And we like to
please them."

The President was interested. He asked Ball if he thought
the diplomats would mind if he dropped in on them later—
in dinner coat. Ball assured him that he would be welcome,
and then hastily departed to change into formal dress for
the dinner.

At the end of the congressional reception, the President
asked Vice President Humphrey to accompany him to the
State Department; and, since the hour was late, they decided to go as they were—in business suits. The envoys
greeted the pair with a thunder of applause and beamed
when the President said he had come because he could not
pass up a chance to see them, en masse, "all dressed up."

In succeeding weeks, Mr. Johnson made a concerted
effort to get better acquainted with his "international con-
stituency." He asked Chief of Protocol Lloyd Hand and
presidential assistant Jack Valenti to invite five or six en-

voys at a time to luncheon at the White House and managed to drop in for an informal talk around dessert time. He initiated across-the-country trips for envoys who wanted to see how Americans solved problems similar to those in their own countries (fifty ambassadors were escorted to desalinization plants in Texas and New Mexico; seventy-eight attended the launching of Gemini 7). He invited group after group to dine with him on the *Sequoia*. When the First Lady received wives of the envoys at tea, he dropped in to greet them. He established a special rapport with several ambassadors by complimenting them in the presence of visiting dignitaries from their homelands.

Diplomatic exposure to the "Johnson treatment" worked better than anyone expected—except, perhaps, the President himself. But LBJ, like Kennedy and Eisenhower before him, ruffled diplomatic sensitivities occasionally when his crowded calendar kept him from accepting the credentials of new envoys promptly and allowed him a minimum of time with them when meetings were finally arranged. Fledgling ambassadors of emerging nations were especially concerned about due courtesies. Veterans in diplomacy also complained, as had several of their colleagues during previous administrations. A number of emissaries were annoyed by the delayed and perfunctory reception they had from President Eisenhower.

An envoy retiring from Washington in 1959 recalled a fairly typical experience. "I waited three weeks for the President to return from a vacation, and then another week, before he received me," he said. "He spent exactly five minutes with me. There was no apology for the delay, and no special ceremony, such as there were on eight other occasions when I have presented credentials to chiefs of state. I expected better treatment in a country of such importance as this."

In his book *Mandate for Change: The White House Years*, Dwight D. Eisenhower wrote:

In the quieter days of the past it was quite convenient for the President to arrange periods during the week when he could, in appropriate formal clothes, and with reasonable pomp and circumstance, receive the credentials of the personal emissaries of the chiefs of state. I am not certain when the President abandoned the custom of receiving ceremoniously those ambassadors from nations with whom we have diplomatic ties, but it happened before my time. Except for a few special occasions, I received diplomats in my office, in simple, informal meetings.

Such informal meetings began in the Truman administration when the foreign missions began to multiply and the busy President was heavily involved with pressing postwar problems. However, Harry Truman made it a point to receive each new envoy as promptly as possible and to spend at least thirty minutes talking with him after credentials were presented.

The mushrooming of new countries in the last fifteen years resulted in such a rapid inflow of new envoys that the White House accreditation ceremonies have bogged down from time to time; but since an ambassador-designate is in a state of social and official limbo before he has met the president, he naturally resents any delay in being received at the White House. Austria's Ambassador Ernest Lemberger, who waited for some time to be fully accredited in 1965 because the President was ill, said, "Only by presenting credentials to the Chief of State can an ambassador be fully recognized by other ambassadors who have had that honor in the host country." At the same time, Nigeria's Ambassador N. Ade Martins and Jordan's Ambassador Farhan Shubeilat, also delayed in being fully accredited, declined all social invitations, forwent all public appearances and were, as the Nigerian put it, "officially invisible."

Apprised of their plight, President Johnson asked Secretary Rusk to accept their credentials on his behalf and learned that though Rusk had already received them, the White House ritual was also necessary, according to "the Rules of Vienna." Subsequently, arrangements were made for all three envoys-designate to present documents at the White House reception for the chiefs of mission in November 1965. This policy, initiated by John F. Kennedy, was followed on two occasions by LBJ. Four ambassadors presented their credentials to him at the January 1965 reception; eight, at the December 1967 reception. The plan worked nicely. The new envoys were pleased to be in the spotlight, during a brief ceremony for each, as cameras clicked.

Through the last two years of the Johnson administration, the President found that even the assembly-line accreditation at the annual reception did not dispose of the problem. New envoys continued to arrive in number, and working in appointments with each of them jammed the White House calendar. Finally, he began telescoping the schedule, receiving two or three envoys at one session, in his office.

At any time more than one envoy presents his credentials to the president, however, the order of precedence is of extreme importance. The envoy who reaches Washington first is entitled to be received first, and so on, in similar sequence. If two designated ambassadors arrive on the same train or plane, the one who precedes the other off the carrier also precedes the other in the White House ceremony and on the official *Diplomatic List*. The latter is of special importance to the nimble-footed envoy; it places him a notch higher in rank than the one who follows him and one step nearer the possibility of becoming dean of the diplomatic corps.

This honor is achieved solely by seniority except in Catholic countries, where the ambassador of the Vatican is always the dean, and the position of the highest-ranking member of the foreign corps is prominent and powerful in any national capital.

Nicaragua's ambassador, Dr. Guillermo Sevilla-Sacasa, has been dean since 1956. When, at the age of thirty-two, he presented his credentials to Franklin D. Roosevelt in 1943, the President said, "You're too young, really, to be an ambassador, but I predict you'll be successful."

He has been successful enough to serve as emissary from six Nicaraguan presidents to five presidents of the United States and has dealt with nine secretaries of state. In addition, he has headed his country's delegations at the United Nations and the Organization of American States for a number of years.

A person of enormous energy, he has long negotiated a calendar that would tax the strength of ten men. A heart attack some years ago called a halt to his prodigious schedule for a time, but in a few weeks he had fully resumed his accustomed rounds. He has been called the "party-goingest man" in Washington. For almost a decade he has attended an average of more than 500 luncheons, dinners, receptions and conferences a year and traveled to innumerable international conclaves. In April 1968, Brazil's Ambassador Vasco Leitao da Cunha presented the badge of the order of Rio Branco to Sevilla-Sacasa, bringing his total to more than fifty honorary awards from forty-odd countries. His collection includes a number of grand crosses, stars and bejeweled sunbursts, some of which in miniature festoon his full-dress suit every time he has a chance to wear it.

He enjoys his job. "I do what I like because I like what I do," he has said. "And I know any diplomat's success depends largely on his enthusiasm, his esteem for the host country, good health, and the ability to take in stride any problems that arise. I don't mind problems, because I love to work out solutions."

Problems are as much a part of his life as parties. As dean

of the diplomatic corps, he is the official spokesman for several thousand diplomats; and he is often guide, sometimes mentor and occasionally father-confessor to new envoys, all of whom pay their first calls on him after having presented their credentials to the secretary of state and the president. He works closely with the State Department and the White House and figures prominently during official visits of foreign dignitaries. He also frequently serves as adviser to the State Department, for he is a well-informed envoy who keeps a practiced finger on the pulse of world trends. (He was one of the first diplomats to warn gullible United States officials that Fidel Castro was a dedicated communist.)

Sevilla-Sacasa's greatest source of pride, however, is his family. He is the father of nine sons and daughters ("a full baseball team," in his words). His wife, the former Lillian Somoza Debayle, is an amusing, relaxed individual, who skips parties when she can and devotes her time to her family, her spacious embassy residence and her personal friends, many who have known her since her school days in Washington. Her brother Anastasio Somoza Debayle was elected President of Nicaragua in 1967. Her late father and a late brother also served in that post.

4

Uncle Sam's Bulging Guest Book

AN EXASPERATED WASH-
ington taxicab driver, barred from crossing a twelve-block
downtown area during a flag-flying, band-playing parade for
a visiting king and queen, ground his brakes to a jolting stop
and growled to his passenger, "All this commotion about
foreign nabobs sure louses up the traffic! And they're coming in droves, one after the other—each one after something, usually money. Wouldn't it be easier and cheaper
just to send 'em a check?"

It would be easier and certainly "cheaper," but with
other major governments, ours is sold on the "new diplomacy," which enables key men to confer with one another
at key moments and to get acquainted even when there is
no emergency.

Ambassador Angier Biddle Duke as chief of protocol had been in charge of planning and managing the
Washington meetings between almost eighty world leaders
and the president of the United States, when he said: "As a
'traffic manager' for this kind of diplomacy, I have seen
suspicions dissolved, fears dispelled, friends reassured, opponents disarmed and even persuaded. This kind of top level
confrontation is a success."

Duke's immediate predecessor, Wiley T. Buchanan, chief
of protocol for four years of the Eisenhower administration,

was equally impressed with the value of personal contact between our president and other national leaders. In his book *Red Carpet at the White House*, Buchanan mentioned as "probably too low" the estimated tab our government pays for each official visitor ("$100 for every hour he spends in the U.S.A.") and answered the question "Is it worth it?" as follows:

> I would say yes, the time and effort and money are well spent. We live in the age of the hydrogen bomb, and whether we like it or not, membership in the grim society of bomb-owners is expanding. This means we need all the friends we can get, and it also means that we must keep in close touch with the uncommitted nations that someday may hold the balance of power on this uneasy planet.

The new diplomacy is calculated to work both ways. During the past thirty years, our presidents and vice presidents have called on many notables abroad, but the fact that our leaders have more frequently been hosts than guests is prestigious for Uncle Sam—a reliable indication that heads of well over half the nations feel they have something significant to gain in face-to-face meetings with our chief executive and other officials in Washington.

So long as the making and receiving of high-level calls can be mutually valuable, our leaders will travel to meet other leaders as often as possible, and our State Department will continue rolling out its 140-foot red carpet to VIPs from around the world.

Embassy Row figures importantly in the planning and execution of visits to the United States. The country's ambassador is generally active in promoting the invitation in the first place, and thereafter he works closely with the State Department in programing social events, appointments, public appearances and the itinerary for his leader.

Security, protocol, transportation, logistics, press coverage, music, flowers, seating arrangements, hotel accommo-

dations, sight seeing and honor guards have to be coordinated. The Office of Protocol is in charge, but always with
full cooperation of the White House and the embassy.

Administrative arrangements cover everything from floor
plans and pronunciation lists to instructions to officials and
organizations—not only in Washington but also in other
cities which will welcome the notable. A typical compila-
tion, prepared for the April 1962 visit of the Shah of Iran
and Empress Farah, included a detailed minute-by-minute
resume that covered 234, single-spaced, mimeographed
pages.

Always taken into account in the overall planning are
dietary habits of the visitor. The Office of Protocol keeps an
itemized list of general taboos (no intoxicating spirits for
Moslems, no beef for Hindus, no web-footed fowl for
Coptic Christians, no pork for Jews), but both the ambassador and his foreign office are consulted about personal
food preferences of the prospective guest.

The arrangements pamphlet prepared before the 1957
visit of Tunisia's President Habib Bourguiba, for instance,
included the reminder, confirmed by his son, the Tunisian
ambassador in Washington, that both the chief executive
and his wife preferred short, simple meals and that, being
Moslems, they should not be served pork, pork products or
alcoholic beverages.

The guidance miscellany for the 1957 visit of Britain's
Elizabeth II and Prince Philip stated: "Her Majesty drinks
sherry, ginger ale and Rhine wine, while Prince Philip likes
Scotch-and-soda and gin-and-tonic; also they prefer simple
meals, always with distilled water."

General Charles de Gaulle goes for distilled water, too,
but only the bottled-in-Paris brands, as the Quai d'Orsay
informed the Office of Protocol before his 1960 visit. Furthermore, it was suggested that all meats served to the
French President be broiled.

Before King George and Queen Elizabeth, the first reigning British monarchs ever to visit the United States, arrived in June 1939, a memorandum as to their sleeping habits was sent to the State Department—not through the British ambassador, Sir Ronald Lindsay, who had already failed to relay several suggestions, but straight from Buckingham Palace. The confidential dispatch specified the kind of sheets to which Their Majesties were accustomed and the color and weight of the down-comfort the Queen preferred for June nights.

Since the King and Queen were scheduled to stay at the White House—there was no presidential guest house in those days—the communiqué also indicated that the royal "plateman" would not have to be accommodated there; he would stay at the Canadian legation.

When reports that a "plateman" would be part of the royal retinue leaked out, many Washington residents learned for the first time that British kings and queens, since the days of Elizabeth I, have never traveled without a "plateman" to look after the silverware that always accompanies them.

But the "plateman" was off duty while King George and Queen Elizabeth ate at the White House. Their Majesties made do with Uncle Sam's knives and forks, and there were no royal complaints.

Prior to their first visit to the United States in 1960, the food habits of King Mahendra and Queen Ratna of Nepal were the subject of intensive research. Accordingly, instructions were that fish or lamb rather than beef or pork was to be on any menus planned for Their Majesties in Washington and everywhere else on their month-long tour of the United States. A similar directive went out before their second, shorter, visit, in 1967.

Mrs. Mary Farr Wilroy, the unflurried manager of the president's guest house (Blair House), checks with each embassy and with the Office of Protocol as to the next high-placed visitor's dietary habits. By the time the dignitary arrives, the Blair House kitchen is amply stocked with provisions carefully calculated to please his distinguished palate.

Occasionally, Mrs. Wilroy's job is complicated by extraordinary precautions as to exactly what the visitor can, or will, eat. Accompanying Saudi Arabia's King Faisal to Washington in 1966 were his royal chef, royal waiter, a royal interpreter to act as liaison between His Majesty and the chef and waiter, and a royal valet.

Politely explaining that their monarch suffered from stomach ulcers and had to be wary about what he ate, they appropriated most of Blair House chef William Dallas' kitchen for the two-day stay. They brought along enough rice and other nonperishable staples to last through the visit; but the Blair House staff kept the royal chef supplied with every food item he requested, including a beef filet, chicken, cornish hen, squash, carrots, green beans, apples, bananas, yogurt and cheese.

Chef Dallas, working in cramped quarters, cooked all meals for King Faisal's attendants—they ate heartily and often and took a particular liking to his pancakes—but not one morsel for His Majesty.

The royal chef of Saudi Arabia prepared everything the King ate in Washington, even when he dined at his own embassy and at the White House. On the night of President Johnson's dinner for His Majesty, the faithful foursome trooped over to the White House kitchen to reheat the food they had already cooked at Blair House. And while other guests enjoyed a gourmet meal, His Majesty, served by his royal waiter in native robes, had unseasoned broiled lamb, boiled potatoes, green beans, carrots, custard and stewed apples.

The fluster around King Faisal at Blair House did not compare with the commotion on the same premises when his father, Ibn Saud, was a state guest in 1957. The entourage then numbered seventy, in contrast to a mere forty in 1966, and because only eighteen could be accommodated at Blair House, the others stayed in nearby hotels and at the embassy. However, they rotated with the eighteen so that everyone in the party could have the privilege of being under the same roof with the monarch part of the time at least. Armed with daggers, bodyguards slept on the floor outside His Majesty's bedroom. Tasters bustled in and out of the kitchen, hovered over all food as it was prepared and sampled each viand before it was served to the King. Demands for more and more lamb bedeviled the Blair House staff, which was also bothered by the constant brewing of coffee in a big brazier brought over from the embassy and installed on one of the finest antique tables in the mansion.

Mrs. Victoria Geaney, Blair House manager at the time, was frantic when one of her staff reported that a live coal from the brazier had landed on a chair, which was in flames. She put in an agonized call to the fire department and prevented further conflagration, but table and chair were damaged.

Nobody was happier than Mrs. Geaney when King Saud and his retinue left, and she had a chance to air out the heavily incensed rooms and to estimate needed repairs on upholstery, draperies and furniture. The bill came to more than $5,000, which was, in any case, somewhat less than a fifth of what the tab was for the reception at which Ambassador Sheikh Mohamad Al-Kahyyal entertained some 1,500 guests in honor of Ibn Saud.

At any rate, all things considered, the visit was the most exorbitant ever recorded in Uncle Sam's guest log. It cost our government $30,000. It was also one of the longest—in Washington. It lasted five days because the King's lame little son, Prince Mashur, was undergoing treatment at Walter Reed Hospital, by special arrangement of President Eisenhower. The State Department provided ten limousines for the royal party, at $50 a day, and a full-blown schedule of official entertainment accented the sojourn. But if King

Saud was an expensive guest, he was also a generous one. He and his party handed out gold watches, jeweled scimitars and flowing robes by the dozen as thank-you gifts; and Deputy Chief of Protocol Victor Purse, whose attention was especially appreciated, got a $3,000 automobile.

Protocol Chief Buchanan scored his deputy for "bad judgment" in accepting the lavish present, and Purse was finally transferred to a department where there would be no such temptation. The hubbub subsided after the ruling that all gifts from foreign dignitaries were to be turned over to the State Department for indefinite safekeeping. Joseph W. Reap, a State Department news officer at the time of Ibn Saud's visit and a recipient of a gold wristwatch and a flowing robe, got his gifts back a decade later.

Every individual now or formerly in the Office of Protocol is a repository of amusing and sometimes embarrassing incidents having to do with visiting VIPs, but few State Department employees will ever admit that any foreign leader is not the perfect guest, nor that plans ever go haywire—as they sometimes do.

Protocol officers who remember Nikita Khrushchev's 1959 visit are not disposed to talk about some difficulties it caused. They just shake their heads in remembered despair.

Plans for the visit, sparked by Soviet Ambassador Mikhail ("Smiling Mike") Menshikov, were whipped up and completed within two weeks. In the rush, it was not made clear that the party was to be limited. The Chairman of the Soviet Council of Ministers brought along fifty persons, including his wife, two daughters and a son-in-law, as well as 824 trunks and suitcases.

Twenty-three individuals packed into Blair House. Foreign Minister Gromyko and his wife were put up at a hotel. Others stayed at the Soviet Embassy.

Throughout the Washington part of the thirteen-day visit, things went fairly smoothly—until the Soviet Chairman discovered that Disneyland had not been included on his California itinerary. He grumbled considerably about the omission and ordered Menshikov to do something about it. When the word came back that the Soviet secret service was responsible for ruling out the Disneyland visit, Khrushchev stewed more than ever. He calmed down only after he was told that every effort would be made to include Disneyland on the itinerary.

"Every effort" was not enough. West Coast security officers negated it after the Soviet party arrived in California.

The luggage of visiting VIPs often presents problems. Khrushchev and his entourage have not been the only ones to bring along a preponderance of bags and trunks.

King Hassan II of Morocco and his party (137 persons) had 500 pieces of baggage on their 1967 visit. King Bhumibol and Queen Sirikit of Thailand arrived in June 1960 with 80 pieces of hand luggage, three big trunks and six medium-sized trunks.

Apparently, most of those were needed to carry the Queen's $75,000 wardrobe, designed by Balmain. Anyway, her well-dressed appearances made a big hit with the fashion press, which was in ecstasy during her entire visit.

The resulting reams of newspaper copy must have had an unfavorable reaction in Thailand, for during the Thai King and Queen's 1967 visit, Her Majesty's wardrobe could not compare with the stunning one seven years earlier. Only five pieces of luggage carted her apparel for the second United States sojourn, which was a week longer than the one in 1960; and, in answer to a Washington reporter's question as to whether it was true that Her Majesty spent $500,000 annually on her clothes, she retorted, "Certainly not. I couldn't possibly spend that much. I have orphans to look after."

Even though they are shut-mouthed about it, protocol planners are sometimes faced with perplexing, last-minute challenges. One staff member in the Office of Protocol had to go shopping for Greek Prime Minister Papandreou four hours before a White House dinner in his honor.

Arriving in Washington with a wardrobe far too heavy for the late spring weather, he wanted a summer dinner jacket. Barbara Bolling, an assistant to the chief of protocol, was dispatched to purchase one for him—size 43, long. He liked her choice.

Mrs. Angier Biddle Duke, wife of the chief of protocol, was the one summoned to personal service when the wife of a visiting chief of state discovered less than an hour before a White House dinner that the petticoat for her best evening dress had been left at home. Mrs. Duke rallied by asking a Washington department store owner to allow her into his establishment after hours to select and purchase the needed garment.

Few problems confronting the Office of Protocol have the embarrassing potential that was posed when an African chief of state, accompanied by his wife, also had in tow a delectable secretary.

Through his ambassador, the African president insisted that his secretary be invited to the dinner at the White House. The envoy passed the word to the Office of Protocol, but her name did not appear on the guest list.

The African president was furious. His ambassador appealed to the chief of protocol and was told that the list was limited to ranking members of the visiting party. The agonized envoy asked the protocol chief to inform the visiting notable. The latter, however, was not to be pacified. He said that if his secretary could not be included, he would skip the dinner himself.

The situation was nearing an impasse, when the African dignitary came up with a solution. If only official guests could be invited, he would make his protégé his secretary of state. He did; and she attended the dinner.

At that, the batting average on smoothness of operation

for visits is high. Official guests generally appear to be pleased with the reception in our country; and judging by the regularity with which many make return visits, or would like to, Uncle Sam is a good host.

"It's primarily a matter of laying the proper ground-work," said Deputy Chief of Protocol Sam King, who has toiled endless hours on innumerable visits since he joined the State Department in 1961. "When the planning is what it should be, successful execution follows. And these guests are usually superior, dedicated—and often delightful—people. Difficulties seldom arise."

Despite all the careful planning, an occasional mix-up threatens to mar if not maim a state visit. There was, for example, the flag confusion that was corrected on the Washington streets minutes before the noontime parade arranged for Ireland's President Eamon de Valera in May 1964.

An alert protocol officer noted that the bright banners fluttering from lampposts beside the Stars and Stripes were not Ireland's at all. The colors—green, white and orange—were right, but the arrangement was different. Flags of the Ivory Coast were snatched down and replaced along the route moments before the parade began.

Joseph Parlon, head of the Highway Department's sign shop, which stores and supplies flags of all foreign countries, tried to explain, "Since the flags of Ireland and the Ivory Coast are the same color, somebody put them in the same bin. It was just one of those things."

Ivory Coast banners figured in a second muddle, in mid-1967, when foreign VIPs were arriving in such rapid sequence that there was hardly time to lower the banners for one before raising them for the next.

The vertically striped flags of the Ivory Coast, put out to honor President Felix Houphouet-Boigny, stayed up for a while after his departure on August 18. Several were still flying shortly before the visit of the Shah of Iran.

Persons with little knowledge of such things naturally assumed that the flags were Iranian, while those aware that the Iranian flag has green, white and red horizontal stripes thought Washington officials had ordered banners in the wrong colors and then doubled the blunder by having them hung sideways.

Queries avalanched the Office of Protocol, which ordered the replacement, a bare five hours before the Shah arrived.

An ambassador who has been *en poste* in two other capitals to which official callers flock was loud in his praise of our protocol office after his chief's state visit. He said:

> I learned a great deal about my president when I had to supply answers to all the detailed questions from your Office of Protocol—such as to whether he preferred a hard or soft bed, what he liked to eat, and what he wanted to see in your capital city and throughout the country. The enormous amount of detailed planning that went into that trip outdid anything of its kind I ever saw. No wonder official visits to the United States are so successful.

With a keen sense of prerogatives and prerequisites, the envoy of each country, first of all, wants assurance that gestures of esteem shown to previous visitors of the same status are duplicated for his VIP. He is apt to take a dim view of suggested variations in the established routine, particularly if he represents one of the smaller or newer countries.

The Office of Protocol is equally concerned about extending equal courtesies to leaders of countries that, in theory at least, are equally sovereign. Ever mindful that an official visit can at best be rewarding—and, at worst, revealing—protocol officers and staff take great pains to plan schedules on the basis of complete equality; in other words, they see to it that the king of a small and impoverished nation is slated for the same treatment as would be shown to the leader of the most powerful and richest among nations.

Visits, therefore, are standardized as much as possible, within well-defined categories. When variations are indicated, they must be acceptable to the ambassador before inclusion on the visitor's capital calendar.

During the first year of the Kennedy administration, Chief of Protocol Duke tried to eliminate the traditional arrival ceremony, which required our chief executive, bands and honor guards to travel miles to greet the visitor with due ceremony at a Virginia or Maryland airport and accompany him in a long parade back to Blair House.

In an effort to save time all around and still have a memorable welcoming ritual, the Office of Protocol came up with the idea of the dignitary's helicopter arrival on the White House lawn, where the president, a corps of foreign envoys and other notables would be on hand for the reception. But no ambassador could be persuaded that such a departure should begin with *his* leader's visit.

At one point there was a faint hope that the envoy of a newly emerged nation might be amenable. He listened patiently to Ambassador Duke's sales talk as to how his president would make long-remembered headlines as the first thus to be received and then evenly replied, "No, my friend. I must refuse to permit my country the first to be downgraded in not having your president meet mine at the airport."

The United States arrival point for that particular caller happened to be a Maryland airport, many miles away from Washington, but President Kennedy went there for the initial ceremonial.

The time-consuming custom prevailed until the autumn of 1962, when an unusual circumstance gracefully led to the proposed replacement. Shortly after Algeria became independent in July of that year, Premier Ahmed Ben Bella was invited to Washington. His prompt acceptance came before he had appointed an envoy to the United States. The Office of Protocol, therefore, unilaterally planned the schedule—and arranged for the Premier to be transported by helicopter from Virginia to meet the President on the White House lawn.

The plan worked. It was a beautiful autumn day, and panoply and procedure were impressive, with an honor guard of troops in dress uniform, a service band, flags flying, a nineteen-gun salute and the red carpet extending across the grass to a raised platform, where the President made a welcoming speech and the visitor replied before a distinguished assemblage and a record turnout of reporters, photographers and newsreel cameramen.

Ambassador Duke said later, "The scene was such as to shake the resolve of the most hardened traditionalist. The watchful diplomatic corps saw for the first time a successful, splendid welcoming ceremony at the White House."

From that time on, our president has never gone outside the District of Columbia to greet arriving notables, but occasionally he does go to Union Station to welcome state and official guests coming by train and then accompanies them in motorcade to Blair House.

The need for more flexibility in visiting routines had been increasingly apparent in recent years. The emergence of new countries, special sessions at the United Nations and such attractions as the New York World's Fair and Expo '67 prompted a steadily growing parade of high dignitaries to this hemisphere, and most of them managed to make it to Washington.

So many have been officially received, in fact, that world leaders have ceased to be novelties on the capital scene, as they were when the influx began in the late 1930s. Continuing through most of the Roosevelt administration, the trend receded for a time after World War II. Compared to the Kennedy years, when almost ninety ranking leaders were guests of Uncle Sam, President Truman received comparatively few—only five in the highest echelon over a period of seven and a half years.

Full-scale state and official visits began to multiply during the Eisenhower administration. The President welcomed, entertained and was entertained by four kings, three queens, ten presidents, a number of prime ministers (including Ghana's Kwame Nkrumah, first head of a new African country to visit the United States), Germany's Chancellor Konrad Adenauer and the Soviet Union's Nikita Khrushchev. Several foreign ministers and crown princes also were received by President Eisenhower before he entertained his last official visitor, Malaya's Prime Minister Rahman in October 1960.

Starting with the February arrival of Denmark's Prime Minister, President Kennedy had thirty-four official callers in 1961, including a long string of prime ministers and four full-fledged state visitors. He received forty-nine leaders the following year, and scores of others eagerly awaited invitations. The official guest book has been filled to capacity ever since.

All such visits to a certain extent are purposeful "working" visits, but they take on different forms for clearly defined reasons, which in turn dictate that they be clearly classified and standardized as much as possible. The differences lie chiefly in the ceremonial field—whether or not there will be an elaborate welcome followed by a parade; whether the White House function will be dinner or luncheon; whether the visitor stays at Blair House or his own embassy; whether or not he is entertained by the vice president, the secretary of state and Senate dignitaries; and the type of return social courtesy, if any, he extends to the president.

For obvious reasons, not more than four or five state or official guests can be received within a year. Other VIPs visit under other classifications.

Each classification, like the top two—official and state—
has a stipulated framework, which governs the type of entertainment, the number of official conferences, and the
program in general. Categories are sometimes revamped,
but the main outline is changed only after long delibera-
tion.

A number of revisions have been made on the list in the
past several years, but at the outset of the Kennedy administration, a thick pamphlet in the Office of Protocol described
four classifications of VIP calls as follows:

1. *State Visit:* A full-scale visit by a chief of state (president, king, queen, emperor) at the official invitation of
the United States president, usually for a three-day stay
in Washington and an additional week in the United
States.

The guest stays at Blair House, has two meetings
with the president, is honored at a White House dinner
and one given by the secretary of state and gives a return dinner to the president.

Other functions in Washington as well as elsewhere
in the country are tailored to the visitor's wishes, when
feasible. Full military honors (including a twenty-one-
gun salute) are rendered on arrival and departure from
Washington. Protocol escorts are provided at all times
during the ten-day visit, and security guards are provided as required.

All air and surface transportation *within the United
States* and all normal expenses for the visitor and
a party up to ten is paid by the United States government.

2. *Official Visit:* A full-scale visit by a head of government
(prime minister, premier, chancellor) at the official invitation of the president, for three days in Washington
and a week elsewhere in the country. Occasionally such
a call is made by a vice president or a crown prince, at

the invitation of our president; and foreign ministers occasionally are invited by the secretary of state to call in this category.

The official visit follows the state proposition in general plan, with a few minor exceptions; for example, a nineteen instead of a twenty-one-gun salute.

3. *Informal Working Visit:* A foreign chief of state or head of government visits for the specific purpose of holding substantive discussions in Washington. Length is determined by the business at hand, and the call pertains to Washington only.

Military honors may be rendered on arrival if the guest travels to the capital in a government or private plane. Guest and party stay in quarters provided by their own government. Entertainment is planned on an ad hoc (for this visit, only) premise and may include an informal luncheon at the White House and a small dinner given by the vice president or the secretary of state.

Although our government *may* provide transportation from New York City to Washington and back, the informal working visitor's expenses are generally defrayed by his government.

4. *Private Visit:* Chiefs of state, government heads and foreign ministers visiting the United States on their own initiative, with or without paying official calls or participating in ceremonial events.

All arrangements for honors and courtesies are worked out on an ad hoc basis by the geographic desk of the State Department and the chief of protocol, often in consultation with the ambassador or a member of his staff.

The visitor stays in his own embassy, and his government underwrites his expenses. Military honors may or may not be rendered on his arrival. When our government transports him to Washington from New York or any other United States city in a government or private plane, protocol and security escorts are provided.

The necessity for streamlining all calendars for a constantly expanding volume of visitors became acutely obvious in 1961. To enable the President to continue to see and talk to as many world figures as his heavy schedule permitted, the State Department added to its list the category of *presidential guest*, to apply to rulers invited by our chief executive for a shorter visit of high prestige.

The reception plan called for two days in Washington and not more than eight elsewhere in the country, two meetings with our chief executive, luncheon at the White House, dinner at the State Department, and either a return luncheon or a reception at Blair House with the visitor as host to our president.

The new category was ushered in gradually. Guidelines were still incomplete in the autumn of 1961, when Finland's President Urho Kekkonen and his wife were invited to visit Washington after a state reception in Canada and were entertained on a two-day schedule very much in keeping with the evolving classification. The same plan was used for Liberia's President William V. Tubman, who arrived later in October.

President Ahmadou Ahidjo of Cameroon and President Sylvanus Olympio of Togo, who came in 1962, were among the first chiefs of state whose visiting calendars adhered completely to the framework for the presidential guest. Soon callers in that category outnumbered all others.

In time, however, the presidential guest definition was to disappear from the official list. The classification had served as a smooth bridge to eventual condensation of all state and official routines, which today stipulate two days in Washington and up to eight in the United States.

In course of the changeover, other modifications were incorporated. Whereas the president had formerly attended dinners given by state visitors in return for White House dinners, the outline for a time designated a luncheon as the return courtesy. Then a reception replaced the luncheon,

and the entire state or official calendar became more flex-
ible.

Despite its brevity or flexibility, however, a tremendous
amount of work is involved in any visit on the highest level,
and arrangements begin far in advance. For example, six
months of concentrated planning on the part of the Office of
Protocol, the Embassy of Afghanistan and the Afghanistan
desk at the State Department preceded the classic state
visit of King Zahir and Queen Homaira in the autumn of
1963.

Ambassador Mohammad Maiwandal instigated the invitation in January 1963 by informing the State Department's
Afghan desk officer, Robert Carle, that King Zahir would
like to visit the United States and by pointing out that no
Afghan ruler had ever done so.

In due course, memoranda went from the Office of Protocol to President Kennedy with a recommendation that the
invitation be issued and a notation as to the general nature
of his expected participation. Secretary of State Rusk was
also informed of the reasons for such a call and its proposed
length. As soon as White House and Department of State
authorization were received, late in March, the Office of
Protocol scheduled the September visit, and plans were set
in motion, in this order:

A cablegram to the United States Ambassador John Mil-
ton Steeves in Kabul requested him to obtain a list of the official party, with exact titles; data as to the proficiency in the
English language of the party; a biographic outline and six
photos of each member; mode of travel desired by the King;
places other than Washington that should be included on
his itinerary; prominent civilians he wished to meet in the
capital and elsewhere; topics he might want to discuss in
official conferences; "any pertinent information that should
be incorporated into public remarks or toasts to be made by
the President, the Vice President, or the Secretary of State."

The cablegram also instructed Ambassador Steeves to

convey to the appropriate persons certain facts about the proposed visit—for example, the official party was to be limited to ten (in addition to the two ambassadors) and expenses for any additional members were to be borne by the government of Afghanistan, which would also take care of living and travel expenses of King Zahir's personal valet and secretary (although they would be housed in Washington); the visit would be limited to two days in our capital and up to eight elsewhere in the United States; the United States government would extend to His Majesty and party the special courtesy of transporting them from and back to Lebanon, where the Afghan national airline terminates.

On receipt of the answer, the White House via cable through our embassy in Kabul issued a formal invitation to King Zahir and Queen Homaira to be guests in the United States for ten days, beginning September 5.

Lengthy conferences at the State Department followed, as details of the program were worked out by a combined team, including Ambassador Maiwandal, Ambassador Duke, the Afghanistan Counselor Ravan Farhadi, Desk Officer Carle and Edward Williams and David Waters of the Office of Protocol.

Ambassador Maiwandal offered three special suggestions: His Majesty desired that any luncheons in his honor be for men only, as they are in his country; he preferred to give a stag luncheon for President Kennedy rather than a dinner; and he hoped to see General Eisenhower, who as president had visited him in Afghanistan.

Arrangements were promptly made for a visit to Gettysburg and for Washington functions to be as His Majesty wished. They would set no precedents. Stag luncheons at the White House had been given for several previous visiting rulers; Hassan II of Morocco had feted JFK at a stag luncheon earlier in 1963; and President and Mrs. Kennedy had attended no VIP return dinners since 1962, when they were honored by the Shah of Iran and Empress Farah at the new Iranian chancery in April of that year.

As usual when a royal state visit is in the offing, the press broke out in a rash of feature stories about the principals and their country. A vast number of readers who had never heard of King Zahir learned something about his leadership in developing woolen and cotton manufacturing in his homeland; in exporting karakul, dried and fresh fruits, nuts, raw cotton and carpets; and in establishing in a country with no railways an air transportation route (Ariana Afghan Airlines).

Queen Homaira also got her share of attention in print, with mention of her seven children and four grandchildren and her assistance in the successful campaign to unveil her countrywomen.

The D.C. Citizens Committee, which under leadership of public-spirited Edgar Morris had for some time been active in whipping up general Washington interest in state and official visitors and helping to welcome them, lined up six bands for the parade and arranged for firemen to bracket the parade route with flags of the United States and Afghanistan, blown-up photographs of the visiting King and our President and hundred-foot aerial arches draped with banners in national colors of the two countries. He also worked with representatives of the armed services on the participation of honor guards and the D.C. Police Department in marshaling into service 700 extra men. In addition, the Citizens Committee looked after the distribution of thousands of pamphlets about Afghanistan to local schoolchildren and promoted the press and network build-up for the royal visit.

The groundwork had been thoroughly laid when Ambassador Maiwandal was transferred as envoy to Pakistan. He left with the full assurance that the welcome would be gratifying. His successor, Abdul Majid, arrived three weeks before Their Majesties with, as he put it, "innumerable confirmations my only pressing duties."

By that time, Washington had become acutely "Afghanistan conscious" and avidly interested in knowing more about the landlocked Asian land—surrounded by Pakistan, Iran and the Soviet Union—which was just emerging from the camel and pony age and where women had been unveiled for only three years.

The *Washington Post* came up with something different: an amusing summary of a capital sojourn as reported in the newspaper in 1921. The visitor was Princess Fatima Sultana of Afghanistan. She had no official position, and the country, although freed from British control, had no diplomatic relations with the United States. The story, as summed up by the *Post* reporter, Elizabeth Ford, in 1963, pointed out that Mohammed Vali Khan, a former Afghan army chief, had been in Washington for months trying to set up a mission when the princess arrived on the scene with three sons and a man she identified as "Prince Zerdecheso of Egypt." Khan steered clear of the unexpected visitors; he said he had never met the princess and implied that she was not typical of the high-born women—or any others—in his homeland.

She was unveiled. She was a champion of equal rights for women, and the enormous diamond she wore in a nostril quivered as she dilated on prospects of women's suffrage throughout the world.

She needed no help from Khan in getting noticed and getting around. She was received by President Harding in the Red Room and posed for photos on the White House lawn. Senator Medill McCormick took her on a tour of the Capitol, and she called on Secretary Charles Evans Hughes at the State Department. But she made headlines only at a private dinner at the Willard Hotel when she discovered a cat under her table, promptly extricated him and fed him from her plate.

Next day, the *Washington Post* carried a purported interview with the cat and his tribute: "What I want to say is that the Princess Fatima Sultana knows how to spread her bounty with a lavish hand. I'll tell the world she gave me a square meal and a square deal. She knows how to feed the kitty."

The Princess' departure after four days in Washington brought an audible sigh of relief from Mohammed Vali Khan, who wondered openly whether his cause had been irreparably obstructed by her visit.

Almost two decades elapsed before diplomatic relations were established between Afghanistan and the United States, and the visit of King Zahir and Queen Homaira was twenty-one years after that.

In 1963, the classic state schedule went off without a deterrent ripple. Even the elements cooperated. Their Majesties arrived in a downpour, which is a lucky omen in Afghanistan; and a sizable assemblage at the White House witnessed the welcoming ceremony with full military honors.

Since Blair House was undergoing repairs, the King and Queen stayed at the interim presidential guest house at 1743 22nd Street, and their bags were hardly unpacked before their crowded calendar began.

It got under way with a bang, literally, when the first fireworks display ever produced for visiting dignitaries followed a White House dinner for 116.

The event had been arranged with the Rose Garden as the setting. Because of the weather the dinner was shifted inside, but the skies cleared in time for the combustible exhibition, which the company watched from the South Portico.

The last state visitor received by President Kennedy was Ethiopia's Emperor Haile Selassie I, in October 1963. His Imperial Majesty's ambassador in Washington was ebullient Berhanou Dinke, who for months had worked tirelessly on arrangements for the three-day sojourn. He had talked frequently by telephone from Washington to Addis Ababa, reporting every detail of the royal schedule as it developed; he had spent endless hours planning His Imperial Majesty's luncheon to honor President Kennedy at the Woodmont Country Club and, as the grand finale of the visit, a reception at the Shoreham Hotel.

Haile Selassie flew to the United States, but he arrived in Washington by train from Philadelphia. The President and a large party met him at Union Station, and the twenty-minute ceremony, climaxed by a twenty-one gun salute, was followed by a parade up Pennsylvania Avenue. The Lion of Judah was no stranger to Washington. Thousands had cheered his ceremonial arrival in 1954, when, in keeping with the custom for state visitors at the time, he spent a night in the White House before moving on to Blair House.

Frail in appearance, His Imperial Majesty proved his iron stamina by negotiating jam-packed programs on both visits. On the last afternoon of the 1963 state schedule, he shook hands with more than a thousand reception guests.

Dinke's obvious devotion to his ruler throughout the visit, and also when he returned a month later to attend President Kennedy's funeral, was mentioned by many in April 1965, when the envoy announced his resignation—in protest to the regime of Haile Selassie. The news took Embassy Row by surprise and precipitated a fiery exchange of charges and counter-charges in the press. A published report that Dinke's exit had been prompted more by his "financial, marital and career difficulties" than by his dissatisfaction with his government brought a reply from the former envoy in a letter to the editor of *The Washington Post* in November 1965. Dinke insisted that he had an ample private income and cited impressive figures to prove it. He also laundered his domestic linen in public. His wife, he wrote, had returned to Addis Ababa in 1962. She had fallen in love with a member of the Emperor's Service, the letter continued, with the result that a high commission had found the two guilty of adultery, and Dinke had been granted a divorce in 1963.

The final portion of his missive pointed out that "Correspondence from the Emperor was always full of glowing praise of my work for the Ethiopian Government" and then concluded: "It is imperative that the people of the United States appreciate fully the oppressive and all-pervading nature of Haile Selassie's personal rule. If change is not fostered in Ethiopia now, violent and radical change can be expected when the Emperor disappears from the scene. All of us will be many decades picking up the pieces."

By the time the letter was published, Dinke had disappeared from the capital scene, his whereabouts clouded in mystery. Half his staff had resigned with him. The second secretary had flown back to Ethiopia. The military, naval and air attaché had taken off without saying where he was headed. Another secretary and the educational attaché stayed to assist the new charge d'affaires, Dr. Getachew Abdi, who had been transferred from Nigeria, but they all declined to discuss the former envoy. The State Department also kept mum.

Subsequent unauthorized reports were conflicting. One line of gossip had it that Dinke had returned to Addis Ababa and was once more in the good graces of Haile Selassie: another circulated that he was spearheading a growing antigovernment movement in Ethiopia. But by then, Washington had lost interest in "L'Affaire Dinke."

Other envoys at odds with their governments have resigned, but generally without airing details of their dissatisfaction. Greek Ambassador George Melas pulled out of his country's service in September 1958 but left his friends—and he had many in the United States—wondering exactly why. He and Mme. Melas departed with the memory of an avalanche of farewell parties and the usual token of high regard, a handsome gift purchased by contributions from a sizable number of acquaintances.

Italian Ambassador Sergio Fenoaltea was less tight-lipped about his resignation in 1967. His disagreements with his country's foreign office had been an open secret in State Department circles for some time, but he clinched his popularity with the Washington establishment by turning in his papers just after Italy's Foreign Minister Amintore Fanfani blasted the United States stand in Vietnam. A steady series of dinners for the retiring ambassador and Signora Fenoaltea followed and were climaxed by a reception and a gift of two exquisite antique mirrors tendered by more than a hundred staunch Washington admirers.

Fenoaltea had been at the embassy helm on January 1964 when Antonio Segni, the second Italian president ever to visit America arrived with Signora Segni. Called a "modified state visit," in deference to the death of President Kennedy less than two months before, the schedule was limited by request of President Segni to Washington and New York, but it made history as the first top-level call to the capital in the Johnson administration.

LBJ previously had received two official visitors elsewhere. He met the first, Prime Minister Mohamed Shamte of Zanzibar, in New York in December 1963. Later that month, in Austin, Texas, he welcomed Germany's Chancellor Erhard, on a working visit.

By the end of his administration, President Johnson had established a record in welcoming government leaders. At the White House or his Texas home, he had entertained more than two hundred ranking dignitaries, including forty-two chiefs of state and thirty-two prime ministers (some of them, several times) and had conferred in his office with a number of other lesser officials on working visits to Washington.

5

Big Bashes and Bold Intruders

Traditionally honored at a series of luncheons and dinners at the highest official level in Washington, the visiting chief of state or head of government generally polishes off his capital calendar with a reception planned by his embassy.

The pattern of such entertaining, although prescribed by protocol, changes from time to time, but the dual purpose—to accentuate the distinction of the visitor and the importance of his country—is immutable.

A cost-no-obstacle embassy reception at the ambassador's residence, the Pan American Union or a hotel admirably suits that purpose. It gives the foreign dignitary a chance to meet and impress the largest number of persons in the shortest possible time, and it generates the kind of publicity that sometimes skyrockets his stock in his homeland and often bolsters his envoy's prestige in the United States.

With these goals in mind, a steadily increasing number of emperors, kings, presidents and prime ministers, as well as other official guests, have shaken hands with countless persons at these affairs in the past quarter of a century. Results have been worth the expense and effort. An embassy gala by or for a foreign leader rarely fails to promote interest in the visitor, his country and his embassy in Washington.

Occasionally, the main problem has been to keep these functions within smoothly operable bounds. It was not unusual that more than 1,500 eager souls, including several hundreds uninvited, thronged the Brazilian Embassy to meet Brazil's President-elect Kubitschek on his semiofficial visit in 1956, nor that engraved admittance cards later were to become the only guarantees for entry at similar receptions.

Always alert to Embassy Row's social calendar, intruders crash many national-day celebrations, but only climbers with a high tolerance for probable rebuff head for parties tied in with official visits.

Since few ambassadorial residences are spacious enough to take care of more than a thousand guests, such functions frequently are held elsewhere. The Pan American Union, with its great, flag-draped hall can accommodate a multitude and is occasionally used for fetes given by foreign notables. More often they greet their guests in hotels that have enormous ballrooms and are geared to the business of providing bounteous buffets for wall-to-wall crushes, with a minimum of strain on hosts and embassy staffs.

The splendor that can be attained in a hotel setting was illustrated at galas given by Hassan II of Morocco on two trips to Washington. The first, during his 1963 state visit, was a distinctive stimulant to increased awareness of opulent Arab hospitality, which already had begun to impress habitués of Embassy Row. Wearing a royal *djellaba* and a fez with a dented crown, His Majesty and his sister Princess Lalla Nezha, in an elaborately embroidered caftan, looked as if they might have stepped straight out of the "Arabian Nights" to join Moroccan Ambassador Ali Bengelloun in the Chinese Room of the Mayflower Hotel. Receiving with them were Mme. Bengelloun, also in caftan, and members of His Majesty's official party.

In the adjoining ballroom, a sixteen-foot buffet and adjoining tables offered a sumptuous buffet, including French, Arab and American specialties, ranging from *canard ravennais au foie gras* (duck in aspic with foie gras) and *chaud frois de paisana plummage* (pheasant with feather embellishment) to whole roast lambs stuffed with rice and pancakes with Southern fried chicken, along with seven kinds of cheese and an assortment of salads. The hors d'oeuvres table featured melon with prosciutto, caviar, jumbo shrimp, salmon, herring and stuffed eggs, and the dessert table was loaded with Arab sweets around a sugar mosque. Case after case of vintage champagne, bonded liquor and soft drinks, supplied by the embassy, supplemented the feast for 2,000 invited guests. The party cost the Moroccan government fifteen dollars a head.

An orchestra played softly throughout the party. Masses of gladioli, carnations and greenery sprouted from urns around the rooms and towered in three bouquets on the long buffet table. A cordon of newsreel and still photographers, reporters and spotlights focused on the King as he arrived at 6 A.M. to welcome the diplomatic contingent and a galaxy of United States officials, while other guests in a steadily lengthening queue waited outside to be received. But only those admitted in the vanguard—a couple of hundred at most—had a chance to meet His Majesty. Others, if they saw him at all, merely glimpsed him as he left the receiving line and took off with the ambassador toward the ballroom, followed by a retinue of Moroccans and photographers.

Guests already clustering around the buffet were hardly aware of His Majesty's presence as he surveyed the central buffet and then stopped at the dessert table. Presently, he selected a walnut-sized ball of *el majoun* (honey-nut sweet), which he munched as he proceeded to the nearest exit—at 7:10.

Ambassador Bengelloun returned to the Chinese Room to continue receiving with Princess Lalla Nezha and Mme. Bengelloun and to explain that His Majesty had to get back to the embassy "to receive an important message from Rabat."

When King Hassan, after an even shorter stay, left his

second Washington reception in February 1967, disappointed arrivals began to catch on that he was not inclined to endless handshaking, even when the ranking guest—in this instance, Vice President Humphrey—had not yet arrived.

This reception, even more dazzling than His Majesty's first in Washington, was given in the vast Regency Room of the Shoreham Hotel. Beneath a red and green striped pavilion banked with flowers and set off with flags of Morocco and the United States, along with his own larger-than-life photograph, the royal host received with his sister Princess Lalla Aicha (Morocco's ambassador to Britain) and his new ambassador to the United States and Mme. Laraki.

An enormous center table groaned beneath an array of Moroccan delicacies, including the national dish, *couscous*, lamb bulging with saffron rice, and rich confections, as well as a full complement of French and American dishes.

Music of violin quartets emanated from each corner of the ballroom, and eight Moroccans in native garb seated on the floor at the far end poured tea from silver samovars and enlightened the curious with the stock statement: "We are down from our mission in New York to serve our king and his guests."

The party got off to a late start. Invited to be there at 5:30, foreign envoys and wives had assembled in the salon across the hallway, had lined up according to precedence and had waited half an hour before the doors to the Regency Room opened and they filed in to be received.

The host had finished with them and had welcomed a few of the remaining 1,500 guests, when the parade stopped, presumably to give His Majesty a brief reprieve. Within five minutes, receiving was resumed by Ambassador and Mme. Laraki. The King had disappeared—at 6:55.

When the Vice President coasted in, twenty minutes later, whispered queries rippled through the crowd. Had

His Majesty known the Vice President was to be there? If so, why the premature departure? Was it a royal snub? Was a royal apology expected?

Not at all, according to genial Hubert H. Humphrey. "I'm the one to apologize," he said to Ambassador and Mme. Laraki as they welcomed him. "I spent an hour and a half with His Majesty this afternoon and told him my jammed schedule might keep me from getting here. He said he probably wouldn't stay long after receiving the diplomats." The Vice President added that when he found he could make it, his office called the hotel to inquire whether or not the King was still on hand. He was, at the time, but apparently he was not informed that the Vice President was on his way.

If the ranking guest had been prompt, the royal departure would have caused little comment, if any. Unless he is honoring the President of the United States, the visiting luminary rarely lingers after the hour set for his ambassador to take over as host.

In any case, the reception was a sensational success, with the Vice President in the spotlight for thirty minutes, and hundreds staying on, and on. The ravished buffet was finally abandoned around 9:45, three quarters of an hour after the music had stopped and most of the embassy staff had gone.

The Moroccan monarch's hospitality, with and without his presence, may never be surpassed in Washington, yet for plausible reasons neither of his big soirees had the headline attractions of a number of receptions given by visiting chiefs of state in recent years with our President and First Lady as honor guests.

The chief executive's presence at such events is contingent on factors within what is called "the frame of reference," meaning what is expected at the time of the visit and the category of the visit. Since the Roosevelt administration it has been customary for state guests to entertain the president in return for the White House dinner honoring them. But the type of return function has varied in recent years.

State visitors, after being feted at the White House (or Blair House), entertained President and Mrs. Truman at dinner. The same routine was followed during the Eisenhower administration. Several foreign leaders similarly honored President and Mrs. Kennedy, but in time embassy luncheons sometimes replaced dinners as the return social courtesy for dinners at the White House.

JFK was entertained at a luncheon by Hassan II on his state visit in 1963, but the pattern had changed and his call was under a different category when he returned in 1967— on an informal working visit "for the specific purpose of holding substantive discussions." He was honored at a White House dinner, but no return party for President Johnson was expected.

Had His Majesty been on a state visit the second time, his Shoreham gala would have been in honor of President and Mrs. Johnson; for, by then, the reception had replaced the luncheon as the customary return entertainment by state or official guests.

The change was initiated in the spring of 1962 in connection with a new classification—the Presidential Guest, invited for a two-day visit; and the new pattern included a reception for our chief executive with the visitor as host.

Norway's Prime Minister Einar Gerhardsen and Mme. Gerhardsen were the first presidential guests thus to honor President and Mrs. Kennedy. The 5:30 reception took place at Blair House, and the company of 400 largely comprised foreign envoys and high United States officialdom.

The locale for similar parties shifted within a few months. Presidential Guests in February 1963 were Venezuela's President Rómulo Betancourt and Señora de Betancourt, who had warmly welcomed President and Mrs. Kennedy in Caracas the previous year. On the evening of their arrival in Washington, the visitors dined at the White House. The following day, they honored their White House hosts at a reception at the Venezuelan Embassy.

It was a two-part affair, with the two Presidents and First Ladies in line to greet diplomats and officials for the first hour and new Venezuelan Ambassador and Señora de Tejera-Paris receiving several hundred others after the Kennedys had left.

State guests generally continued to entertain President and Mrs. Kennedy at dinner; but there were more visitors at other levels in 1963, and the President began to make headlines by unscheduled appearances at their late afternoon parties. The week after the Venezuelan to-do, he happily surprised hundreds, including the news media, by dropping in at the Embassy of Laos for the reception given by Laotian King Sri Vatthana, who was on a private visit to Washington.

Other chiefs of state who bid successfully for JFK's impromptu presence at their receptions included President Mwalimu Julius K. Nyerere of Tanganyika (later Tanzania), in July 1963. The newly independent African country had not yet acquired an embassy residence, and Blair House was being renovated. The visitor stayed at the Foxhall Road home of Protocol Chief Angier Biddle Duke, and it was there that the forty-two-year-old son of a Zanaki chieftain welcomed President Kennedy and with him received African and Commonwealth diplomats and State Department officials and their wives.

As such parties go, this one was small—there were fewer than 200 guests—but it made headlines for Tanganyika, and also for Dr. Martin Luther King, who arrived ten minutes after the President had departed. Immediately surrounded by African diplomats and the press, Dr. King stayed for an hour, talked at length about the scheduled August 18 March on Washington and predicted that it would be "the greatest peaceful demonstration ever held."

By the time President and Mrs. Kennedy appeared unexpectedly with Ireland's Prime Minister and Mrs. Sean Lemas at the Irish Embassy's mammoth reception at the Mayflower in October 1963, partygoers bidden to receptions given by or for visiting notables began arriving well in advance of the scheduled hour with high hopes of meeting the President of the United States.

JFK set a popular precedent; Johnson continued and expanded it. With Mrs. Johnson, he attended receptions given by state visitors, standing cheerfully with his hosts to receive hundreds, amid the hubbub of grinding television cameras, glaring lights, photographers jockeying for position and swarms of reporters. Later, he often mingled with the crowd and stayed well past the hour when he might justifiably have left.

"He's never happier than when surrounded by a jam such as this," said one of his intimates, observing LBJ, arm in arm with Israel's Premier Levi Eshkol as they moved through the mob at the latter's Mayflower reception in June 1964. "He'll probably hold a conference with his host before he leaves." He did just that. Joined by Mrs. Johnson, Mme. Eshkol and Israeli Ambassador and Mme. Harman, the President stopped in the middle of the ballroom and discussed Israel's water problem with the Prime Minister, as reporters hovered around and cameras clicked.

The staid social script bored LBJ, and his talent for the ad lib resulted in some startling social performances. The Indian Embassy was the setting for one, during Prime Minister Indira Gandhi's visit in March 1966.

Mme. Gandhi's call was labeled as official, but it was very much a working visit. She stayed at Blair House but spent much of her time in conferences at the White House and the State Department, in addition to attending social functions.

The White House dinner for her was one of the most brilliant ever given by President and Mrs. Johnson. The following late afternoon, she received ambassadors and their wives at the Indian Embassy and then greeted several hundred other guests with Ambassador and Mme. Nehru as hosts. A dinner in honor of Vice President and Mrs. Humphrey was set for 8:30.

President and Mrs. Johnson had been invited to the reception, but since LBJ the evening before had told Mme. Gandhi that they probably would not be able to attend because of his tight working schedule, she did not expect them.

She was visibly surprised, therefore, and so were Ambassador and Mme. Nehru, when the President and his daughter Luci arrived at 7:30. "I got caught up with my work," he said to Mme. Gandhi. "I wanted to come to talk a while and tell you good-by. Lady Bird sent Luci in her place." After the reception ended and dinner guests began to arrive, the President was still there, talking to Mme. Gandhi, while Luci entertained Mme. Gandhi's two sons.

Most of the dinner company had gathered by 8:20, and President and the Prime Minister, now comfortably seated, continued their conference. At 8:25, Mme. Nehru invited him to stay to dinner.

"No," he said, dejectedly. "It wouldn't be right, with everybody but me in black tie. But may I stay a little longer?"

At 8:40, when all the dinner guests had arrived, dressed to the nines, he told Mme. Nehru he would like to remain for dinner. Luci, he added, would "go along home and take the boys with her."

"Shall I call Mrs. Johnson and ask her to join us?" asked Mme. Nehru.

"Don't bother," he replied. "Lady Bird's not feeling well. She has already gone to bed. She won't mind if I stay."

Happily flabbergasted embassy aides rallied to the emergency, and the seating was rearranged so that the President could be in the place of highest honor, on Mme. Gandhi's right. Meanwhile, one invited guest had disappeared. He was India's deputy commissioner to London, and he had volunteered to drop out because the embassy dining room seats only forty.

The event marked the first time a president of the United States wearing a business suit had ever attended a black-tie embassy dinner. He made the most of the precedent. Concluding his toast to the Prime Minister, he said, "I'm the man who came to talk and stayed for dinner."

He stayed on for coffee and liqueurs and continued talking until shortly before midnight, when he took his leave, saying he had "never attended a better party."

He had called signal attention to Mme. Gandhi's visit. The Indians loved it. "It was a courtesy, indeed, to our Prime Minister," said Ambassador Nehru, later. "And having the President as a dinner guest was a pleasure for all of us."

LBJ's flair for working embassy receptions on a relaxed basis, and staying around for quite a while, was evinced early in his administration when he and Mrs. Johnson were honored in 1964 by their first royal visitor, King Hussein of Jordan. The party at the Mayflower was planned along the usual lines, with foreign mission chiefs invited to His Majesty's party at half past five and others from six to eight o'clock, as guests of the Jordanian Ambassador and Mme. Juma.

President and Mrs. Johnson joined His Majesty in the Chinese Room, which resembled a Hollywood set with cameras and lights trained on the principals. A battalion of reporters, kept just out of earshot by security men, noted every gesture of President and King as the ambassadorial corps and a few officials were received.

Then the spotlights went off, and newsreel and still photographers were asked to leave. As they carted out their equipment, the President drew the King aside and engaged him in an apparently serious conversation. The exchange continued for ten minutes, while Ambassador and Mme. Juma chatted with Mrs. Johnson and hundreds waited to be received. Dozens of others, already inside, gave up hopes of being welcomed and made for the buffet. Suddenly, the President, with the King following, plunged into the crowd en route to the ballroom, shaking hands with everyone in his path—waiters, musicians, old friends, casual acquaintances and utter strangers.

The spontaneous presidential tour ended at seven o'clock, when the honor guests were escorted to their limousine by His Majesty, Ambassador and Mme. Juma and Chief of Protocol Duke. But the Johnsons' departure was not immediate. The President had promised a couple of old friends that he would take them home, and they were nowhere in sight. He insisted that his hosts return to their party. They stayed until after the tardy pair arrived and the White House car pulled away.

It was 7:20 and King Hussein had a private dinner ahead. He asked for his limousine and left for Blair House, while Ambassador and Mme. Juma returned to the reception.

It had grown considerably during their absence. Some 300 persons had crashed the party and were mingling with the 800 invited guests. The Jordanians, diplomats to the core, appeared not to notice, but press comment on the unbidden inflow prompted envoys planning similar parties in the future to arrange for rigid collection of admittance cards at the door.

President and Mrs. Johnson, from then on, attended receptions given by U. S. government guests in the state or official category. Occasionally, LBJ also made unscheduled appearances at parties tendered by high-level dignitaries who visited Washington unofficially.

King Mwambutsa IV of Burundi was such a visitor in May 1964. The one big event slated for him was a reception, planned by his son-in-law and daughter, Burundi's Ambassador Leon Ndenzako and H.R.H. Princess R. Ndenzako. The President was not expected; but arrangements were made to transport the Royal Burundi drummers and Watusi dancers from the New York World's Fair to entertain the King and his guests at the Shoreham Hotel.

Things got off to an unpropitious start when the airline engaged to transport the troupe to Washington reneged after taking into account their long spears and outsized drums. Vexed at having to travel by bus, drummers and dancers were livid when the Secret Service negated their plan to accompany the King to his ceremonial welcome by President and Mrs. Johnson on the White House lawn. Ambassador Ndenzako was openly distressed. There were rumors that even His Majesty was miffed.

United States functionaries hastened to make amends by inviting the Burundis to perform in the State Department courtyard and by promising that Secretary Rusk and guests invited to Undersecretary Ball's luncheon in honor of His Majesty would be present. Up until an hour before the show, set for 12:15, there was no definite promise that the ruffled performers would cooperate. But there they were, with tribal drums throbbing, when Secretary Rusk, after welcoming the King on the State Department's brand new red carpet upstairs, arrived with him to join the assemblage.

A preview of the performance planned for the Burundi Embassy reception, the forty-five-minute spectacular featured ten drummers in red and white togas and eleven towering Watusis in raffia-fringed leopard skins, monkey fur headgear and anklets of jingling bells. The only Western touch to their African garb were American tennis shoes. "Their bare feet can't take the cement," said an embassy spokesman. "They're used to dancing on the grass."

Shortly after the performance the President sent word to the King that the White House had been deluged with enthusiastic reports about "the dancers." His Majesty promptly invited the President to accompany him to the reception, where they would perform again.

There the President was at six o'clock, standing with His Majesty, as envoys and their wives filed by and a platoon of surprised photographers went into action.

The reception had gone on for perhaps fifteen minutes when drums at the far end of the room sounded an ear-splitting staccato that deepened into a steady, hypnotic throb. It was a signal that the show was ready to begin. The receiving line dispersed and proceeded to the area within a few feet of the frenetic performers.

The President did not stay through the entire exhibition. He missed the latter half—the Watusi dancing—but he stood spellbound while the royal drummers punctuated their jungle rhythms with dramatic vaults and whoops. Then he took a deep breath and whispered something to the King, and the two chatted amiably as they made for the door. Within minutes, His Majesty returned, wreathed in smiles, and the Watusis lunged into the spotlight.

The President had accomplished his purpose. Along with his subjects, King Mwambutsa was visibly pleased. "Naturally, we were delighted that the President of the United States came to our party," said the Burundi ambassador. "Who wouldn't be?"

An embassy aide added, "The President is a charming man, and a thoughtful one. He has soothed some bruised feelings. All is forgiven. And our *Mwame* is happy."

King Mwambutsa had reason to be "happy"—not only because the President attended his party but also because his kinetic performers made his reception unique in the annals of Washington. (However, had a crystal ball been available to the *Mwame*—and could he have interpreted its portents—he would have known that his lively party was his last as a king visiting our country; for a little more than a year later, while on a trip to Switzerland, he was displaced in a coup d'état that put his nineteen-year-old son on the throne—but not for long. Both the new King and the monarchy were deposed in November 1966, when

Colonel Michel Micombaro became president of the Republic of Burundi.)

Most receptions tendered by or for foreign visitors—particularly state guests—feature no special entertainment at all. The accent is on personages and a palatable repast, in the best possible surroundings.

As we have seen, such events often proceed with a fine flourish in hotel ballrooms, but an embassy mansion is an even more elegant setting.

Let us go behind the scenes for highlights on the planning and execution of a state visitor's reception in his own Washington embassy, a few years ago.

It was a Big Day in an ambassador's household. A 5:30 to 8:00 P.M. reception, with the envoy's visiting president as host and President and Mrs. Johnson as honor guests, was scheduled; and at 10 A.M. the household was in the final buzz of preparation for its grandest party of the year.

The logistics for such an event are as complicated as for an invading horde on the march, and its success involves multiple details, anticipated far in advance and discharged with timetable precision. Weeks before official announcement of the visit, the reception date had been set and plans were under way. Embassy personnel and wives had been individually assigned to explicit services and the domestic staff alerted as to necessary extra chores. Most important of all, a capital caterer, long experienced at big-time party operations, had been engaged.

The guest list and menu posed the first problems. A speculative head count, based on previous receptions, indicated that in addition to "must" guests, several hundred others could be included. By judicious selection in which the ambassador and his wife, the embassy staff and the United States Office of Protocol took part, the initial list of 1,400 names was drawn up. In succeeding weeks, it was to be revamped several times.

Restrictions other than space govern invitations on Embassy Row. The one hundred-odd nations having missions in Washington are constantly involved in feuds, rivalries, racial and religious prejudices and, sometimes, states of war. Theoretically, an envoy planning a party to honor our president is free to invite even antagonists and combatants among his colleagues—anyone, in fact, whose name appears in the State Department's *Diplomatic List.* In practice, an ambassador officially entertains only mission chiefs from countries with which his own has passably pleasant relations.

For this party, the diplomatic contingent, wives included, totaled 220—all to be received at 5:30, half an hour before the remainder of the company. On the "must" list, also, were the fourteen members of the visitor's official party, the Cabinet, the chief justice, congressional leaders and State Department officials who deal directly with the embassy— all with their wives. Additionally included were high brass from the military, personal friends, and the press.

From the moment news of the prospective visit hit the headlines, the ambassador and his wife were inundated with invitations, callers and telephone calls. The sudden outcrop of popularity was not unusual. From a socially ambitious sea it rises around an embassy every time a stellar event is in the offing, and the attention can swell into a tidal wave when a state visit is involved.

Shortly after the handsomely engraved invitations, with admittance cards carefully enclosed, had been posted and several hundred lucky persons began talking about their bids, complications multiplied.

Every able-bodied recipient who expected to be in town accepted "with pleasure" or, more properly, had "the honor to accept," but dozens asked to bring house guests with them. Within a week the initial list had increased by 150 names.

Concurrently to be dealt with were the hangers-on, the

has-beens and the never-wases, perpetual banes of a ranking diplomat's existence, who seldom if ever entertain and
yet manage to wangle enough embassy invitations to make
a complete set, year in and year out.

Through three harassed weeks, the social secretary was
swamped with passionate pleas and besieged with demands. An old hand at the game, she complied with plausible requests, pretended to ignore veiled threats and fielded
innumerable ploys by promising to take the matter up with
the ambassador. "You'd better," replied one persistent
climber. "If you don't, I'll take it up with President Johnson!"

As the invitation problem intensified, the ambassador's
wife ("Madame" to embassy and household staff), the
caterer, the embassy butler and cook were working on the
menu. Their lengthy conferences had been fraught with conflicting suggestions and uncertainty. For a week, butler and
cook had held out for "specialties of the homeland," such
as had been voraciously consumed by guests at the national-
day reception six months before. Madame wondered
whether repetition would be appreciated. The caterer mentioned that an "international" buffet might have more appeal to the majority.

Madame finally called in the ambassador and asked him
to make the decision. He sided with the caterer. Accordingly, an order went out for 7 Smithfield hams, 6 turkeys, 8
beef tongues (to be served with Cumberland sauce), 150
pounds of strip loin of beef, 4 20-pound salmon, 24 pounds
of galantine of capon, 20 pounds of lobster (for lobster
Newburg), 15 pounds of pâté de foie gras in aspic, 10 gallons of vegetable salad, 1,000 raspberry tarts, 50 dozen as-
sorted cakes, and 20 gallons of ice cream.

The embassy had a complete table service to take care of
a seated dinner for 60 and a reception for 500. The caterer
was instructed to provide additional china, serving dishes,

glassware, flatware and napkins and to employ 12 waiters, 2 captains, an announcer, a pantry girl, 3 cloakroom attendants and a doorman (still called a "carriage man" in nostalgic Washington).

During the month prior to the event the embassy's social calendar had included a tea for 200 women, 4 small luncheons and 3 dinners for 40 guests each. But with the presidential reception in the offing, innumerable special duties had devolved on the domestic staff of 7—butler, cook, 3 maids, valet and chauffeur.

They handled their extra chores as expected. By the morning of the big day, the entire mansion was the high-shine result of endless hours devoted to the black and white marble entrance hall, six enormous chandeliers, carpets, heavily carved Sheffield candelabra, Sèvres vases, bric-à-brac, draperies and ornate staircase.

Meanwhile the embassy staff had concentrated on numerous assignments. Secret Service agents had been consulted and shown through and around the embassy. Arrangements had been made for four District police officers to be posted in the area at least an hour before the party and to stay there for its duration. A chart of the drawing room had been made to indicate location of the receiving line, spotlights and camera and newsreel equipment.

A florist and two helpers, after spending four hours at the embassy, had determined how many bouquets and how much greenery would be needed and where it should be placed to give the rooms an extraordinarily festive air.

In the mansion's amply stocked cellar, the butler had set aside 20 cases of champagne, 40 cases of Scotch and bourbon and 6 cases of gin and had ordered 20 cases of soft drinks and 10 gallons of tomato juice. He had also supervised the placement of the four bars and figured out how they would be manned, supplied and replenished.

At noon of the reception day, terminal chores were

being checked off on various individual lists. Someone's list had on it refrigeration and handling as the last food supplies arrived. Someone's list noted extending the dining room table full length, setting up another big table in the adjoining room and covering both with damask cloths. Another list called for placement of plates, flatware, napkins and serving dishes; another, the installation of lights and other television equipment in the drawing room and at the entrance.

The invitation list continued to plague the social secretary. With entries carefully marked "accepted," "regrets," "with guest" or "uncertain," the total changed at every ring of the telephone. At 12:30, she shut off the instrument and closeted herself with a typist to make the final list, in triplicate.

At midafternoon, the caterer was in command of a battalion, handling last-minute chores in kitchen and dining room. Fresh flowers and greenery, in twelve enormous arrangements, were in place—four as background for the receiving line in the drawing room, two flanking the staircase, four filling corners of the large reception salon and the others centering the buffets.

At 4:45, when the ambassador left for Blair House to collect his president and official party, everything was ready. Television cameramen were checking equipment; photographers and reporters were already arriving. A quarter of an hour later, Madame, freshly coiffed and trimly turned out in a street-length frock of blue brocade, was in the drawing room, where the embassy counselor was giving directions to the announcer.

At 5:15, a flurry in the crowd outside the embassy heralded the arrival of the visiting president and his party. As they proceeded to the drawing room, the ambassador waited at the entrance to welcome the honor guests. Other guests were already there in number, and envoys and wives, lined up according to precedence, were also waiting when the White House limousine pulled up to the entrance, and cameras went into action. Within a few minutes President and Mrs. Johnson had been ushered into the drawing room and were in line with the hosts, to receive the foreign corps first and then the hundreds of others in the company.

The embassy production resulting from two months of tedious planning and concentrated teamwork was on.

6

Tiptoe Diplomacy

Aᴌᴛʜᴏᴜɢʜ ɪᴛ ɪs ᴀɴᴀᴛʜᴇᴍᴀ to United States taxpayers, expected to obey laws that some 6,000 privileged foreigners in and around the District of Columbia can break without fear of prosecution, diplomatic immunity goes back a long way.

Charles W. Thayer in his book *Diplomat* suggests that the first person to which the system applied probably was a caveman who visited a neighbor to arrange a truce and managed to get home alive. Homer wrote that the Trojans were appalled when Antimachus suggested the slaughter of emissaries sent to negotiate the return of Helen; and, although questionably regarded in the host country, peace legates from Hittite King Khetesan to Ramses II of Egypt were protected by immunity and sent home safely in 1272 B.C.

Violation of diplomatic immunity has even caused war. According to the Second Book of Samuel, King David waged war on the Ammonites because the envoys he dispatched to King Hanum's coronation were seized as spies, had half their beards shaved off and were publicly stripped to the buff.

Greek and Roman rulers through the earlier centuries after Christ took pains to protect diplomats from prosecution, and by the sixteenth century it was fairly well established that monarchal representatives were to be accorded the same privileges and protection as would be given their rulers when visiting on foreign soil.

The generally persisting practice eventually gave rise to an international law, passed for the specific purpose of safeguarding the "function" of the diplomat. This was to ensure his freedom to conduct his affairs unhampered by impeding and perhaps embarrassing lawsuits.

Since the founding of the Republic, the United States has observed diplomatic immunity according to the English statute of Queen Anne, which was enacted in 1708, after a Russian representative in London was thrashed by merchants to whom he was indebted and then imprisoned.

The law today, established by the 1815 Congress of Vienna and reaffirmed by eighty-four nations at the Second Congress of Vienna in 1961, simply means that a diplomat is not subject to local law enforcement, civil or criminal. It does not give him the right to break the law, but it guards him from prosecution.

Solid penalties are set out for immunity violations, including a $5,000 maximum fine and three years in jail for assaulting a diplomat and a $10,000 fine plus a ten-year sentence if the assault is with a deadly weapon. There is also a maximum sentence of three years in jail for anyone who *attempts* to sue or prosecute a diplomat or who tries to attach his possessions. Immunity covers not only the envoy but also his aides and family, and sometimes his servants, and extends to his residence and chancery, which cannot be invaded and searched under any circumstances.

Hand in hand with immunity—indeed, an integral part of it—are special diplomatic privileges. One is duty-free import. During Prohibition in the United States, even mediocre diplomatic staffs rode a high wave of popularity when they kept an ample supply of the very best liquor and served it freely at their parties. Of course, the privilege that has become a constant source of irritation to the traffic-harassed American is the special license plate to which the diplomat is entitled: DPL in the United States and CD (*Corps Diplomatique*) in other national capitals.

Citizens with little or no conception of the actual need for diplomatic immunity constantly complain about the DPL limousines that pull up to curbs restricted to their own vehicles and sometimes even block driveways to their residences. They are naturally incensed when their lives are endangered by privileged foreigners who ignore traffic lights and drive at breakneck speed.

The basic reason for diplomatic immunity, with all the privileges it implies, is obvious. It is a guarantee for comparative protection and privilege for the host nations' own representatives abroad. Violations can bring swift retaliation in other countries. Washington police, well aware of this, for years did not dare do more than give polite warnings to DPL traffic violators. The average effort was no more effectual than was that of an officer who hailed an Ecuadorian attaché and reminded him that he was leaving his car squarely in front of a "No Parking" sign on downtown Connecticut Avenue. "Well, it's none of *your* damn business!" retorted the offender and took off in a huff, leaving the policeman angry—but helpless.

By comparison, in the early 1930s, an Elkton, Maryland, constable who was unversed on diplomatic immunity precipitated an international incident by taking an Iranian envoy, his wife and chauffeur into custody after stopping their speeding limousine on the highway.

The portly emissary invoked diplomatic immunity by screaming that he was the Iranian minister. The constable countered that he had "heard of Baptist ministers and Presbyterian ministers, but never an Iranian minister" and hauled him and his companions off to the station.

Within minutes the envoy was telling it to the police judge, who, after a telephone call to Washington, released

the indignant trio. Profuse apologies from the secretary of
state and the governor of Maryland followed, but the diplomat was inconsolable and insistent that the "rude policeman" be dismissed. Elkton's Town Council promptly fired
the constable, only to reinstate him a week later.

After voicing dire hints of retaliation from his government, the minister secluded himself in his legation and
pouted, but his shah did not take up the squabble. Instead,
his imperial majesty recalled the minister and left an attaché as head of the legation.

Washington had a field day with "L'Affaire Elkton,"
while the new chargé d'affaires promptly busied himself by
sending out 700 invitations to a reception in honor of the
shah's birthday. Two days before the party, the invitations
were recalled with the explanation that the prospective host
was ill. Six days later, the legation furnishings were put up
for auction and the chargé and his small staff departed, on
order of the shah, who also closed all his diplomatic installations in America. Iran did not send another envoy to the
United States for almost ten years.

The intelligent emissary, ever mindful that his prime job
is to make friends and develop the confidence of those with
whom he deals in the host country, generally abides by
local laws and is quick to apologize when he happens to
transgress. Lord Lothian, British ambassador in 1940, made
a friend and established a bond with a state trooper when
his DPL car broke the fifty-five-mile speed limit on a Virginia highway. The agitated chauffeur was spluttering
about diplomatic immunity, when the envoy shushed him—
and profusely apologized to the trooper. The lengthy conversation that ensued touched on other topics, and by the
time Lord Lothian left the scene, he and the trooper were
virtually relatives, having discovered that they had a common
forebear among the earliest English settlers in Virginia.

The 1961 Vienna Convention of Diplomatic Relations, clarifying the 1709 law, specifies in Article 41 that "without prejudice to their privileges and immunities, it is the duty of the person enjoying such privileges and immunities to respect the laws and regulations of the receiving State. They also have a duty not to interfere in the internal affairs of that State." When a chief of mission flagrantly abuses diplomatic courtesy, particularly in regard to interference in internal affairs, the host government has stringent recourses. It can ask the offender's country to recall him, declare him *persona non grata* or "hand him his passport," which means he is dismissed without notice. These measures usually are taken only in cases of improper political activities, but they can also be invoked for personal reasons. Whatever the cause, if the dismissed diplomat refuses to leave the country, his usefulness ceases, for he no longer has access to the State Department.

In the early days of our Republic, several envoys were declared *personae non gratae* for unseemly behavior. The first was French Minister Genêt, who in 1792 became "unwelcome" because he had openly solicited funds in America to underwrite privateers against the British.

One of the most notorious instances of enforced withdrawal had to do with British Minister Sir Lionel Sackville-West, during the 1888 presidential campaign. A purported letter from an American friend to Sackville-West asked advice on how a United States citizen should vote in the coming election. The reply advised "for Grover Cleveland because he is a conciliatory President" (meaning, to the British) and enclosed a newspaper clipping bearing out that impression. Cleveland's Republican opponents published the minister's letter, much to the President's embarrassment. He demanded Sackville-West's recall and, without waiting for a reply from London, handed him his passport.

Disparaging remarks about President McKinley in a personal letter written by the Spanish minister came to light in

Havana in 1898, and the diplomat departed from Washington shortly afterward, *persona non grata.*

Before the proliferation of nations following World War II, less than fifty envoys at most, with their staffs and families, made up the diplomatic corps in Washington. DPL-licensed cars posed comparatively few problems in a city still unperturbed by traffic congestion. Friction between the diplomatic community and United States citizens has intensified in the past generation in direct proportion to the increase of residents, cars and government installations, both foreign and domestic.

With a diplomatic corps more than twice the size it was a generation ago, the hazards of diplomatic immunity as it applies to traffic infractions, and sometimes traffic disasters, have been sharply pointed up in recent years. There have also been numerous salutary indications that trustworthy diplomats have due consideration for local laws, take care to obey them and expect their relatives and aides to do the same.

If for no other reason than that the wise diplomat is well aware that his status and influence depend strongly on the regard of those with whom he is personally acquainted, law infringements in the diplomatic corps are far less numerous than they are generally believed to be.

Occasionally, however, there are thoroughly publicized reminders that the internationally protective cloak is not a coverall for deliberate misdemeanors. A case in point pertained to a Belgian officer assigned in 1962 to the Washington staff of NATO, which, like the United Nations, has diplomatic immunity by treaty rather than by international law. Late one evening, the Belgian was driving his DPL-licensed Chevrolet on the wrong side of Kalorama Road, apparently thinking that it was a one-way street. A Volkswagen approached from the Connecticut Avenue intersection and the driver of the smaller vehicle sounded his horn.

The Belgian responded by gunning his car, hitting the other head-on and spinning it forty feet into the middle of Connecticut Avenue. Then he rammed it again, sideways, before speeding off down Kalorama Road.

A taxicab driver who saw the crash had followed the car at ninety miles an hour for eight blocks, when he noted the DPL tag and gave up the chase. But he got the license number for the police.

When they turned up at the Belgian's house at about midnight, they informed him that he had endangered the lives of the Volkswagen occupants and had left the car with smashed headlights, a shattered window and a huge dent in the side. In reply the Belgian reminded the police of his diplomatic immunity. "Besides," he was reported to say, "I didn't do *all that*. The other car was coming at me, and I said to my wife, 'It's a cute little car. Let's give it a nudge and get it out of the way.'"

After the mutilated car was pictured the following day in a newspaper, with a full account of the wreck and a head-line indicating that the accident was caused by a DPL-licensed driver, the Volkswagen owner got swift assurance from the State Department that diplomatic immunity did not cover such deliberate breaking of the law and that the violator would be held responsible for all damages.

He was; and he paid the full cost—$500. He was also promptly recalled.

In 1959, diplomatic immunity saved the Irish minister's son from court action in Washington after the automobile he was driving knocked down a woman and killed her. The broken-hearted father promptly took the boy back to Ireland and shortly thereafter resigned his post.

Several fathers in the diplomatic corps have seen to it that their sons learned early that even minor offenses against local laws should not go unpunished. When the son of a Paraguayan minister skidded his speeding car onto a private lawn while being pursued by police, the envoy apologized, ordered the boy to apologize and to pay full damages and gave the entire story to a newspaper.

A British Embassy counselor, when informed that his son had been ticketed a second time for speeding but had been excused from a hearing on revocation of his driving permit, ordered the boy to turn in his driving license and apologize to the police. The British Embassy promptly notified the State Department of the infraction and of the counselor's insistence that his son be barred from driving until authorization was granted through the normal channels.

Prior to 1965, only diplomatic officers in embassies and legations—envoys down to attachés—had DPL licenses. Other employees had the same kind of plates as local automobile owners. This situation caused confusion when tickets on the illegally parked cars of diplomats were ignored. When warrants were issued and attempts were made to serve them, the police ran afoul of diplomatic immunity.

To clarify the situation, the State Department in 1965 drew up a "blue list" and a "white list" for diplomatic license plates. The blue list comprised names of ambassadors and ministers and their top aides—604 in all—who were entitled to DPL tags with the compliments of Uncle Sam. On the white list were 2,200 others covered by diplomatic immunity but who had to pay for their license plates. These were designated WN, meaning nothing at all except that the holders could not be prosecuted for traffic violations.

For some time before 1965, wrought-up American citizens had been inundating the State Department with complaints of traffic infractions by the diplomatic corps. The State Department then put the foreigners on notice that the issuance of tickets and summonses did not violate diplomatic immunity and that in the future fines would be levied and should be paid.

A press release from the State Department emphasized the "belief that members of the diplomatic missions should be responsible for operating their automobiles in accordance with local traffic laws and regulations," but took note of "a serious shortage of parking space near certain chanceries" and expressed the hope that "these problems will be resolved in the next few weeks." There was an additional softening addendum: "Until this has been done, the Department will not count, under its new policy, parking violation notices received by diplomats from those foreign chanceries lacking sufficient parking space, provided the notices are received during normal working hours and in the vicinity of the chanceries where these diplomats work."

In meetings with the dean of the foreign corps, State Department officials fully explained the proposed policy and spelled out that diplomats who disobeyed would be issued no more license tags. He was asked to convey the information and at the same time to stress that "In no circumstances, of course, will diplomatic officials be subject to arrest or detention for failure to pay such charges." Then the State Department officially notified all missions that the policy would go into effect in the near future.

Howls of protest resounded through the diplomatic community and precipitated pointed hints of retaliation to American diplomats abroad. Suggested reprisals included everything from ticketing cars of United States personnel to draining of the embassy swimming pool in an African country where the water shortage is acute.

African envoys were particularly annoyed. Meeting with the dean of the African diplomatic corps, Dr. Mostafa Kamel, ambassador of the United Arab Republic, they appointed him, along with the ambassadors of Liberia and Sudan, to call upon the dean of the diplomatic corps with the request that he register protest with Secretary Rusk.

Three days after the announcement of the policy, United States diplomats in the Philippines felt the retaliation lash. Manila's Mayor Antonio Villegas ordered police, "as a matter of reciprocity," to concentrate on American traffic offenders and a motorcycle squad was posted outside the

American Embassy gates to trail cars and hand out tickets. United States Minister Richard M. Service received one.

Back in Washington, DPL traffic infringement continued to bring swift invocation of diplomatic immunity and repeated reminders of possible retaliation abroad. One incident in April 1964 involved a Nigerian Embassy attaché whose speeding car was observed on Georgia Avenue and followed by a couple of police scout-car privates. When they caught up with the diplomat and motioned him to the curb, he responded by stepping on his accelerator and whipping away at ninety miles an hour. After pursuing for fourteen blocks, the privates managed to stop the car. When they noted its DPL license, they summoned two officers to the scene, and the four went into a huddle to determine what could be done. The prompt answer was nothing, since the lawbreaker had diplomatic immunity. One of the officers simply drove him home.

Later, when newspaper reporters asked the attaché what had happened, he referred them to the Nigerian second secretary, who said that his colleague had been in Washington only a year and had become "nervous" when he lost his way in an unfamiliar section of the city. The spokesman further observed, "Diplomacy is a reciprocal thing. And don't forget that the United States also has representatives in Nigeria."

A few diplomats who had been habitual traffic violators fell into line with the law and caused no more trouble. A member of the Indian Embassy made history in May 1964 when he voluntarily appeared before Chief Judge John Smith, Jr., of the District Court and offered to pay for all the parking tickets and warrants he had received.

Impressed and surprised, Judge Smith complimented the Indian on his "forthrightedness," dismissed the warrants and told the repentant he could settle with the Central Violations Bureau for seventy-seven dollars, the charge for the tickets.

The plan to withhold new DPL plates from diplomats already at odds with traffic authorities was tested in June 1964, when the director of the Department of Motor Vehicles stated that the Paraguayan military and naval attaché would not be issued new tags. The director added that his office had refused to issue plates to thirteen other diplomats who had been involved in accidents and carried no insurance. His position regarding the Paraguayan pertained to an incident in 1962 when the diplomat was driving on an icy street in Chevy Chase and skidded into two parked cars, with a resultant $700 damage. The attaché had argued that a broken fire hydrant, for which the city was responsible, caused the slick pavement. He was uninsured; he posted no bond.

Traffic authorities were still vexed by the problem of DPL lawbreakers in 1965 when, early in the year, it was noted that fifty-four diplomats (or their chauffeurs) from twenty-seven countries had received an average of ten parking tickets each and had not paid for them.

None of the fifty-four offenders was an envoy. The State Department sent out a polite letter to the effect that it "would be grateful if Their Excellencies and Messieurs of the Chiefs of Missions would take whatever steps are necessary to insure that these (54) persons avoid such violations in the future" and indicated that issuance of free diplomatic license plates for 1966 would not be authorized "for those persons who were issued an excessive number of citation tickets in 1965."

Ensuing grumbling from annoyed American citizens prompted a reminder from Richard T. Salazar, assistant chief of protocol for special services, that the 54 violators were "less than one per cent of the 6,000 diplomats and their families who drive cars with DPL license plates. We used to get a lot of complaints about diplomatic cars parked in front of hydrants or blocking driveways; but in the last year, we have had very few complaints from the public."

Statistics compiled by the Central Violations Bureau seemed to bear out Salazar's statement. Certainly they indicated a marked improvement over the 11,000 "warning notices" that had been posted on illegally parked DPL cars in a previous year.

But although the situation in Washington was better, the number of diplomats caught speeding on highways outside the city was still causing serious concern on Capitol Hill.

In April 1965, the chauffeur-driven limousine bearing the ambassador of Sierra Leone had been clocked at ninety miles an hour on the Jersey Turnpike when it was stopped by a state trooper who told the chauffeur that he was breaking the speed limit. According to the officer, the envoy bellowed from the back of the car, "You do not tell me! I have made a note of your discourtesy and using my time. We are in a hurry."

Mindful of diplomatic immunity, the trooper allowed the car to proceed but followed it all the way to Newark and recorded its speed at ninety-five miles an hour. Turnpike Director Thomas J. Flanagan dispatched a report to Chief of Protocol Lloyd N. Hand, who had another version of the incident from the ambassador. When his car was stopped, said His Excellency, he had told the trooper to speak to his chauffeur, who had been subsequently dismissed. "It is preposterous to accuse me of abusing my diplomatic privileges," the envoy insisted. Apparently Hand took him at his word.

In any event, the matter would have ended there had Flanagan not appealed to New Jersey's Senator Clifford P. Case. By that time, the latter's concern had been heightened by reports of several similar incidents, including one in July, when the Senegalese ambassador's car, going eighty-three miles an hour, was escorted off the Jersey Turnpike by a state trooper. The reprimanded envoy, in high dudgeon, complained to the State Department; and when Hand questioned New Jersey traffic authorities as to whether the action

had been "discriminatory," they appealed again to Senator
Case. He asked for a summation of previous offenses and
learned that within the preceding nine years state troopers
had noted forty-four serious violations by diplomats from
thirty-two countries.

Senator Case's report to the State Department brought
results. In August 1965, a letter signed by an assistant secretary of state went to the Senate (where it was read and
applauded), indicating that unless traffic laws henceforth
were heeded by diplomats—and fines paid—certain steps
would be taken. Included was the reiterated policy of with-
holding future DPL license plates from offenders. The letter
also clearly stated that persons guilty of "persistent or more
serious traffic infringements" might be declared *personae
non gratae*.

Diplomatic traffic infractions were becoming fewer by
1966. No 1966 license tags had been withheld, but the State
Department pointedly requested twenty-six violators to pay
fines. Six did, to the total of $300. The others promised to
pay.

Immunity remained inviolate, of course, and compliance
with traffic laws continued to be largely up to the diplomats
themselves—but only for the time being. By 1967, even the
State Department was in a no-nonsense mood about offenders. In that year, the issuance of six DPL license plates was
withheld until violators from four nations, with a total of
106 parking tickets, paid long overdue fines.

Members of the Soviet Embassy consistently got more
parking tickets than other diplomats, but with some reason
they laid the responsibility to the lack of adequate parking
space near their embassy at 16th and L Streets.

"We simply do not have room for the cars necessary to
carry on our business," said Soviet Ambassador Anatoliy
Dobrynin, after the crackdown on parking infringements
was announced.

He had a talking point there. District regulations allow a

maximum of sixty yards for DPL cars in the area of a diplomatic installation. Such space will take care of not more
than three standard-sized cars and, at most, seven smaller
vehicles. With the largest diplomatic staff in Washington,
the Soviet Embassy has more than fifty cars to accommodate daily. The mammoth living-and-working operation on
a jammed thoroughfare had long posed an apparently un-
solvable parking problem. The Russians met it for years
by ignoring no parking signs on a wholesale basis and ac-
cumulating 1,500 parking tickets in the six months immediately before the State Department's injunction.

The State Department at that time teamed with District
officials to provide additional parking facilities for the Russians and came up with space for five or six more cars on
nearby L Street, which was promptly designated "RESERVED
—CARS ONLY U.S.S.R." Nevertheless, Soviet diplomats got
1,700 parking tickets the following year, and the annual
average since has been about the same.

"The only answer is more space, a lot more space," said
Ambassador Dobrynin. "We must have larger working and
living quarters and an adequate area for our cars."

Looking for a new location, he was soon to discover another perplexing situation: embassies and chanceries were no
longer welcome in select residential neighborhoods of Washington.

7

Housing and Other Headaches

Until the end of 1935, 16th Street was the recognized "Embassy Row," with the majority of diplomatic missions ensconced in the area extending the seventeen blocks from the Soviet Embassy to the Mexican Embassy. But Massachusetts Avenue, for some time bidding for the title, had its claim significantly strengthened in 1931 when the British Embassy, then the largest diplomatic establishment in the city, moved to its new million-dollar headquarters on upper Massachusetts Avenue.

Little Latvia tipped the scales in December 1935, when it opened its legation on Massachusetts Avenue and brought that thoroughfare's total to an even dozen diplomatic residences. "Sixteenth Street lost another place in the race of the two streets for diplomatic honors," the *Washington Post* observed at the time.

Less than thirty years later, streets were no longer vying for "diplomatic honors." With 107 missions in the city in 1963 and a dozen more expected in the succeeding two years, residents of Massachusetts Avenue, along with those in other choice sections, wanted no more embassies in their midst.

The disenchantment, growing steadily since World War II, applied particularly to chanceries, the foreign missions' office buildings, which caused general traffic congestion, as well as parking problems for United States citizens.

"I can't have a 'No Parking' sign in front of my house," complained a capital dowager whose Massachusetts Avenue mansion is in the same block with two embassies. "I'm going to put up my own sign reading: 'No Parking: U.S. Taxpayer's Home.' "

The outcry against more embassies in sections where mission chiefs preferred them took no account of the fact that diplomatic business has much to do with the capital's reason for being and the need for conveniently located premises on which that business can be transacted.

When Thomas Jefferson and Pierre Charles L'Enfant were working out plans for the City of Washington, they recognized the new Republic's essential obligation to offer suitable quarters to foreign representatives and envisioned diplomatic establishments along the Mall, with easy access to the White House, the Capitol, and other United States government installations. On May 3, 1797, the Commission of Public Buildings and Grounds dispatched the following letter to English, Spanish, Portuguese and Dutch envoys:

> We are happy to have it in our power, with the approbation of the President of the United States, to offer to your nation a convenient site in the City of Washington for the residence of its Minister near the United States government buildings. Should your government be disposed to accept such a grant, it will give us great pleasure to accommodate you agreeably, both in point of situation and quantity of ground, wherever it may suit you to make the selection.

There were no takers. Foreign emissaries, then living in Philadelphia, were not enchanted with prospects of living, anywhere, in the fledgling capital; but they were at least polite enough to profess interest. Robert Liston, the British minister, on behalf of his diplomatic colleagues, discussed the matter with President Washington and on two occasions visited the suggested locale on the Potomac. Presumably, the diplomat was unimpressed. There is no record that he or any of the other three envoys to the new Republic seriously considered the proposal.

Later city planners took no account of providing for diplomats at all. Thomas Jefferson would have been appalled at the confusion in recent years, when the capital of the free world would not acceptably accommodate many of those who figure in the ever more important business of international relations.

In earlier decades, leading local citizens were eager to have diplomatic missions in their neighborhoods. Consequently, a number of the older countries established embassies and legations in select residential communities. From the late 1950s on, however, diplomats of new nations struggled to locate missions in desirable sections. At the same time, embassies that had outgrown their excellently situated establishments found it increasingly difficult either to enlarge them or to build new chanceries in comparable areas.

This was no problem before 1958, when there was virtually no regulation as to diplomatic real estate. A nation with money enough could establish its mission almost anywhere it chose. As a result, several mansions that might have been demolished in the wake of rising taxes and the servant exigency became embassies and legations, and choice tracts were purchased as sites for complexes to accommodate adjacent or combined diplomatic homes and offices in elite residential communities.

However, with the increase of independent nations, American home owners began to be disturbed. They saw that additional chanceries in their midst would bring the nuisance of expanded traffic, carelessly parked DPL cars and a commercial atmosphere that threatened the residential tone.

To quell residential Washington's growing resentment against additional chanceries, the District government in 1959 authorized the Board of Zoning Adjustments to exercise the "city's local prerogatives" in issuing permits for new embassies and legations. In other words, for the first time, foreign nations had to obtain approval of the board before locating missions.

The dual task of placating the American community and avoiding insult to foreign governments from then on has been a bone of contention between the State Department, which has the responsibility of keeping diplomats reasonably contented, and the District government and the Congress, which tend to think first of the United States taxpayer.

The situation became acute in 1960, when fourteen nations were combing the city for locations. One country after another chose a propitious place, only to arouse the ire of organized citizens in the vicinity.

By the autumn of 1963, Sweden, Canada, Spain, Algeria and Dahomey were among the countries sedulously seeking properties for chanceries, while several new African envoys could not find premises that were both suitable and within their budgets.

For eighteen months Australia had been looking for a convenient new chancery site. But Australian Ambassador John (later Sir John) Keith Waller endeared himself to Cleveland Avenue neighbors when he moved his office to a temporary location at 17th and I Streets and declined to rent the vacant building to another government. "I wouldn't particularly like to have an office structure right next door to my home," he said—and won the undying approbation of the neighborhood. In time, his own search was rewarded. He found a location at Scott Circle and proceeded with plans for a new chancery.

A few months before Malawi became the 35th independent state of Africa and the 114th in the world, David Rubadiri, who was slated to become the country's first ambassador to the United States, arrived in Washington to look for a residence and a chancery. Four months later, he and his two-member staff still were operating in a suite at the Shoreham Hotel ("Which our government cannot afford," he said), and prospects of finding permanent living quarters and an office were dim. His unhappiness was accentuated by the fact that he had wanted, particularly, to be established in a residence so he could entertain at a reception on July 6, 1964, his country's independence day. His plight came to the attention of John D. Rockefeller IV, who loaned his house for the event.

With the aid of the Afro-American Institute, Ambassador Rubadiri leased a residence on 28th Street a month later; but when he applied for a permit to have a chancery on Q Street near Massachusetts Avenue, area residents protested on the grounds of "traffic congestion." His Excellency saw the opposition as reflecting an attitude that had repeatedly confronted him in his housing search—that of United States citizens who correlated pigmentation with property deterioration.

"While looking for a house and an office, I was told over and over again that Asian and African diplomats ruin any place by dirtying the walls, starting fires, throwing loud parties," he said. "When I left each place, my blood would be boiling."

However, on July 21, 1964, the zoning board approved his application, and Malawi opened its chancery on Q Street.

The diplomatic-offices problem intensified when Senator J. William Fulbright, chairman of the Senate Foreign Relations Committee, introduced an amendment to the city's zoning law, to prohibit establishment of any new chancery in a one-family, detached residential district. Walter N. Tobriner, president of the D.C. Board of Commissioners, went further and proposed that new chanceries be barred from all residential areas and that all existing chanceries be treated as "nonconforming users"—prohibited from enlargement.

Pedro A. Sanjuan, of the State Department's Office for Special Representational Services, opposed Fulbright's amendment on the grounds that it would be interpreted as "discriminatory" against African diplomats, who were having the greatest difficulties in establishing their missions. He added that while he, along with many others, personally favored chanceries in commercial areas, some of the smaller, newer countries could not afford the high rentals in office buildings and hotels.

He did not mention that diplomats themselves were generally averse to offices in commercial locales on several other counts. Obviously, missions in residential areas are more prestigious. "There's no place even to fly our flag in front of a hotel or office building," said an envoy. He also pointed out that reserved parking space is provided for installations occupied solely for foreign governments but it is forbidden in front of public buildings.

Senator Fulbright's amendment, signed into law in October 1964, was a bombshell, shattering the hopes of more than twenty nations, eight of them African, still wanting chanceries in desirable residential areas. At the same time, it left the field open for locations in medium high-density apartment areas but required nations to conform their new designs with the height and architecture of nearby structures and also to provide adequate off-street parking space. Exempted were all governments that had filed chancery applications before May 1, 1964.

Algeria was one of several countries that missed the deadline, and Ambassador Cherif Guellal, an articulate and handsome bachelor adored by distaff Washington and highly respected by his diplomatic colleagues, was among those who felt especially put upon by the new law. Accredited to Washington in 1963, he and his staff had tried to buy an embassy residence and lease a chancery for almost a year. Finally, they settled on a Massachusetts Avenue townhouse near the chanceries of India, Uruguay, the

Malagasy Republic, Chile, Austria, and Pakistan; but the Algerian application was not filed in time. Guellal and his staff complained that they were victims of discrimination, an impresson that bore some weight after the staff director of the zoning board was quoted in a newspaper as saying, "The Algerians are smelly, messy people; unclean in their habits." The director declared he had been "grossly misquoted" and worried District officials attributed his remark, "if he made it at all," as merely repeating the comments of residents who protested the proposed location.

The New York Times Washington bureau, which broke the story, did not retract it; but the State Department issued a formal apology to Ambassador Guellal and stressed that the alleged remarks did "not in any way represent the opinion of the U.S. Government." The District commissioners came through with an even more abject apology. However, the Algerians' irritation did not subside until their chancery was established on R Street, not far from Massachusetts Avenue. Meanwhile, the country had purchased The Elms, the 34th Street house that belonged to President Johnson and had been his home when he was vice president. Immediately after Guellal moved in, he declared that the restrictive covenants attached to the house were "racially and religiously discriminatory" and filed suit to have them eliminated. The District government complied, and then followed through by removing restrictive covenants on all Washington properties.

In September 1964, the announcement by the Swedish Embassy of plans to construct a chancery on Edgevale Terrace brought unusual repercussions. Senator A. S. Monroney, carrying Senator Fulbright's proxy, appeared as a star witness for home-owning protestors and insisted that such a structure "would open a Pandora's box of real estate speculation in the area." Additional surprise opposition came from another source. An administrative attaché of the Canadian Embassy took the witness stand and insisted that the proximity of the proposed chancery would reduce the value of the nearby Canadian property.

On the other hand, some embassies staved off vocal opposition to proposed chanceries by the simple process of getting neighborhood approval on building plans before they were completed. Thus, with applause rather than clamor from the residential contingent, the Netherlands Embassy opened its modern office complex on Linnean Avenue, near Mrs. Merriweather Post's estate, in the summer of 1963. The German Embassy launched its battleship of a chancery on Foxhall Road the same year.

"Yes, it does dominate the neighborhood—on all four sides," a neighbor said of the German office building not long ago. "But at least it went up with our permission. Besides, it's beautifully kept, and it has its own parking area. And it's not too commercial; it's not entirely given over to business affairs. The Germans have many big parties there." Not long afterward, the chancery was awarded a prize for the excellence of its landscaping.

The manner in which Netherlands Ambassador J. H. van Roijen enlisted neighborhood support for his country's new office building set an all-time high example for his housing-bedeviled colleagues. As with many diplomatic ventures, this one began on a social basis. Shortly after the purchase of the four and a half acre tract in 1960, Van Roijen invited prospective neighbors to his residence, plied them with delicious food and drink, told them he hoped to build a chancery in their vicinity and answered the chief objection by promising that it would not be "just another office building." Subsequently, after one opponent got a court staying order against the proposed chancery, the ambassador came up with blueprints for a rambling structure that would blend beautifully and unobtrusively with its verdant setting and would have a large parking lot. He asked area citizens to approve and even gave his word that the venetian blinds would be closed at night, so that any office lights needed for business would not detract from the residential atmosphere of the area. The staying order was dropped; the majority of home owners approved; the few who did not, kept quiet.

The chancery opened for business late in 1963; and the following January, neighbors were invited to the dedication ceremony, at which Netherlands State Secretary of Foreign Affairs Leo de Block thanked the home owners for "the sacrifice of accepting an office building in your midst" and called the structure "a symbol of cooperation between two countries and a place where people can work to promote still better understanding between two nations." The residents loudly applauded; and the Netherlands Embassy staff, which had been inadequately accommodated since World War II, happily settled into its spacious new quarters, while more than two dozen missions continued to battle the disheartening housing problem.

The Soviet Embassy, intent on moving from their cramped, noisy headquarters on 16th Street, began canvassing the city and nearby areas for a site on which they could construct a residence-and-chancery complex. For a time they considered Merrywood, the forty-six-acre, McLean, Virginia, estate where former First Lady Jacqueline Kennedy lived as a girl, but the property lost its appeal for the Russians when they learned that Virginia laws do not always take into account diplomatic immunity. Then the Russians tried to buy six acres of the Naval Observatory grounds between the residence of the chief of naval operations and the British Embassy. The U.S. Navy turned them down.

Their subsequent frustrated attempt to purchase property in Chevy Chase precipitated a battle royal and had international repercussions. The chosen site was the Bonnie Brae estate, which has a handsome Tudor-style fieldstone and white brick house surrounded by 16 acres, commanding a magnificent view of Rock Creek Park.

Two thriving citizens' associations combined forces and

managed to block the zoning variance that would have been necessary for construction of the chancery.

Ambassador Dobrynin, who was visiting in Detroit at the time of the decision, was asked how he felt about it. "How would *you* feel?" he countered. "You have a residence for your ambassador in Moscow. I live with the whole embassy staff in Washington. Your embassy in Moscow is four or five times bigger than ours."

The portent of his remarks did not escape the State Department, which was well aware that our government for some time had been looking for a new property to house our overcrowded embassy in Moscow. Shortly afterward, just before Dobrynin took off for the Soviet Union with the scrapped Bonnie Brae blueprints in hand, he drove the reciprocal point home by casually observing, "Of course there is no direct connection between your plans to build a new embassy in Moscow and our needs here . . . but . . ."

Tregaron, the twenty and a half acre estate of the late Joseph E. Davies in Cleveland Park, was the next Washington property considered by the Soviets. The Cleveland Park Citizens Association raised no objections to the proposed embassy complex there but urged that the tract be divided, with one side for the diplomatic establishment and the other for a city park. The Russians began to look elsewhere.

When, in 1965, they tried unsuccessfully to buy a thirteen-acre site between Massachusetts Avenue and New Mexico Avenue, across from American University, the State Department redoubled its efforts to help. In July 1966, concurrent with a request for a long-term lease on a comparable site for construction of a new American Embassy in Moscow, the Russians were offered a piece of federal property—the thirteen-acre Mt. Alto Hospital site on Wisconsin Avenue. The Soviet government got around to accepting the offer in August 1967, thus ending a protracted deadlock in negotiations.

By that time, twenty-seven other governments were pressing to relocate their facilities, while several newer nations were having to take what they could get. To meet the problem, the suggestion that the city set aside a diplomatic enclave, similar to that in New Delhi, came up time and again, as it had, periodically, since 1960. But the idea of being segregated into what several envoys termed "an international ghetto" had little appeal to the majority of the diplomats, particularly those whose countries could afford individual establishments.

When a sizable area in Southwest Washington came up for consideration as the possible site of an "international center" in 1964, even the envoys who had experienced the most distressing housing difficulties argued that it was too far from "the big embassies" and the State Department. Others said they did not wish permanently to share space with other countries in high-rise buildings. A few envoys were privately dubious that Southwest Washington was prestigious enough for the conduct of diplomatic business— even after Vice President Humphrey took up residence there.

In 1967, President Johnson requested legislation to establish a diplomatic center in an acceptable area. Several proposals suggesting various locations had gone by the board when, in September 1968, the House and Senate passed a bill for an enclave of thirty-four acres on the old Bureau of Standards location, Connecticut Avenue at Van Ness Street, N.W. The bill authorized the United States government to turn over eight acres to the OAS as a site for headquarters, provided that sixteen acres could be leased or purchased for chancery buildings and reserved the remaining property to give the new structures a park-like setting. Even before President Johnson signed the bill, emissaries of twenty countries had indicated interest in having chanceries there.

Diplomatic housing problems were not the only ones that involved the State Department in the early 1960s as a host of newly independent countries began establishing their missions in Washington. Most of the emissaries were nonwhite, keenly aware of racial tension in America and quietly determined not to be victimized by it.

Constantly aware of their sensitivity, as well as of communist efforts to turn every trace of discrimination into a political asset, the State Department was especially attentive to Africans, as well as East Indians, who complained about the rude treatment they received in hotels and restaurants in several sections of the country and at beaches along the Eastern Seaboard.

A flagrant example concerned the envoy of one of the larger African countries who made a reservation at a hotel many miles from Washington. When the management learned that he was not white, the reservation was canceled. State Department officials spent hours persuading the manager to rescind the decision.

The refusal of restaurant facilities to a representative of an emerging West African country had disturbing repercussions abroad. En route from Washington to Pittsburgh, the diplomat was told flatly that persons of his "color" could not be served in the roadside establishment at which he stopped. The incident made headlines in Africa, and State promptly launched an investigation, with the result that the restaurant soon opened its doors to all customers, regardless of race, and local authorities invited the offended emissary to make a return visit.

Humiliating episodes continued elsewhere. An African ambassador, on his way from New York to Washington to present his credentials to the president, was ejected from a highway restaurant, and the first secretary of a Caribbean country was treated similarly in Virginia. An East Asian counselor was told that he could dine only in one section of a cafe in a Southern city. An African envoy aired his grievance after he, his wife and their eight-year-old child were denied a glass of water at a Maryland lunch stand. In a

letter to Secretary Rusk, the diplomat wrote that he had
been an officer in the French army in World War II and
that even under battle conditions he had shared water from
his canteen with thirsty children of the enemy.

After a Southeast Asian government official and some of
his diplomatic colleagues were refused admittance to a
Maryland beach and an African ambassador reported that
he was turned away and then pelted with stones, State Department officials investigated the racial policy of the re-
sort. Its racial ban was lifted.

The management of Beverly and Triton beaches on the
Chesapeake Bay in July 1963 notified the State Department
of its new policy "to refuse admission to any person who
possesses or claims to possess diplomatic immunity from
arrest and to all persons accompanying any such person."
The manager said further, "We don't want to be subjected
to those who feel they're above the law. But if a particular
embassy wants to assure us that they'll abide by the laws,
that's a different story."

Even such assurance could not ease the way for African
and Asian diplomats, for the resorts had a long-standing
policy—and a sign posted at the entrance—that only persons of north European ancestry would be welcome.

The State Department could do nothing to break the
racial barriers at Beverly and Triton beaches because they
were privately owned, but it moved quickly, with sharp
insistence that diplomats of every race, color and creed be
courteously treated in places of public accommodation.

The situation, widely publicized abroad, came up for
lengthy discussion when the African heads of state met in
1963 in Addis Ababa, and delegates unanimously condemned racial discrimination "especially in the United
States" but approved the role of United States federal
authorities in "attempting to combat it."

Meanwhile, insults to dark-skinned diplomats prompted
them to stay as much as possible within the confines of the

District of Columbia or to solicit specific assistance from the State Department before making any trips.

"I definitely feel that life in Washington is like living on an island, and if I ever travel, it will be only to New York," said an African ambassador. "But, even in Washington, things have not been easy." Another African envoy, after having been advised that he would receive proper treatment in public establishments if he would identify himself, replied, "If I have to announce that I am an ambassador in order not to be subjected to humiliation, anywhere, I will request that my government recall me."

Scores of similar threats and complaints had bothered the State Department and had reverberated to Capitol Hill, when Secretary Rusk, on July 10, 1963, appeared before the Senate Committee on Commerce in regard to Senate Bill 1732, which included a provision to eliminate racial bars in public establishments. Secretary Rusk dwelled at length on the situation as it affected diplomats "because," as he put it, "they are the special concern of the State Department." But he also expressed the hope "that Congress would join the Executive and the Judiciary in declaring it to be our national policy to accord to every citizen—and every person— the respect due to him as an individual."

Senate Bill 1732 did not become law, but its proposed provision to remove racial discrimination was covered by the Civil Rights Act of 1964, which ordered equal access to any place of public accommodation "without discrimination or segregation on the ground of race, color, religion, or national origin."

Thus, for the first time, the State Department had legal support for its efforts to ensure that the United States would abide by an important enunciation of the 1961 Vienna Convention on Diplomatic Relations: "A diplomat shall be treated by the receiving State with respect, and that State shall take all appropriate steps to prevent any attack on his person, freedom or dignity."

Concurrently, the civil rights act liquidated what had been a compelling Soviet commentary on racial tension in the United States: namely, that "inaction by the U.S. government is tantamount to support of the racists."

The State Department has been called "the most apologetic agency in America," and the regularity with which its officials have to soothe affronted feelings in the foreign corps gives authenticity to the description. Hardly a day passes in Washington without an official demur, palliative statement or extenuating gesture to placate discomfited diplomats.

Capitol Hill solons sometimes precipitate the displeasure, as did Senator Allen J. Ellender of Louisiana in a June 1963 television debate when he referred to those responsible for racial tension in the D.C. school system "as well as Liberia, Ethiopia and Haiti" as providing ample evidence of lack of governmental ability. "In other words," Ellender declared, "when people cannot qualify to do a job, they contend that they are being discriminated against because of color."

The State Department promptly assured the indignant ambassadors of Liberia and Ethiopia that Ellender spoke for neither the United States government nor the American people. Ellender shot back, "I'll be damned if I believe that. I think I speak for the bulk of the American people."

Liberia's Ambassador S. Edward Peal in a broadcast cited Ellender's assertions as "an apparent crusade to stigmatize us as inferior human beings" and wound up by saying, "The gist of the matter is this: Are we willing to come to grips with the overriding realities of our times, as brothers belonging to the same family, or are we to go our separate ways—with our own pride, our own prejudice, our own pigmentation—to our very certain and very fatal doom?"

By that time, aroused envoys of twenty-seven African nations had appointed the ambassadors of the United Arab Republic, Sudan, Nigeria, Morocco, Somalia and the Mala-

gasy Republic to call on Acting Secretary of State George
W. Ball with a letter requesting a policy declaration from
President Kennedy. Caught between the irrepressible Louisiana lawmaker's unyielding stand and the wrought-up
African corps, Ball quietly promised to look into the
matter, reiterated that Ellender's views were not those of
the United States government and the majority of the
American people and persuaded the envoys to abandon
their plan to take the protest directly to the President.

The following month, Senator Thomas J. Dodd of Connecticut took up the cudgels against Ghana. In a 163-page
document released by the Senate Internal Security Committee, Dodd stated that Ghana under President Kwame
Nkrumah "has become the first Soviet satellite in Africa"
and cited it further as "the focal point for the subversion of
Africa, just as Cuba is the focal point for subversion of the
Americas." Dodd's attestation also pointed out that even
though Nkrumah had consistently followed the communist
line, Ghana had continued to benefit from generous United
States aid, including $113 million in 1962 for the vast Volta
River project.

The Embassy of Ghana labeled Dodd's charges as "base-
less and a travesty of the truth," and, mindful that many
Ghanaians might take Dodd's charge as United States policy, the State Department said that "information available
does not support the suggestion that Ghana has become a
Soviet satellite" and added that United States aid to Ghana
"is tangible demonstration of our friendship for the Gha-
naian people."

Concerned as it always is about assuaging wounded feelings in the foreign corps and safeguarding diplomatic immunity, the State Department draws the line on the latter
when a mission employee counts on the protective cloak to
cover not only relatives and servants but also the animal
kingdom. A Belgian Embassy secretary, living in Arlington,

Virginia, made this discovery a few years ago, after neighbors asked the police to confiscate her pet ocelots Sabu and Elizabeth. She insisted that they had diplomatic immunity.

Temporarily stymied, the police took the case to Arlington Commonwealth's Attorney William J. Hassan, along with the reminder that it is illegal to import any "undesirable species" in Virginia. Hassan, in turn, dumped the balls of fur squarely into the lap of the State Department, and Pedro Sanjuan came up with the dictum: "Ocelots don't have diplomatic immunity." The Belgian Embassy secretary disposed of them.

Complaining neighbors do not get the results they want, however, if their charges are aimed at possible court action against a diplomat. One incident frustrated an Arlington, Virginia, housewife who told the police that a Turkish attaché had attacked her with a broomstick after she took the part of her sons, aged seven and eight, in their squabble with his ten-year-old daughter. She charged him with felonious assault. He denied the accusation and invoked diplomatic immunity to block a warrant. Authorities appealed to the State Department, which referred the matter to the Turkish Embassy. The attaché must have made his denial convincing enough there, for a year later he was still on the staff and residing at the same Arlington address.

Ever alert to counteract disagreeable incidents against foreign missions, the State Department promptly orders restoration of diplomatic property damaged by irresponsible persons. In March 1965, for instance, a complete sandblasting of the front of the Soviet Embassy was underway the day after a group stormed the establishment and splashed paint on the entrance. Our government paid the bill.

Any act, in fact, that threatens diplomatic security places the State Department in an amends-making posture, but, fortunately, few have been as serious as the catastrophe that shook Washington's Kalorama residential section at 3:50 A.M. on a Sunday morning in January 1967, when ten carefully placed sticks of dynamite exploded in the Yugoslav chancery on California Street.

At approximately the same time, the Yugoslav Embassy in Canada and four other consulates elsewhere in North America were bombed. The coordinated attacks, according to Cvijeto Job, Yugoslav counselor in Washington, were obviously arranged by "Yugoslav Quislings" now living in the United States. He added that his embassy had repeatedly asked the State Department for "protection aganst such terrorist elements."

No one was injured in the blasted chancery, but a four-foot hole in the wall, shattered windows and impaired ceilings added up to a damage of several thousand dollars.

Yugoslavia's Ambassador Veijko Micunovic formally protested to the State Department and was assured that our government would bear all restoration expenses. Secretary Rusk expressed his regret and deplored "the outrageous and senseless acts of terrorism that can only be condemned by the American people." Protocol Chief James W. Symington and several other State officials called at the embassy to proffer apologies in person, and Ambassador Arthur Goldberg told the Yugoslav delegation at the United Nations that "full resources of the U.S. government will be employed to apprehend those responsible."

Ambassador Micunovic accepted apologies and promises graciously and with incredible calmness. At a reception two days after the bombing he spoke of it as "simply a criminal act" and continued, "Certainly, we can't blame any responsible person, and certainly not the U.S. government, which is deeply disturbed by the action."

Within two weeks, subpoenas had been served on suspects and the Justice Department had begun a grand-jury investigation that turned up a Yugoslav-American, living in Chicago, who admitted participation in the conspiracy "to call attention to the fact that Yugoslavia is a communist country and an enemy of the U.S."

When other suspects also were apprehended, Ambassador Micunovic publicly declared that "the attempt of a small, noisy group to work against the good relations of America and Yugoslavia has not succeeded." And five months later, just before transfer to another post, he spent a friendly half-hour with President Johnson and Secretary Rusk and expressed his gratitude for the manner in which the unpleasant incident had been handled.

For months after the bombing, however, guards were on around-the-clock duty at the Yugoslav chancery.

In March 1967, when the border problem between Jordan and Israel began to intensify, Jordan's Ambassador Farhan Shubeilat reported to the State Department that he was being increasingly harassed by telephone calls from persons who said that they were Zionists and vowed they were out to kill him. The envoy said further that Mme. Shubeilat was ill and that most of the calls came through at all hours of the night and unduly disturbed her. During the day the telephone often rang but there would be no reply when it was answered.

The State Department solicited help from the police. The night telephone calls ceased, and an officer assured the ambassador, "Don't worry. We'll be circling your house regularly as long as threats against your life reach you at any time."

When an American publication or motion picture portrays any nation, historically or currently, in an unfavorable light, protests from the foreign mission concerned barrage the State Department. Frequently, apologies are forthcoming, either from State or, at its behest, from the medium involved—but not always. For example, after Haiti's Ambassador Arthur Bonhomme attended a private screening of *The Comedians*, a 1967 motion picture set in Haiti under the Duvalier regime, he filed a complaint in a three-page letter to Secretary Rusk and then dispatched a sizzling objection to Metro-Goldwyn-Mayer. The missive to Rusk insisted that Haiti would never permit "such aggressions or assaults to take place on its territory against the prestige and dignity of the noble American people, government, or President." The protest to MGM labeled the motion picture "a libelous assault on the island republic." Neither State nor MGM publicly responded, and the film was shown throughout the country.

By comparison, a reception scheduled at the State Department to precede the Washington premiere of *America, America*, in March 1964, was canceled after the Turkish government charged that the film was critical of Turkey and contained pro-Greek overtones that might aggravate the Cyprus situation. And when *Newsweek* magazine in November 1967 hinted that King Bhumibol Adulyadej of Thailand was too apprehensive to leave his helicopter on a tour of the southern part of his country, the reaction was so adverse in Thailand and at the Thai Embassy in Washington that the magazine, at the urging of State, apologized for its parenthetical aside in regard to His Majesty.

On the other hand, Thailand did not wait to launch its protest through the State Department early in December 1967 after the *Washington Star*, the *Washington Post* and the *New York Post* carried comments that Premier Thanom Kittikachorn considered erroneous, to the effect that Thailand was trading Hawk missiles for troops going to Vietnam. In Bangkok both Kittikachorn and Foreign Minister Thanat Khoman charged that the reports were completely false. Khoman went further. He called American newspapers "a sewage press" and declared:

> It was only because of delays and procrastination on the part of the U.S. Government that the decision to respond to the Thai request for additional means of defense was reached at the time when we of Thailand also decided to send troops. The Hawk missiles have not arrived yet, but in the meantime, the *New*

York Post, the *Washington Post* and the [Washington] *Evening Star* are attacking Thailand.

All three newspapers published the statement.

Freedom of diplomats to travel within a host country has been widely regarded in modern times as a right based on courtesy and international law, but it has been a thorny problem for our State Department since 1941. It was then that the Soviet Union, deviating from the practice, first set up restrictions that spread to other countries in the communist bloc and started a chain of reciprocal measures by Western nations.

The initial issuance of rules regulating travel for all foreigners within the Soviet Union was followed periodically by additional restrictions. The State Department, even when forced to impose retaliatory measures, pushed for the removal of all travel bans in the interest of normal diplomatic relations. Rumania, the first Eastern European nation to follow the Soviet Union's example, closed about two-thirds of its country to the personnel of foreign missions in April 1949 and required prior notice to the Ministry of Foreign Affairs each time a diplomat wanted to travel outside of Bucharest. The United States retaliated a year later by restricting Rumanian diplomats in Washington to an area within twenty-five miles of the District of Columbia and requiring that they obtain permission from the State Department to go elsewhere.

Patently in retaliation, State approved some Rumanian travel requests and rejected others. Thus, Rumania's Minister Mihai Magheru and his wife were granted permission to vacation in Maine in the summer of 1950, but two other members of the Rumanian legation who wanted to visit Delaware the same summer were not allowed to do so.

A January 1951 executive order in Hungary confined all

members of foreign missions to a radius of thirty kilometers from the center of Budapest, with permission given by the Foreign Ministry for travel beyond that zone only "for adequate reasons." The State Department responded by restricting Hungarian diplomats to an area within an eighteen-mile radius of the White House, with prior permission granted for travel beyond that zone, "in accord with the consideration given to our diplomats in Budapest."

The Soviet Union continued to intensify its travel restrictions, while pressure in the United States executive and legislative branches mounted toward imposing stringent counterbans on Soviet diplomats in America. Finally, in March 1952, State announced that members of the Soviet Embassy, the personnel of Tass News Agency and AMTORG (the Soviet trading agency) would be expected to stay within a twenty-five mile radius of Washington and New York and would be required to give a forty-eight-hour notice of plans to travel beyond the restricted zones.

State stressed at the time that the retaliatory measure was issued "reluctantly" since "such treatment of foreign representatives by a receiving state is not necessary, customary or correct, nor is it conducive to the proper conduct of relations between countries."

When eight other Western nations also reciprocally imposed travel bans on Soviet diplomats, the Soviet Union, in June 1953 amended its previous restrictions and opened about two-thirds of the country to traveling diplomats. But the following year bans more stringent than ever specified that foreigners could not take photographs or make sketches of border zones; communications, military or industrial installations; seaports; hydroelectric plants; railroad junctions; tunnels; bridges and power stations. The directive also listed newly barred vicinities that had no plants or installations of strategic importance.

Retaliating in early 1955, the United States closed off

comparative areas to all resident Soviet citizens, other than those employed by the United Nations Secretariat. Most of the Mexican and Canadian border zones were placed off limits, as were sixteen cities and counties in thirty-five states.

In each instance, when the United States announced restrictions, it made it clear that it would be willing to eliminate all travel barriers on a reciprocal basis. The Soviet Union remained largely unreceptive to the idea, even after the 1961 Vienna Convention on Diplomatic Relations ruled under Article 25 that "the receiving state shall ensure to all members of the mission freedom to travel within its territory." The one major exception was that specific areas might be closed off "for reasons of national security."

With little hope of getting Soviet cooperation toward promoting free travel, the State Department began to encourage the Eastern European countries to join America in eliminating barriers wherever possible. The campaign had some effect. In July 1963, Hungary announced that United States diplomats would henceforth be at liberty to move throughout the country—except to certain sensitive areas— and that advance notice of travel plans would no longer be required, if America would reciprocate accordingly.

State wished to comply, but by then there had been a significant change in the attitude of other United States agencies. In the spring of 1963, two communist military attachés had taken a "sightseeing trip" near some missile installations and had aroused the apprehension of air force officials.

Similar visits by communist diplomats disturbed the Department of Defense, which suspected that a number of East European representatives were engaged in undercover operations for the Soviet Union and should not be allowed to roam as they wished. And, in November 1963, a major change in United States policy, which previously had supported the removal of travel bans, barred diplomats from

Bulgaria, Czechoslovakia, Hungary, Poland and Rumania from 355 areas in the continental United States "for reasons of national security."

Affected for the first time was the free movement of emissaries from Poland and Czechoslovakia, the only communist-bloc members that had not been included in the twenty-mile radius restriction imposed earlier by the United States. Poland promptly retaliated by barring corresponding areas to American diplomats.

The Cold War went on, with reciprocal travel bans—and concurrent travel harassments in the communist countries —increasing the tension in East-West relations. By the end of 1963, twenty-six percent of our country was off limits to the Russians and about 10 percent to diplomats from other nations in the communist bloc.

Enforcement required additional personnel and caused countless headaches in the State Department, which had the responsibility of telling communist diplomats exactly where they could travel; of processing requests for special trips; of granting permission for some applicants and declining others; and, most of all, of keeping a watchful eye on the movements of suspicious military attachés.

On July 22, 1967, the picture became slightly more promising when the Soviet Union enlarged its open-travel area, and the United States responded by easing restrictions for the Russians by 3.5 percent and those for the Poles, Czechoslovaks, Hungarians and Bulgarians by 36 percent. Still remaining in effect, however, were requirements that Soviet diplomats, as well as military attachés of all communist countries, notify our State Department forty-eight hours in advance of a proposed trip outside open areas.

Too many communist agents had been apprehended and expelled in the preceding fifteen years for Uncle Sam to relax his vigilance over spies with diplomatic passports.

8

Russian Tapestry

Like most other envoys sent to Washington in its earlier days, Russian emissaries were maintained in the new Republic primarily for prestige. Diplomats generally disliked the assignment because the United States was not a great power and decisions made on the Potomac seemed unimportant to Old World eyes. But at least it was a comparatively easy, if not always a comfortable, tour of duty. Representatives of foreign governments had little to worry about except the mounting thermometer in summer and an occasional housing problem. For nine months of the year, they could devote themselves to giving parties and going to them and then enjoy vacations abroad or in cooler American climates from June to September.

Imperial Russia's first minister to the United States, Prince André de Daschkoff, presented his credentials to President James Madison in 1809, at the same time that John Quincy Adams was making his bow at the court of Alexander I in St. Petersburg. The Russian envoy did not try to find a house for himself and his legation staff. With a resplendent, gold-braided entourage, he took up residence at a hotel near Lafayette Square, posted a Cossack in full uniform at the entrance, installed his own chef in the kitchen and proceeded to treat social and official Washington to the excellence of Russian cuisine.

But before he departed less than a year later, he selected a three-story residence for his successor, Count Pahlen, on

K Street. The best available dwelling in the city, it had served as the first British legation in Washington. And it had certain other distinctions. Originally two dwellings, the structures had been built in 1795 by one of Georgetown's most prominent citizens, Robert Peter. One of the houses had been a wedding gift to his son Thomas and the latter's bride, Martha Parke Custis, a granddaughter of Martha Washington.

There were no permanent diplomatic establishments in the federal city during the first 66 years of its existence. Housing posed an even bigger problem for members of the diplomatic corps than it did for some of their successors 150 years later. Few suitable, or even passably adequate, residences were for either sale or lease; and when one became available, it was quickly taken.

Through the nineteenth century, however, Russian envoys fared better as to housing than did many of their diplomatic contemporaries. One, in fact, managed to lease Decatur House, the Lafayette Square mansion that Benjamin Latrobe had designed for Admiral Stephen Decatur in 1815. A flourishing social center until Decatur's death on the dueling field in May 1820, the dwelling then had a number of distinguished tenants. The first was French Minister Baron Hyde de Neuville, who continued to give the house a cachet of continual social elegance.

In sharp contrast, the next tenant was Russian Minister Baron de Tuyll. He was patently disinterested in society—except as a means toward a purposeful end. With a brilliant background, including service in the imperial Russian army and as czarist envoy to France, he was regarded as one of the ablest representatives of Alexander I, and he had long since learned the value of entertaining small, powerful groups at delicious dinners rather than hundreds of purely social guests at expensive balls and musicales.

He had come to be rather favorably known on his first Washington tour of duty, from 1817 to 1819, when, for convenience in American circles, he insisted on being addressed as Baron de Tuyll rather than by his somewhat complicated name, Major General Baron Vasil'evich Teil'-fan-Seroskerken.

When he returned early in 1823, he was envoy on a very definite mission: to get the United States involved in the Holy Alliance, under the guidance of Prince von Metternich, the Austrian chancellor, and Alexander I.

Baron de Tuyll, therefore, had important reasons for declining invitations from his foreign colleagues and devoting his time to the cultivation of senators and State Department officials at frequent dinners in Decatur House. But all who enjoyed his Lucullan feasts did not digest the propaganda he served with them. Unaware at the outset that he would be battling America's highest surge of nineteenth-century isolationism and insensitive to the fact that Secretary of State John Quincy Adams was a strong nationalist, the Russian minister continued to dilate on the advantages of the international bloc until Adams let him know, in July 1923, that nations of the Western Hemisphere had no intention of being controlled by European governments.

To offset propaganda for the Holy Alliance, which was established to bring Western Hemisphere colonies back under control of European nations, British Prime Minister George Canning openly opposed the international bloc by initiating Anglo-American conversations to examine its plan and purpose. And in July 1923, Adams gave Baron de Tuyll a foretaste of future developments by informing him that the United States "should contest the right of Russia to any territorial establishment on this continent and that we should assume distinctly the principle that the American continents are no longer subjects for any new European colonial establishments."

Baron de Tuyll played his diplomatic cards poorly. "Our Yankee friends shrink from European entanglements," he said, "but they like to have a hand in every pie." And, shortly afterward, when the question of Spanish reconquest of her American colonies reached fever pitch, the envoy visited the White House to present the Russian view, supporting Spanish ambitions. The tart reply that Secretary Adams immediately drafted and dispatched to the Russian minister emphasized that the United States was unequivocally opposed to further European conquests on the American continents. That position, fully clarified, became the Monroe Doctrine, enunciated by President Monroe in his message to Congress in December 2, 1823.

For his remaining three years in Washington, the Russian insisted that he was "a prisoner of the gout" and rarely left his legation. But his dinners for select gourmets continued, and his distinction as an epicure soon overshadowed his diplomatic disappointment. Long after he left the United States, he was to be remembered primarily for his dictum on local food as follows: "Washington with its venison, wild turkeys, canvasback, oysters, terrapin, etc., furnishes better viands than Paris and wants only cooks."

His landlady, Mrs. Stephen Decatur, was to remember him, however, as "an impossible tenant." She complained that he allowed his servants to sell flowers that they dug from her Decatur House garden, that he caused her insurance to be canceled by installing a conservatory on her premises and that his steward furnished a parlor in Decatur House and had the bills sent to her after the envoy refused to pay them.

Baron de Tuyll departed Washington without even attempting to mollify Mrs. Decatur, and when she appealed to the next Russian minister, Baron Mollitz, he disclaimed all responsibility for the transgressions of his predecessor. Secretary of State Henry Clay finally placated Mrs. Decatur by leasing the Lafayette Square mansion himself and promising to remove the conservatory.

A distinguished diplomatic host during the Jackson administration was Baron Krüdener, the Imperial Russian minister, who lived in a handsome red brick house on H Street, Lafayette Square. According to a contemporary observer, he made it "the most hospitable mansion Washington had ever known."

But he had strong social competition in the British minister, Charles Richard Vaughan, who resided in the Monroe House on I Street (today, the Arts Club) and entertained constantly. Vaughan's brilliant coup in 1829, when his ball brought 400 carriages to the British legation, was matched shortly thereafter when Baron Krüdener gave a lavish dinner for Secretary of State Martin Van Buren, followed by a gala ball for 500 guests and a midnight supper. From then on, the Russian envoy managed to maintain his social supremacy; and when he left in 1832, he must have gone with the happy assurance that his opulent hospitality had made a dramatic impact on the capital city.

Fifty-year-old Baron de Bodisco, who arrived as minister of the Czar of All the Russias in 1838, established the Russian legation in the best house he could find in Georgetown and proceeded to impress the natives with his liveried coachman and footman, his white barouche drawn by four black horses and his lavish social calendar. The interior of his house, furnished with expensive pieces from St. Petersburg, was elaborate indeed. The magnificent assemblage of gold plate in the dining room alone prompted a guest to liken it to "a gold mine."

Residing with him were two young nephews, who attended Georgetown College, and it was at a party for them that Baron de Bodisco met sixteen-year-old Harriet Beall Williams and fell in love with her. As his ardent courtship proceeded, there was much gossip about the disparity in ages, and rumors ran that the elegant baron was actually six years older than he admitted. But 500 handpicked guests, including President Van Buren and Dolley

Madison, crowded into the modest home of Harriet's mother for the June 1839 wedding and went on to the reception at the Russian legation; and a few days later, the bridal party was honored at a White House dinner. (The marriage was a happy one. Baron de Bodisco died in the Georgetown house in 1854 and was buried in Oak Hill Cemetery.)

Twentieth-century Russian diplomats have posed serious problems for the United States government, but during the nineteenth century Washington demanded the recall of Count Constantine de Catacazy, minister of the court of Alexander II. He embarrassed President Grant's administration by openly hinting that his emperor and the United States had worked out a secret treaty about rights at the Port of Odessa. Secretary of State Hamilton Fish, aware that both Great Britain and France were annoyed, told the Senate Foreign Relations Committee that the Russian Minister was an "atrocious liar" and declared him *persona non grata*. Through his minister of foreign affairs, Alexander II inquired whether President Grant "would tolerate Monsieur de Catacazy until the forthcoming visit of the Grand Duke Alexis was concluded." President Grant assented.

Although wounded to the core, the envoy shepherded the Grand Duke around Washington, entertained him at a dinner and accompanied him to a White House reception. The beautiful Countess de Catacazy was there, too; but rumors were that she was greeted by President and Mrs. Grant even more coolly than was her husband. By then, however, she must have been inured to such treatment; for fifteen years before, when Count de Catacazy was secretary of the Russian legation, they met at a ball and began a romance that was the gossip of Washington. She was married to a titled Italian diplomat at the time, but she left her husband the next week; and when De Catacazy was recalled to St. Petersburg, she followed him. Although they were later married, with the Czar's approval, and De Catacazy had been an able diplomat in both Paris and London before he was sent back to Washington as envoy, the scandal that rocked the capital was still remembered.

Few diplomats assigned to Washington, however, have been the focus of more unveiled curiosity and gossip than the turn-of-the-century Imperial Russian envoy with the longest name of all: Arthur Paul Nicholas, Marquis de Capizzuchi de Bologna, Count Cassini.

Distinguished on many accounts, he had served his country in a number of high diplomatic posts, including that of minister to China. His appointment to the United States came at an especially prestigious time. Since 1893, the United States had been exchanging ambassadors instead of ministers with Great Britain, France and Prussia. In 1898, Russia joined the "world powers" in thus recognizing the growing importance of the United States. That same year, Count Cassini, dripping with gold braid and decorations, presented credentials as the first Imperial Russian ambassador to the United States.

With his iron-gray hair, a thick mustache and a prominent cleft in his chin, His Excellency looked every inch the aristocratic envoy. President McKinley evidently was impressed, for after the formal reception he asked the envoy to stay on for a lengthy conference.

The first Russian Embassy was a sizable but unattractive brick house at 1634 I Street, and Cassini's entourage included, in addition to the embassy staff, four servants brought over from Paris, a governess, whom he called "Mme. Scheele," and a teen-age beauty, whom he introduced as his niece, Mlle. Marguerite Cassini.

Two weeks after his arrival, he gave a dinner for twenty select guests and astounded them by presenting "Mlle. Marguerite" as his official hostess. Within twenty-four hours, all Washington was agog. Diplomatic wives old enough to be Marguerite's grandmother were openly annoyed that a mere "niece" was slated for position and privileges traditionally reserved for spouses or daughters of envoys. Lady Pauncefote—wife of the British ambassador, who was dean of the diplomatic corps—urged her husband to point out to the Russian envoy that the situation was fraught with embarrassment, but jovial Sir Julian was too clever to involve himself in the sticky situation.

Meanwhile, moving into her exalted role with girlish enthusiasm, Marguerite made little, if any, attempt to placate her critics. She presided gaily at a series of dinners and receptions, accompanied the ambassador to all official functions and gave the town plenty to talk about, besides. She owned and drove one of the first automobiles in Washington and shocked the local citizenry by powdering her nose in public and smoking cigarettes. She started a fencing school, and it was said that she owned twenty borzois and kept them all in the embassy. She wore extravagant, extreme clothes and flirted outrageously; and she had a host of prominent, ardent admirers. She also had voluble detractors, among them Colonel E. D. Mann, publisher of the scandal-mongering *Town Topics* of New York. Regular reports of her escapades and successive romances appeared in it, while the local press closely followed her contretemps with diplomatic wives. Baroness Hengelmüller von Hengervár, wife of the Austrian minister, was one who especially resented her. At a White House dinner when Mlle. Cassini was presented to the President before the Austrian baroness, the latter was furious and complained to Secretary of State John Hay. Although he pointed out that as an ambassador, the Russian outranked her husband as minister and that Mlle. Cassini as her uncle's official hostess had to be presented with him, the baroness was not appeased. She continued to grumble about the vaunted prerogatives of the "young Russian upstart." Several equally jealous diplomatic wives backed the baroness' position, and the situation became so unpleasant that Cassini went to St. Petersburg for a heart-to-heart talk with his Emperor. The visit brought results. Within a short time, there was a formal announcement that Nicholas II had ended the "niece" status by recognizing the nineteen-year-old girl as Cassini's adopted daughter and by bestowing on her the title of countess.

Decades later, Countess Marguerite Cassini in her autobiography, *Never a Dull Moment*, gave a slightly different version. As she told it, Count Cassini confessed to the Emperor that "Mme. Scheele," who lived at the Washington Embassy as governess, was his wife, whom he had married years before in London, and that Marguerite was their daughter. The Czar was sympathetic and immediately issued the ukase to define her status and to give her the title that was rightfully hers.

The imperial edict did not stop wagging Washington tongues, but at least it prompted them to function less openly and with a certain degree of awe. Countess Cassini, with bolstered assurance, determined to quell her critics by the sheer grandeur and frequency of her dinners, balls and musicales. But in order to do that, she needed a more elegant setting. The I Street house was a moderately large, two-story structure with a plebeian front porch and an ugly mansard roof. The dining room could accommodate only twenty-four seated guests, and the Cassinis' handsome Louis XV and XVI furnishings seemed out of place in the square salons with plain walls.

The resourceful young countess set out to find a more resplendent house. She chose the Levi Morton mansion on Rhode Island Avenue at Scott Circle. Its interior included a marble staircase, a spacious dining room and a rectangular ballroom with ornately paneled walls picked out in gold. The palatial dwelling became the Russian Embassy in February 1903, but plans for a social splurge there were short-lived. Ambassador Cassini soon became too involved with demanding diplomatic affairs to encourage his daughter's social aspirations; he was working day and night to wangle United States support for Russia in her troubles with Japan and was having no luck at all; and the outbreak of the Russo-Japanese war finally brought down the curtain on the Cassinis' social calendar.

The envoy was transferred to Spain in 1904. His successor, Baron Rosen, was not particularly interested in society as such, and neither was his wife. They preferred the I Street house, and it once more became the Russian Embassy, managed with quiet elegance by an efficient Russian staff, complete with a towering doorman who wore a lethal saber in the belt of his full-skirted Cossack uniform.

The last Imperial Russian envoy to the United States was the only one to reside in Russia's first purchased embassy in Washington. He was George (Georgi Petrovich) Bakhmetev, and he had gilt-edged ties to residential Washington. As a young secretary in the Russian legation years before, he had courted Mary Beale in Decatur House, the home of her parents, General and Mrs. Edward Fitzgerland Beale. Solely on the grounds that Bakhmetev was a "foreigner," the parents opposed the romance and declined consent to the marriage; but in time they were reconciled to it, and the wedding took place in Vienna shortly after General Beale became minister to Austria. The Bakhmetevs had been happily married for thirty years when he was appointed ambassador to the United States and they returned late in 1911.

It was a most propitious time for them. Mme. Bakhmetev's sister, Mrs. John R. McLean, was the acknowledged social arbiter of Washington. Her nephew Edward Beale McLean and his wife, the former Evalyn Walsh, resided in a Massachusetts Avenue mansion that was the scene of the most elaborate parties of the era. An example was the lavish dinner given there for the Bakhmetevs shortly after their arrival. According to Evalyn Walsh McLean's autobiography, *Father Struck It Rich*, the dinner for forty-eight was a $40,000 affair "with orchids and four thousand two-dollar yellow lilies from London." But what pleased the new Russian ambassador and his American-born wife most in Washington was the magnificent house that Nicholas II bought to serve as the Imperial Russian Embassy.

Known to this day as the Pullman Mansion by old Washingtonians who remember its origin, the palatial residence on Sixteenth Street was commissioned by Hattie Sanger (Mrs. George) Pullman, widow of the Pullman car tycoon, in 1909. Nathan C. Wyeth, of the architectural firm of Sullivan and Wyeth, designed the limestone, granite and Roman brick structure in the French Renaissance tradition and made it one of the finest houses ever built in Washington. It would have admirably fulfilled the purpose for which it was reputed to have been planned—to serve as a distinguished setting for the Washington career of Mrs. Pullman's son-in-law, Representative Frank O. Lowden, of Illinois, and his wife. When the house was commissioned, Lowden had his heart set on a seat in the Senate and his political future seemed assured; but by the time the house was finished, his aspirations were shattered and he had returned to Illinois.

Mrs. Pullman put the mansion on the market at a time when expensive houses were difficult to sell. John Hays Hammond, the multimillionaire mining engineer, agreed to help. With his numerous international contacts he finally interested the Imperial Russian government in the property, and the sale was completed in October 1912.

The purchase of the sixty-four-room house included most of its fine furnishings, to which the Bakhmetevs added their own effects; and for four years, they lived luxuriously in the majestic edifice. With a sense of what Washington expected of a czarist ambassadress, Mme. Bakhmetev presided over the house as though it were an imperial palace. A French chef with a dozen assistants made the embassy cuisine famous. An additional staff of forty ran the place in the grand manner and took great care with the Caen and Bottecini marble foyer, the magnificent stairway, the gold and white ballroom inspired by Versailles, the dining room paneled in Circassian walnut and the priceless Louis XV and XVI antiques from Paris and St. Petersburg. Ambassador Bakhmetev's bons mots, tossed off as he adjusted his monocle at exclusive soirees, were widely quoted, establishing him as the wittiest envoy in Washington. Mme. Bakhmetev, by all odds, was Embassy Row's leading hostess.

That glamorous world collapsed late in February 1917 when news reached Washington that Nicholas II had abdicated and, with his family, was confined to the imperial palace at Tsarskoye Selo. Three days later, the embassy was notified that the new provisional government's ambassador to the United States would leave Petrograd for Washington within a week.

His name was Bakhmetev also, but he was no relation to George Bakhmetev, as the latter was to make clear on his farewell visit to the White House. "This Bakhmetev who is being sent over here to represent the Russian people in your place—he is a relative?" President Wilson asked the retiring czarist envoy. The ambassador replied, "He is related to me in just the same way that Booker T. Washington was related to George Washington."

By the end of March, George Bakhmetev and his wife and most of the embassy furnishings were on their way to France. The retiring Imperial Russian envoy offered no apologies for stripping the mansion. The Louis XV and XVI sofas, chairs and tables and the rich Oriental rugs certainly did not belong to the provisional government, he said; and besides, he and his wife planned to build a replica of the 16th Street house in Paris and the furniture would be needed.

Boris Aleksandrovich Bakhmetev, a smooth-shaven, stocky man, with a twinkle behind his rimless eyeglasses, arrived to find an almost bare residence. He acquired some modest wicker and walnut veneer replacements for the priceless antiques that had graced the mansion for four years. They served his needs. He had neither the desire nor the funds to carry on the lavish social pattern set by the last czarist emissary. Instead, he spent much of his time in conference at the State Department, where he impressed those he met as a highly intelligent man and a convincing talker. He also impressed audiences outside the capital and was on his way to fulfill a speaking engagement in Memphis, Tennessee, on November 7, 1917, when news of the "Great October Socialist Revolution" broke. (Then, as later, the idea of an October revolution in November caused some confusion in the United States. The old Julian calendar, still used in Russia at that time, was ten days behind the Gregorian, or New Style, calendar, which had been followed in most Christian countries for centuries.)

By telephone from Tennessee, Bakhmetev instructed the first secretary, Jean Soukine, to issue a statement blasting the "Maximalists" (revolutionaries) and clarifying the position of Kerensky's diplomats. Soukine immediately complied. "The Maximalists are in no way representative of the whole of Russia," he declared. "If they have succeeded in seizing power and have formed a Maximalist government, such a government cannot express the will of the nation. Consequently, the Russian Embassy in Washington will refuse to accept its authority."

Shortly afterward, when Moscow announced that Leon Trotsky had been named commissar for foreign affairs, Bakhmetev reaffirmed his position in a letter to Secretary of State Lansing, as follows: "In the future, I will continue in not recognizing a 'Bolshevik' or any other similar government which would break loyalty to Russia's allies and aid the country to non-participation in the war."

Communiqués and orders from Trotsky soon began to bombard the embassy. They were ignored. The United States, which had lent vast sums of money to the Russian provisional government, declined to recognize the Soviet Union, and confusion soon enveloped the frenetic embassy staff without a country. Both the first secretary and the second secretary resigned and tried to enlist in the United States army. In time, Bakhmetev himself gave up and went to New York to teach hydraulic engineering at Columbia University; but for five years, his name appeared in the *Diplomatic List* as the Russian ambassador to the United States.

Meanwhile, Alex I. Krymstky, a Kerensky appointee who was registered at the State Department as "custodian," was in charge of the embassy without government. The brocaded and gilded walls of the mansion were covered with cheesecloth, and he and his family lived on the sparsely furnished third floor. M. Serge Ughet, Kerensky's former financial agent, administered the building from New York and appeared in Washington for occasional conferences at the State Department. Finally, Krymstky became an American citizen and a metallurgist at the Bureau of Standards.

For almost sixteen years, the 16th Street embassy had stood dark, virtually deserted and tax free, an anomalous property of a government unrecognized in Washington, when Franklin D. Roosevelt was elected President of the United States.

9

Kremlin Carousel

SHORTLY AFTER THE "GREAT October Socialist Revolution" of 1917, Leon Trotsky took over what had been the imperial Russian Foreign Ministry and became the first people's commissar for foreign affairs. He planned a drastic change in the routine of dealing with other countries and announced that he would issue "some revolutionary proclamations to the peoples of the world" to take care of foreign relations, once and for all. In other words, Trotsky envisioned a steadily increasing number of nations rallying to triumphant communism and a global policy that could be decided in Moscow. Thus, diplomacy along traditional lines would no longer be necessary.

Trotsky's tenure as foreign affairs chief was short-lived. When, despite his objections, the Soviet Union signed a separate peace treaty with Germany at Brest Litovsk in March 1918, he resigned, broke with Lenin and precipitated a power struggle that eventually resulted in his own political demise. The Soviet government apparently became resigned to the fact that world revolution was not imminent and that workable diplomatic relations had to be established with capitalistic governments.

The Soviet Foreign Ministry—today one of the largest in the world—was from its inception significantly different from that of any other country. Emphasizing the necessity of spreading the communist doctrine by any means—even espionage—Soviet diplomatic installations abroad were propaganda centers staffed by mediocre emissaries sent out by a commissar for foreign affairs who had little influence on Soviet policy and with a complement of secret security agents—also called diplomats—to spy on the other diplomats, and keep them in line.

Rules for the foreign service were spelled out by the Kremlin. Personnel were ordered to mingle as infrequently as possible with inhabitants of the host country. Their children were to be schooled by Soviet teachers and were to associate exclusively with communist children. All representatives below the ambassador could attend concerts, the theater and motion picture houses only with permission of superiors. Living quarters had to be within easy access of the security agents. Diplomats could have their own homes —although it was preferable for as many to live under the same roof as possible—but they could not entertain foreigners or go to any except official parties or those given by other communists.

With those restrictions enforced, Soviet diplomats had no chance to make friends for themselves or their country abroad. Soviet diplomacy, therefore, was at low ebb in 1930, when Maxim Maximovich Litvinov became commissar for foreign affairs and began preaching the importance of international cooperation.

The plea was not a new one for Litvinov. Since 1921, when he was deputy commissar for foreign affairs under Georgi Chicherin, he had tried to promote an about-face in diplomatic policy; but the constantly changing leadership in the Kremlin was at first too much concerned with the power struggle at home to worry about improving relations abroad. The Soviet Union's diplomatic plight had become so depressing by 1930, however, that something had to be done. And Litvinov was prepared to take charge to initiate changes.

He began by completely restaffing his embassies with more dynamic personalities and relaxing the rules that had so sharply restricted the movements, contacts and even living quarters of Soviet diplomats. By the time those reforms were in force, he had moved toward obtaining United States recognition of the Soviet Union.

Concentration on that effort began in earnest the moment Franklin D. Roosevelt was elected president in 1932. Shortly after the 1933 inauguration, Litvinov arrived in Washington with a sizable party that included Constantine Oumansky, a stocky man with prominent gold teeth and an aggressive personality. Calling himself "press officer," Oumansky turned up at every important conference with Litvinov. President Roosevelt and Secretary of State Cordell Hull were puzzled that the commissar permitted himself to be so constantly shadowed by an ostensible underling; but along with a number of other high United States officials, they were to learn later that Oumansky was high in the GPU, the Soviet secret police, and was in Washington for the express purpose of keeping Litvinov under close surveillance.

As the talks with Litvinov continued, another Soviet agent was working quietly behind the scenes, very much as he had been for almost twelve years in Washington. Boris Skvirsky was a nondescript man with a quiet, mild manner. He had first appeared in the city in the early 1920s to attend a preliminary disarmament conference as delegate from the Far Eastern Republic (located in eastern Siberia and then independent of the Soviet Union). At the end of the sessions, however, the Far Eastern Republic had become a Soviet possession, and Skvirsky and his wife stayed on in Washington, leased a modest house on Massachusetts Avenue and established the Russian Information Bureau, presumably to aid prospective tourists to Russia by arranging for passports and a hospitable reception in Moscow. He had become a kind of unofficial Russian ambassador in Washington by the time Litvinov and his entourage arrived for conferences. With his many contacts among prominent

Americans, Skvirsky was able to be a tremendous help to his countrymen. He was soon to be amply rewarded.

United States recognition of the Soviet Union again focused attention on the 16th Street mansion. Eugene Schoen, the noted New York architect, was commissioned to put the house in order for the new ambassador, Alexander Antonovich Troyanovsky.

The Soviet government's original intention was to have the interior of this first Soviet Embassy in the United States drastically transformed into a setting suitable for modern, functional furnishings. But Schoen soon realized that replacing the rococo marble effects and the gilded and paneled walls would be more expensive than restoring the Eighteenth- and Nineteenth-century periods of the house. He suggested, therefore, that if everything had to be modern, it would be advisable to buy some other structure and start all over again. There were tentative efforts to sell the mansion; but when no buyers were forthcoming, Schoen was commissioned to proceed with the refurbishing, using as much as possible of the $100,000 allotment to install a stainless steel main kitchen and smaller kitchens on each floor and to modernize the fourteen white-tiled bathrooms in the house.

"Other than putting in new kitchens and baths, I am doing only what is absolutely necessary in renovating the house," Schoen said shortly afterward. "The Russians hope someday to sell the place and build an embassy more to their tastes and needs."

When the commission was completed, the mansion was as resplendent as it had been in the days when the last czarist ambassador ran it like a palace. The double-eagle motif of Imperial Russia was still on the magnificent bronze doors at the entrance, a mute symbol of the vanquished Romanovs. Russian Imperial museum pieces and effects purchased from the Edith Rockefeller McCormick estate were tastefully arranged in the spacious rooms. Red velvet draperies in the Versailles-inspired ballroom set off the white walls with their ornate decorations and fluted columns picked out in gold. Louis XV medallions and long mirrors glistened above marble mantels, and light from elaborate eighteenth-century crystal and ormulu chandeliers spilled on rich Bokhara rugs, gold-inlaid candelabra and exquisite Byzantine vases. In the Circassian walnut-paneled dining room, a handsome, century-old mosque rug covered most of the floor. China cabinets held a complete dinner service of Popoff and Imperial porcelain and table jars that were gifts from Louis XV to Catherine the Great.

The first reminder that the embassy was no longer a czarist possession was the oval picture gallery off the dining room. There, a huge plaster bust of Lenin shared the spotlight with colorful modern Russian paintings.

The chancery, which had been added to the mansion shortly after Nicholas II bought it, was also refurbished for the new envoy, along with the ambassador's simply furnished office on the ground floor of the main structure, his family living quarters on the third and a sitting room and several bedrooms on the fourth.

With periodic minor changes, the addition or subtraction of huge portraits of Soviet leaders from time to time, the house was to be the anachronistic setting of official Soviet hospitality in Washington for more than three decades. The atmosphere was occasionally gay but often grim, and the annual reception, celebrating the "Great October Socialist Revolution" was to be an accurate barometer of the accord, or lack of it, between the United States and the Soviet Union. When relations between the two countries were harmonious, notables flocked to the November observance of the historic October upheaval. When Moscow and Washington were at odds, distinguished Americans stayed away from the party, and the crowd jamming the 16th Street mansion was a heterogeneous mixture of foreign envoys, left-wing authors and scientists, reporters and employees of the Soviet trading agency in New York, summoned to Washington to fill the vast embassy reception rooms.

On a bright morning in January 1934, however, optimistic Americans anticipated a long period of uninterrupted friendship with the Soviet Union as a new flag with the hammer and sickle fluttered on a long black limousine en route from the 16th Street embassy to the White House. On the back seat sat a man with dark pendant brows and a square, swarthy face. He wore a tall silk hat, and his striped trousers and cutaway were models of sartorial elegance. Alexander A. Troyanovsky, as he usually signed himself, the first Soviet ambassador to the United States, was on his way to present his credentials to President Roosevelt.

As his automobile glided through the White House gates, His Excellency waved gaily to the crowd that had gathered to catch a glimpse of him. Five minutes later, he was inside the executive mansion.

Less than two months earlier, Roosevelt had announced termination of sixteen years of nonrecognition of the Soviet Union, and the Kremlin had been given a fresh lease on international prestige. In return, Litvinov, with Oumansky at his elbow, had signed an agreement with some significant provisions, including a guarantee against subversive and propagandistic activity of any kind in the Western Hemisphere.

Liberal Democrats enthusiastically hailed the rapprochement, while many of the old guard deplored it. Alarmists throughout the country pictured Washington as about to be taken over by bearded Bolsheviks. Capital drawing rooms echoed surmises that the new envoy and his wife would be generally ostracized by the Best People.

Reporters who converged on the embassy in numbers for Troyanovsky's first press conference waited nervously for him in the embassy foyer. They were greeted by an affable, immaculately dressed little man who for half an hour answered their questions politely in fluent English and, as one correspondent put it, "acted just like any other able envoy— only he was more pleasant than most."

Readers across the country avidly picked up threads of Troyanovsky's background in lengthy newspaper accounts, which covered his life from the days when, as the son of a czarist colonel, he attended the Imperial cadet school and later served as an artillery officer in the Russo-Japanese War. Accounts of his first press conference indicated that he glossed over his career as a revolutionist and his months with Stalin in exile, but talked at some length about Japan, where he had been Soviet ambassador just before coming to the United States. On the personal side, he said that he was happy to be in Washington and that his mission would, he hoped, "promote world peace." He added that his wife was pleased with the redecorated 16th Street mansion ("she chose the draperies and some of the furniture") and that their teen-age son Oleg had enrolled at Sidwell Friends (Quaker) School.

Standing by Troyanovsky's side through the conference and introducing him to several reporters later was Skvirsky, who had just been appointed counselor of embassy and, with his wife, had moved into the 16th Street mansion with the Troyanovskys.

On April 10, in a blaze of patrician glory, the first Soviet ambassador to the United States and Mme. Troyanovsky, a genial, well-educated woman, showed capitalistic Washington how to give the party of the year. Scheduled at 10 P.M., the white-tie reception precipitated much excitement. A thousand persons received engraved invitations bearing the gold crest of the hammer and sickle. Several hundred called the embassy and boldly asked for invitations. Refusals were polite but firm. The list, unfortunately, was closed. So sorry . . . another time, perhaps. On the evening of the event, a few resolute individuals who were thus turned down put on their best evening clothes, anyway, and appeared at the embassy promptly at ten o'clock; but a platoon of door checkers barred the uninvited proletariat, and the rebuffed contingent had to make an embarrassed exit through a throng of the curious spectators jamming 16th Street.

Inside, a distinguished cross section of officialdom and capital society climbed the marble stairway to greet the Soviet envoy and his wife and to enjoy their lavish hospitality. "Mr. Ambassador, this is the most capitalistic show I've ever seen," said Assistant State Secretary Walton Moore, by way of greeting his host. Troyanovsky grinned broadly and shot back, "What else did you expect?" Cabinet members, senators and residential notables mingled in the crowd, admired the decor of the mansion, commented on the geniality of the hosts and enjoyed the elaborate buffet.

The reception was an epic in the social and diplomatic history of the nation's capital, but it shared newspaper columns the next day with a startling revelation before a congressional committee. Dr. William Wirt, a Gary, Indiana, educator, told about having heard of a communist plan to overthrow the democratic system. The plot was discussed at a Washington dinner he attended, said Wirt, and six capital residents were involved, with Dr. Rexford Tugwell, the New Deal brain truster, as the head and President Roosevelt as the "Kerensky" of the revolution.

The testimony caused a brief uproar in Washington and resounded throughout the country. The right-wing press, still convinced that recognition of the Soviet Union was a dire mistake, pointed out that Tugwell had attended Troyanovsky's reception and that the ebullient Texas Representative Maury Maverick by way of greeting Tugwell there had teased, "Well, Rex, looks like you've found your way home!" But the New Dealers liquidated the Wirt testimony with ridicule, and within a week, reference to the "Wirt Revolution" was good for a guffaw in almost any capital gathering.

For seven months after their highly successful house-warming, the Troyanovskys gave no other big parties, but the envoy and the forty-one other members of his embassy staff got around and got acquainted where contacts could count. For the time being, bars were off on mingling with Americans, and Soviet diplomats went out of their way to be courteous to United States officials and the press. Troyanovsky acquired a number of powerful friends and frequently entertained them at small, off-the-record dinners, with bridge afterward. His card-playing cronies soon included Joseph E. Davies, who was slated to succeed William Bullitt as ambassador to the Soviet Union; Jesse Jones, director of the Reconstruction Finance Corporation; Representative Royal Johnson of South Dakota; and Eugene Meyer, publisher of the *Washington Post.*

In the fall of 1934, after a pleasant summer in the Blue Ridge mountains, the Troyanovskys resumed their demanding social calendar. Their embassy was inundated with calling cards left by persons in officialdom as well as countless others who hoped to be invited to the next big Soviet Embassy party. One ambitious dowager dispatched her chauffeur to the 16th Street address on three successive Friday afternoons to leave her card for Mme. Troyanovsky. Finally, she had an unexpected response. A DPL-licensed limousine pulled up to her house on Friday afternoon, and a liveried chauffeur alighted and left an envelope at her door. Inside, on paper with an intaglio of the hammer and sickle, was a note that read:

> Dear Comrade,
>   Thank you for your cards. Mme. Troyanovsky knows of them, and they have been filed. When our embassy resumes its social schedule, we will repay your kindness.

There was no signature; but the kindness was repaid within a few weeks, when the dowager received an invitation, bearing the hammer and sickle gold crest and inviting her to the Soviet Embassy reception "In celebration of the Seventeenth Anniversary of the Great October Socialist Revolution, 1917–1934."

Invitations to this, the first anniversary celebration of its kind in the United States, went out to 1,200 persons throughout the country. For the next five years, with varying degrees of success, the annual party was to follow much the same pattern: hours, from 5 to 7 P.M.; admission cards demanded at entrance; the ornate stairway hidden for two solid hours beneath masses of guests ascending to the second floor to be received by the host, hostess, military attachés in full uniform and their wives; masses of red roses decorating the main salons and sprouting from silver vases on the long and heavily laden dining-room table; a miniature papier-mâché Kremlin in the center of the table, flanked by yards of sturgeons and sterlets, *en jellee*, from the Volga, huge bowls of caviar from Astrakhan, Russian salad, *piroskie* (pastry filled with meat, rice, cabbage or jam), an assortment of hot and cold hors d'oeuvres, ham, turkey, breast of pheasant, a wide variety of sweets and a huge square cake decorated with a sugar hammer and sickle; another buffet in the picture gallery, and one each on the third and fourth floors; six bars dispensing vodka, Russian brandy (*Zybrovska*), martini and manhattan cocktails, Scotch and bourbon; an orchestra screened by palms on the reception floor and a string trio on the third floor.

Forty waiters and ten dishwashers were on duty during and after the first revolution reception, and a hundred cases of champagne and thirty of vodka were consumed.

Proof that the Troyanovskys had successfully mitigated prejudice against the Soviet Union was borne out by the appearance of several prominent persons who might not have been expected to attend. The president of the Daughters of the American Revolution defended her attendance as follows: "Since our government now recognizes the Soviet Union, it is our duty to get better acquainted with Soviet representatives in our country. Besides," she blurted in conclusion, "*these don't look like Bolsheviks!*"

Two days after the reception, a tactless Washington woman met Troyanovsky at a dinner and complimented him on giving "a marvelous party" and then added, archly, "although I must say, it seems odd to celebrate a revolution."

"Why?" he asked softly. "You celebrate your Fourth of July, don't you? Wasn't that a revolution—just a little more than a hundred and forty years before ours?"

Both the ambassador and his wife were music lovers, and in the spring of 1935, their social calendar took a cultural upswing. Dinners for up to 50 guests with 200 or 300 more asked in afterward for music accented their calendar frequently. Efrem Zimbalist was the featured artist at one event; Giovanni Martinelli, at another; Sergei Prokofiev and his wife, Lina Luberia, at still another.

By August 1935, the 16th Street mansion had begun to lure even those capitalites who had vowed "never to set foot in the communist embassy." Then an international turn of affairs ended the Soviet-American honeymoon. An exchange of notes between Washington and Moscow bared the fact that the Soviet Union was reneging on its promise not to diffuse Russian propaganda in the Western Hemisphere. From Moscow had come the announcement that speeches of the World Congress of the Communist International (the Comintern) would be distributed throughout the Americas. Secretary Hull dispatched a stern protest to the Kremlin. The Kremlin rejected it, declaring that the Soviet government could assume no obligations for actions of the Comintern.

From that time on, Soviet diplomats periodically were to

find themselves on precarious footing in the United States. Because of his personal popularity and the feeling of confidence that he had carefully cultivated among Washington officials, Troyanovsky weathered the first squall, but it was a mere portent of the stormy climate of Soviet-American relations in the future. Meanwhile, blusters within his own embassy were to keep him involved, and unhappy, for his remaining time in Washington.

Skvirsky, his able counselor of embassy, was appointed envoy to Afghanistan early in 1936. Shortly thereafter, Constantine Oumansky appeared on the scene as counselor and became Troyanovsky's constant companion. Soon it was apparent to the ambassador's intimates that the former official of the dreaded secret police had been sent to keep close watch on Troyanovsky—as he had watched Litvinov in 1932—and to report to the Kremlin whether or not Troyanovsky was likely to succumb to the life of bourgeois freedom and comforts. The ambassador's cronies soon noticed that he accepted invitations less readily, had fewer bridge games at the embassy, appeared somewhat aloof and preoccupied and rarely laughed.

Then he and Mme. Troyanovsky departed for Moscow, presumably on a vacation, leaving Oumansky as chargé d'affaires. Months later, when they returned, Troyanovsky was a changed man. His characteristic exuberance had disappeared; his smile was thin and fleeting. Even with his bridge-playing friends, he was nervous and ill at ease. Finally, with no prior notice, he and his family departed from Washington late in 1938.

Friends who tried to get in touch with the Troyanovskys in the following months were unsuccessful. Oumansky as chargé d'affaires was vague as to his chief's whereabouts and about when he would return to Washington.

The only Troyanovsky ever to be seen again in Washington was Oleg, who served as interpreter for Nikita Khrushchev on his trip to the United States in 1957. Former

Sidwell Friends schoolmates remembered him as "Mickey," a soccer star who was also voted the most popular member of the class of 1937. He had attended Swarthmore College the following year, but when his parents left Washington, he transferred to Moscow University. Subsequently, he served in the Soviet Embassy in London before becoming Khrushchev's interpreter. When Khrushchev was ousted, Oleg Troyanovsky's name appeared among the "pro-American advisers" who went with him. If that report was true, however, Oleg was soon reinstated, for he was appointed Soviet ambassador to Japan in May 1967 to fill the post held thirty-eight years earlier by his father, and in June 1967 he was on leave to serve as Soviet Premier Kosygin's personal interpreter and unofficial adviser on his trip to the United States. Still charming, Oleg appeared delighted when former classmates got in contact with him, although he consistently pleaded that his crowded and unpredictable schedule gave him no time to renew acquaintances.

Oumansky was appointed ambassador to the United States early in 1939, a week after Molotov relieved Litvinov of his portfolio as commissar of foreign affairs. Oumansky's promotion had a lukewarm reception in Washington. The suspicion that he had undermined the popular Troyanovsky worked strongly against him, as did his record in Moscow. Several foreign correspondents had come to dislike him heartily in Moscow, where he had given them a hard time for five years as chief of the press section of the Foreign Office and virtual censorship dictator of the Soviet Union.

Oumansky was nothing if not determined. He set out systematically to court approval with his proficient English and his mastery of the American idiom. He had an easy smile and flashing gold teeth that gave the impression that he was something of a Soviet country bumpkin, eager to make friends.

An attractive diplomat with more finesse might have been able to overcome initial handicaps, but with every move, Oumansky became more unpopular. He gave luncheons and dinners constantly, and when persons he invited said they had previous engagements, he complained to Undersecretary of State Sumner Welles that the Soviet Embassy was not being treated with respect by Washington officialdom.

Several drastic changes in policy for the staff took place while Oumansky was envoy. The ruling as to the education of Soviet Embassy children had been relaxed while Troyanovsky was ambassador. Then Molotov ordered a return of the old edict: children of Soviet diplomats abroad, henceforth, were to be taught by Soviet teachers in Soviet schools; English was to be banned; all children past the sixth grade were to be sent back to Russia for further education. Concurrently, Oumansky informed his own subordinates that they were to mingle socially with Americans as infrequently as possible.

When Molotov summoned his ambassador in Washington to return to Moscow for conferences in the autumn of 1939, Oumansky was lucky, for he was allowed to stay long enough to miss being host at one of the grimmest soirees ever to take place in the capital. The Soviet chargé d'affaires, Dimitri S. Shuvakhin, and Mme. Oumansky greeted guests at the reception to celebrate the Twenty-second Anniversary of the Great October Socialist Revolution. It was a disaster.

The Soviet Union and Nazi Germany had signed a nonaggression pact in August. In late October, Poland was partitioned by Russia and Germany, and Russian troops were massed on the Finnish border by early November. President Roosevelt had expressed strong sympathy for threatened Finland, and Molotov had blasted Roosevelt as a "meddler."

Some 1,400 invitations went out to the reception, scheduled for November 7, 1939; but visions of Soviet caviar, sturgeon and vodka were no longer tempting. Almost a thousand "regrets" poured into the Soviet Embassy. The

Russians took no chance on having their spacious salons virtually bare during the scheduled party. A call to AMTORG in New York brought numerous Russians and acquaintances to the capital in time for the reception. More than 800 persons, the majority of whom were strangers in Washington, were at the party by six o'clock.

Reporters, having posted themselves at vantage points in and around the embassy at five o'clock, waited in vain for any high American officials to arrive. Not one Supreme Court justice, Cabinet member, senator or top-ranking State Department official appeared.

British Ambassador Lord Lothian and French Ambassador Count de Saint-Quentin were not there. The only Latin American envoy who attended was Ecuadorian Ambassador Capitán Colon Eloy Alfaro. Count Jerzy Potocki, the Polish ambassador, was not present, but making an unexpected appearance—and headlines—was Finland's minister, Hjalmar Procope, who stayed exactly five minutes. Every embassy and legation that had diplomatic relations with the Soviet Union was, of course, represented by some staff member— as is always the case when a national holiday is being celebrated on Embassy Row but most ranking diplomats were missing.

Missing, also, was the lavish menu for which the "Revolution Affair" had become noted. The dining room buffet was not dominated by yards-long lots of sturgeon, and the huge bowls of caviar were no longer there. An adequate but not unusual array of appetizers and other viands surrounded a big cake, elaborately iced with the Soviet flag motif. Two bars were amply stocked with Scotch and bourbon, but there was no champagne. Vodka flowed, but not freely, dispensed from a small bottle on request, at only one bar.

Arriving in New York two days later, Oumansky was met by a battalion of reporters, who bombarded him with embarrassing questions he declined to answer. Finally, he was asked whether or not he was a member of the GPU, the Soviet secret police.

"No! No!" he cried. "I am not a member! What *is* the GPU, anyway?" He had been rescued by Soviet colleagues and disappeared before there was an answer. Actually, he was not a member of the GPU at the time. The name of the agency had changed to the NKVD, and in that organization he was a high official.

Back in Washington, Oumansky resumed an active social schedule. He honored Leopold Stokowski at luncheon. He gave a series of dinners, at which the presence of capital notables described a consistently descending scale. Then the scrapping of the German-Soviet nonaggression pact brought a noticeable reversal in attitudes. The Soviet Union, all at once, was a fast friend of the allied powers, and the euphoria that had swept over Washington during Troyanovsky's tenure as envoy again was evident.

Despite the changing attitude toward the Soviet Union generally, however, there was still little regard for Oumansky personally when he returned to Moscow late in 1940. However, he was to continue to be listed as ambassador to the United States for many months; and it was not until shortly before Pearl Harbor that Maxim Maximovich Litvinov arrived to replace him.

Washington welcomed the appointment of Litvinov. His opposition to the Nazi-Soviet alliance and his widely publicized advocacy of cooperation with England, France and the United States had prompted his expulsion from the central committee of the Communist Party. But after the German attack on Russia in 1941 and the United States Lend-Lease extension to Russia, his political status vaulted. His assignment to the United States was logical recognition. Washington was in a mood to receive with open arms the representative of the world's biggest country at a most crucial time.

In his sixties and with thinning hair, a pudgy physique and a robust face that radiated common sense, Litvinov looked more like a retired American businessman than a Soviet diplomat. He was personable, intelligent and convivial. Like Troyanovsky, he enjoyed bridge and soon had a number of bridge-playing intimates in officialdom. He basked in the approbation of the White House; the press hailed him as a staunch friend of America; and he was soon the most widely discussed and the most popular envoy in Washington.

Big, abrasive and Argus-eyed, Mme. Litvinov had been a controversial figure in London and Moscow for some time. The former Ivy Low, born in England, she was daughter of Walter Low, and a niece of Sir Sidney Low, the famed historian. She first attracted attention with her radical writings during the prerevolutionary decade when Litvinov was, by turns, a salesman, clerk, teacher and communist pamphleteer in London. Press correspondents who had known her in the early 1930s in Moscow described her as "extremely talkative, opinionated, and undiplomatic"; but they also pointed out that in 1937 she had been temporarily exiled in the Urals because of her loyalty to a friend who had been purged that year.

Her penchant for making startling remarks, saying exactly what she thought, when and where she pleased, soon was the talk of Washington. She deplored "the silly questions" asked by reporters and preoccupation of American women with style and charm. Her own wardrobe was obviously chosen with a fine disregard of fashion, but its dowdiness somehow suited her. Typical of her attitude about clothes was a remark she made to a society reporter who was making notes on Mme. Litvinov's costume at one of her receptions. "Why on earth would your readers *care?*" she asked. "*I* certainly don't."

She was an omnivorous reader of American newspapers and a ruthless critic of their contents. "They tell everything

—but the facts," she complained. "Why, every time I read an article about myself, I find out something new, and it's usually a lot of bosh! Don't American journalists believe, at all, in the law of diminishing returns?"

There were few "diminishing returns" in Mme. Litvinov's flair for making news, and she often made it from the platform with uninhibited speeches. "Your wife is one of the best public speakers I've ever heard," a club woman once told Litvinov. "Is that good, I wonder?" asked the envoy, with a grin. "But," he added brightly, "I can always depend on Mama to keep things lively."

Had Ivy Litvinov not been the Russian ambassadress during an ascending period in Soviet-American relations, it is doubtful that her strong personality would have been palatable to Washington, but as it was, she crested the wave of Soviet-American accord and for two years got more attention than any other woman in the diplomatic corps.

One of the most memorable parties ever given in Washington was the annual Russian celebration on November 7, 1942. A capital wag arriving at the embassy that afternoon whispered to a companion, "I guess the Russians have dusted off their biggest sturgeons for *this* shindig!" America was at war, the valiant Red Army was routing Nazi forces at Stalingrad and Washington was beside itself with admiration for the Soviet Union, its indestructible ally. Ambassador and Mme. Litvinov greeted 1,500 guests, including Vice President and Mrs. Wallace, the entire Cabinet, heads of all the wartime emergency agencies, 80 senators and dozens of celebrities from out of town, including playwright Lillian Hellman, and Cyrus Eaton, the Ohio industrialist and outspoken advocate of increased trade and understanding between the Soviet Union and the United States.

By the spring of 1943, Litvinov's time in Washington was nearing the end. In May, he was recalled to Moscow. Rumors spread that Stalin and Molotov were fed up with his popularity in the United States and annoyed at American sympathy toward anti-Soviet rumbles abroad. While Roosevelt and Churchill were conferring in Quebec in August, the Soviet ambassador to Britain and the Soviet minister to Canada were summoned to Moscow, and Litvinov's replacement in the United States was announced. Thirty-four-year-old Andrei Gromyko, chargé d'affaires in Washington, whom Litvinov had once described as a Kremlin messenger boy, had been appointed ambassador.

Typical of the tough young Russians who grew up after the Bolshevik revolution and who were educated entirely under the Soviet government, Gromyko had been a Communist Party member since 1931 and was recruited into diplomacy after the Great Purge of 1936–1938 depleted the Soviet foreign service. In 1939, he was sent to Washington as counselor. He knew little English at the time, but he had mastered it by the time he became ambassador.

Although he had been on duty in Washington for several years, few Americans knew Gromyko, even by sight. Until he moved into the 16th Street embassy, he and his wife and their two children had lived quietly in a remote suburban area and had not mingled with even their closest neighbors.

As ambassador, Gromyko was distinctly different from his gregarious predecessors. Tall, dark and taciturn, he barricaded himself behind embassy portals most of the time and was aloof and enigmatic, even when he was host at the annual revolution receptions.

He created a ripple of interest at one, however, when he and members of his staff appeared in their own new diplomatic uniforms, the first worn by Russians in Washington since Imperial days. Of blue serge, with wide gold-braided cuffs and lapel trim, the attire for eleven ranks from ambassador to attaché made quite a hit. Gromyko's was set off with the Order of Lenin, the highest Soviet decoration.

By the time Gromyko had been envoy for two years, his

embassy's social standing had noticeably diminished, and United States official participation in even the annual revolution reception had dwindled to brief appearances by lesser members of the State Department. The 16th Street diplomatic establishment had become one of the biggest puzzles in the city.

For the next six or seven years, the steady deterioration of Soviet–United States relations isolated the Soviet Embassy staff into the deep freeze it seemed to prefer. Nikolai Novikov became ambassador in May 1945, to be followed by Alexander Semenovich Panyushkin, appointed ambassador in 1947. Panyushkin was tagged as "another Soviet mystery man," but on the surface he was as colorless as a glass of vodka and was unprepossessing enough to pass unnoticed in even a small gathering. The only oddments of interest that could be pried out of his embassy before he arrived was that he was forty-two, had been envoy to China from 1939 to 1944 and after that assigned by the Kremlin to "unspecified duties" before being appointed emissary to the United States. Panyushkin's problems as envoy were monumental. The communist coup in Czechoslovakia, the suicide attempt of Oksana Kasenkina, the Russian consulate schoolteacher in New York, and Soviet spy hearings before congressional investigating committees were only a few of the troubles that involved him on his United States tour of duty.

On arrival as Soviet ambassador in 1952, Georgi Nikolaeyvich Zaroubin appeared to be the diametric opposite of his elusive forerunners Gromyko and Panyushkin. He was pushingly affable, talkative and eager to ingratiate himself with other foreign envoys and Americans. He was a party-goer and the first Soviet ambassador since Litvinov to move without the constant accompaniment of some member of his staff. He was particularly courteous to the press and passed up no opportunity to observe that he was "always happy with Americans." But his record was not conducive to confidence. He had been linked with two startling espionage cases. He was ambassador to Canada when a giant communist spy network was discovered and destroyed, and he was ambassador to Britain when Klaus Fuchs confessed to stealing atomic energy secrets for the Kremlin. He arrived in Washington when suspicions were spreading that the Soviet Embassy had become little more than a propaganda outlet and espionage headquarters.

However, he was a determined diplomat and an active one; and he was not deterred. Host at the first black-tie reception at the Soviet Embassy since World War II, he followed through with a series of musicales featuring famous artists. He was beginning to make a slight impact on the social capital when Soviet oppression of Hungary aroused the free world, and the slim attendance at the November 7, 1956, reception indicated widespread resentment against the Soviet Union. Of the 1,500 persons invited, only 450 appeared. Not one ranking member of the State Department showed up. Justice William O. Douglas was the only high United States official there. Envoys of England, France, Spain, Germany and Italy were conspicuously missing.

On October 4, 1957, however, the launching of the first earth satellite, Sputnik, zoomed the Soviet Embassy into a prestigious position again, and the November 7 reception that year created renewed interest. Zaroubin, wearing his gold-trimmed diplomatic uniform, received well over a thousand guests, including a ranking representation from United States officialdom and the diplomatic corps. The beluga caviar, red caviar, salmon, roast beef and turkey, washed down with champagne or vodka, went quickly, and the anniversary cake, iced with the inscription "Anniversary of the Great October Socialist Revolution, 1917–1957," was bigger than ever before. It was a gala occasion. Guests, congratulating Zaroubin, were prone to forget that a number of his embassy underlings had been expelled for spying in the preceding year and that several others were under sharp surveillance.

The party was Zaroubin's swan song. His Washington tour of duty coincided with a power struggle within the Kremlin following Stalin's death. Then, with Nikita Khrushchev in power, a notable change of Soviet diplomacy was aimed to liquidate the inscrutable image that had been set by Gromyko and Panyushkin and to add dash and convincing convivality to the illusion Zaroubin had tried to project.

Khrushchev wanted his envoy to the United States to play the diplomatic game as others played it in Washington; to get out and about, entertain and be entertained with as much elegance and charm as possible; to prove generally that the de-Stalinization of Russia perceptibly extended to its foreign policy.

Mikhail Alekseevich Menshikov, silver-haired, handsome and energetic, was assigned to personify the new concept in the United States; and in preparation for his arrival, the Soviet Embassy in Washington was refurbished.

Resourceful Menshikov lost no time in establishing camaraderie with the press. Just after he presented his credentials to President Eisenhower, a reporter asked him how to spell his first name. He complied; then added with a wide grin, "But just call me Mike." He was off to a good start.

That evening, trimly turned out in white tie, complete with a top hat, he arrived at the diplomatic dinner at the White House. There was nothing particularly spectacular about Mme. Menshikov, but she impressed those she met as a pleasant woman who dressed conservatively and appeared to be a quiet foil for her ebullient husband.

The Menshikovs went everywhere they were asked. News cameras constantly focused on the ambassador; reporters sought him out. His affability and his constant grin soon earned him the sobriquet of "Smiling Mike" and he loved it. Although he occasionally mutilated syntax, the story that he clicked champagne glasses with a sedate senator's wife at dinner one night and chirruped, "Up your bottom!" is probably fictitious. But it went the cocktail rounds in Washington and enhanced interest in him.

Menshikov was no mental giant, but he could converse on a wide variety of subjects—and did, although on the social circuit, at least, he generally declined to discuss anything political. At a small gathering one evening, he listened in wide-eyed surprise as an American was sharply critical of President Eisenhower. "You wouldn't hear that kind of talk about your leaders in Moscow, would you?" a woman whispered to him. "I don't think you should hear it—anywhere," he softly, and gravely, replied.

The 1959 visit of Khrushchev must have taxed Menshikov's patience, as it did others who had the responsibility of seeing it to a reasonably satisfactory conclusion; but the envoy ably handled such chores as conveying constant complaints and worrisome requests from his chief to the State Department. He also had to inform the White House that, although the state dinner for Khrushchev stipulated white tie, the honor guest had never been known to wear full dress and would not on that occasion.

An epicure, Menshikov patently enjoyed planning the dinner at which Premier and Mme. Khrushchev honored President and Mrs. Eisenhower at the embassy. The head chef and most of the food had been flown from Moscow in the jet that transported Khrushchev and his party, and the menu was prepared in the kitchen of the Mayflower Hotel. Thirty-three persons were involved in getting it to the embassy and serving it to the fifty-two guests, who were seated at a U-shaped table set in the white and gold ballroom. The occasion marked the first time that President Eisenhower had ever set foot in the embassy, so he did not notice that the portraits of both Stalin and Lenin were missing.

Stalin's was still missing when Menshikov gave his final November 7 reception in 1961; but Lenin's was again in place, and a new painting of Khrushchev hung nearby. "Whatever became of Stalin's portrait?" an inquisitive guest asked Menshikov. "I don't know," he shot back, "but there is no reason to have it here—now."

At his farewell soiree on December 29, 1961, Menshikov appeared deeply touched that so many guests expressed regret that he was leaving. He was going, he said, at his own request. He had been on assignments away from Russia for eight years.

With the exception of State Department officials who deal with them, security men who watch them and tradesmen with whom they do business, comparatively few Washington residents ever have a chance to get acquainted with any of the Soviet diplomats besides the ambassador and the military attachés. So, although Anatoliy Fedorovich Dobrynin had been Soviet counselor in Washington from 1954 to 1955, when he returned to the foreign ministry, he was virtually a stranger when he arrived as ambassador in March 1962. He was forty-three, six feet tall, with a high forehead, a slightly receding hairline and bright blue eyes behind steel-rimmed glasses. Dobrynin looked like an American bank president when he and his attractive wife held an impromptu press conference on arrival and readily answered a barrage of personal questions. They revealed that both were trained airplane designers; that their only daughter, fourteen-year-old Yelena, had stayed in the Soviet Union to finish the seventh grade; that they felt very much at home in the United States, having spent a year in Washington and three years in New York, when Dobrynin was the ranking Soviet member of the United Nations Secretariat.

The capital soon learned that the new ambassador knew how to make the most of his wit and his flair for terse expression, in either excellent English or French. In a short period, he had established himself as a topnotch personality, considered by those whom he favorably impressed as an efficient, genial and intelligent diplomat and by others as a shrewd and dangerously clever Soviet agent.

From the beginning, Dobrynin has fared better than several of his predecessors. He is neither shy nor aggressive. He is a delightful host and an equally delightful guest. And because of his quotable wit, reporters try to get near him wherever he goes. They are not always successful. At parties, he has a way of engaging high officials or diplomatic colleagues in long, apparently serious conversations that admit no intrusion. At White House receptions and other social gatherings, he and Secretary Rusk have engaged in lengthy talks as though they had nowhere else to confer. Dobrynin and former Indian Ambassador Braj Kumar Nehru rarely met at any gathering without retiring to a quiet corner for a chat. Another of Dobrynin's special conversational cronies was former Algerian Ambassador Cherif Guellal. A brief talk that they had at a party in October 1963 brought such a hearty chuckle from Dobrynin that Guellal repeated the tête-à-tête to a reporter. It had to do with an Algerian official who came to Washington to talk to Secretary Rusk about the Algerian-Moroccan border dispute and wanted to report back to his foreign office. When he asked the overseas telephone operator to put him through to Algiers, she asked, patently puzzled, "Algiers? Where's that? In Morocco?"

The personal popularity of Dobrynin has not kept him from being subjected to snubs in protests of actions by the Kremlin. The reception he gave for a delegation of Soviet cultural leaders in November 1963 took place shortly after Yale Professor Frederick C. Barghoorn was arrested in Moscow as a suspected spy. Among the very few invited notables who appeared was Senator Ernest Gruening of Alaska. "I thought it would be rude to stay away," he told a reporter, "but I certainly deplore the arrest as Soviet stupidity!" To Dobrynin, he said, "It's a good thing that guy your people arrested wasn't a Harvard man!" Dobrynin burst out laughing. The Soviet visitors—a delegation of noted artists, authors, scientists and philosophers headed by Professor Nikolai Blokhin, Russia's leading cancer authority—were astounded and chagrined.

The group, all of whom had paid their own way to the United States, had come to celebrate the thirtieth anniversary of United States–Soviet relations. However, after the news of the American professor's protest, many groups—including, in the Washington area alone, the National Gallery, Georgetown University and the University of Maryland—had canceled engagements to receive them.

Spokesman and interpreter for the party, Mme. T. G. Mamedova, who had been cultural attaché at the Soviet Embassy from 1956 to 1959, gave a newspaper interview in which she lashed out at the rude treatment to her countrymen who were "in no way responsible for actions of the Russian government." Her protest had some effect. As the party continued the trip, enough prominent Americans managed to entertain them privately to keep them reasonably happy until the tour ended. The ambassador, meanwhile, declined to discuss the matter.

Dobrynin has weathered a number of storms in Washington. Housing problems that have long beset him now show signs of easing, with the plans under way to build an enormous new Soviet complex on the Wisconsin Avenue site of Mt. Alto Hospital. Vandal-critics have splashed paint on the façade of the 16th Street embassy several times, and a bomb shattered windows and a wall of a first-floor office there in February 1968. United States–Soviet relations have followed a rough course since the war in Vietnam began to escalate in February 1965. Yet none of these situations or developments have seemed to affect Dobrynin's personal standing in Washington. He is still regarded as the best envoy Moscow has sent to the United States since Litvinov.

As with all envoys when the going is difficult, there have

been recurrent rumors that he was to be replaced. Each time he has been asked about them, he has replied with light, noncommittal banter. Typical was his rejoinder in September 1964 when a reporter queried him about the report that he was slated to replace Foreign Minister Gromyko before the end of the year.

"Do you *want* me to leave?" he shot back, with his engaging smile.

"No, no, of course not."

"Then I *won't* leave," he promised, with a twinkle. "And now, shall we talk about something more pleasant?"

Mme. Dobrynin, an unusually attractive woman, left Washington the spring of 1967, presumably to be in Moscow for only a brief time. When her absence was prolonged, the ambassador said repeatedly that she would be returning soon. Then he explained, "Her mother, who takes care of our daughter, is ill, and she must stay longer." She returned in the spring of 1968, bringing their daughter with her.

With little of the lavishness that marked Soviet party giving by the Troyanovskys and Litvinovs, the Dobrynins soon established themselves as charming hosts at the annual celebrations. Guests at several of their receptions have included Cyrus Eaton and his wife, Van Cliburn, the famed pianist who won the coveted Tchaikovsky award in Moscow, and a sizable number of distinguished United States officials.

One of the biggest Soviet Embassy receptions since Dobrynin has been envoy celebrated the fiftieth anniversary of the revolution, on November 7, 1967. Invitations went out in the names of the ambassador and his wife. She was not there, but Dobrynin, in full diplomatic uniform, adorned with the Order of Lenin, and his uniformed military, air and naval attachés, with their wives, received more than 1,300 guests. Very much in the spotlight was Secretary Rusk, who rarely appeared at late-afternoon soirees. Asked why he broke his rule to attend this particular party, he replied, "Well, for a fiftieth anniversary, I make an exception."

As is often the case with Soviet Embassy parties, this one was picketed—but quietly and at a comfortable distance: a couple of blocks down the street, fifty persons paraded with banners urging help for captive nations. Demonstrations are illegal within 500 feet of embassies in Washington.

The heaviest security precautions ever laid out for an embassy reception were in force on February 23, 1968, when the Armed Forces Day reception marked the fiftieth anniversary of the Soviet military. The event took place two days after the embassy was bombed, and District police by the dozens were on guard all around the place. Soviet security men checked invitations at the door. Dobrynin himself was a guest, as was Minister Counselor Yuri Tcherniakov, whose office was blown up in the bombing. With infectious good humor, he joked about it, said it was a very good thing that he was not the type of worker who rushes to duty at an early hour. "If I were, I would have been blown up," he added, referring to the fact that the explosion had been at daybreak.

Meanwhile, a constant release of press statements from the embassy implied that the United States might have been implicated in the bombing—that, in any case, it was negligent in protecting the Soviet Embassy. The old pattern of Byzantine suspicion that periodically appears in Russian dealings with the United States was again in evidence, to be handled in the only way the Soviets seem to understand. Accordingly, the State Department took "serious exceptions" to the Russian charges in a heated conference with Tcherniakov, representing the Soviet Embassy.

Today, the Soviet Embassy is the biggest diplomatic establishment in Washington, with the listing of its 89 official members covering more than three pages in the *Diplomatic List*. Almost half the members have several assistants who are not listed. At least 150 Russians are connected with the embassy, and security sources indicate that a high percentage is engaged in some kind of espionage.

Jean-Paul Mauriat, chief of France's counterespionage service, warned in December 1967 that "of every ten diplomats in certain foreign embassies, from four to six are engaged in espionage." He was referring to diplomats in Paris, but his statement might well apply to Washington, where the "certain embassies" are generally in the Soviet bloc. More than forty Soviet diplomats were accused of spying and asked to leave the United States from March 1950 to February 1968. Eighteen diplomats from satellite countries were sent home for similar reasons during the same period.

Not all espionage cases are brought to public attention. On a quid pro quo basis of reciprocity with the Soviet Union, the United States has quietly ushered many Soviet spies out of the country. But some have played their cards so ineptly that their recalls attracted wide publicity.

The stereotype of the spy as an unkempt, furtive figure who meets his contacts in shabby, dimly lighted taverns is dispelled in Washington, where smartly dressed agents with diplomatic status sometimes operate in the chandeliered drawing rooms in and around Embassy Row. Much of the undercover activity may continue elsewhere—in suburban restaurants, at secretive "drop" points and in offices from which strategic information is extracted—but the cocktail circuit is a fertile field for invaluable espionage contacts.

For example, Colonel Stig Wennerström was arrested in Stockholm in 1963, on charges of spying for the Soviet Union since 1948. Wennerström, Swedish air attaché in the United States from 1952 to 1957, admitted he had gathered information as he moved freely in Washington social circles and had even relayed some of it at diplomatic receptions.

Many Washingtonians remembered the tall, white-haired officer in his middle fifties, who with his wife often entertained at their house on 29th Street. The Wennerströms had a noticeable number of prominent acquaintances outside, as well as inside, the diplomatic corps, and some of them recalled that the flurry of farewell parties preceding the Wennerströms' departure in June 1957 was embarrassingly interrupted by domestic complications, when their sixteen-year-old daughter, Christina, and Huw Williams, a seventeen-year-old congressional page boy, eloped. Mme. Wennerström was openly anguished, though her husband seemed preoccupied and more concerned with getting away from Washington than in retrieving his daughter. In fact, when no trace of her had been found in a couple of weeks, he took off for Sweden, leaving his wife to continue the search.

Colonel Wennerström's espionage activities, which were revealed in a series of testimonies from 1963 to 1966, emphasized that an attaché from a neutral country has an extraordinary opportunity to mingle, unsuspected, with communist diplomats as well as others in Washington's ceaseless party-go-round and to gather intelligence important to opposing sides.

While awaiting sentence on espionage charges, Wennerström said that he had made the most of that advantage in Washington. The ease with which he operated as a double agent before casting his lot with the Russians was stressed throughout the heavily censored transcript of this testimony. His wide acquaintanceship with U.S. Air Force and Navy officers, sedulously cultivated at social gatherings, resulted in his obtaining information easily. His friends often permitted him to borrow classified technical material, which he privately photographed for the Russians and sometimes passed on to them at diplomatic receptions. As described in the testimony, the latter procedure was uncomplicated. Wennerström simply left the roll of film in a pocket of his overcoat when he deposited it in the cloakroom. Then, over cocktails later, he quietly apprised the Soviet agent that he had brought the film and where it could be found.

On the other hand, Wennerström disclosed at his pretrial hearings, "As a temporary agent for the CIA, I agreed to attend Soviet functions regularly and to be on the lookout for a Russian-speaking contact who would make himself known in an exchange of passwords." Other aspects of Wennerström's multiple activities, according to his testimony, were along more routine lines. He made friends with a few people in high places, he said, by complimenting their wives and sometimes paying their parking tickets.

10

Always the British

For years, the British Embassy crested the social wave in Washington, and invitations with the gold lion and unicorn insignia were coveted second only to those from the White House.

However, it was not always so. From Anthony Merry to Sir Patrick Dean, the ambassador who retired at the end of 1968, British emissaries have operated with varying degrees of success in Washington. In the earlier days, Great Britain, like most other countries across the Atlantic, sent inexperienced or second-grade diplomats. Nevertheless, some succeeded brilliantly; several were popular; only three—all in the nineteenth century—were expelled.

The Merrys, who irritated Jefferson, probably would have fared better in any other post. Dr. Manasseh Cutler, in 1804, described Merry as "a well informed, genteel man, extremely easy and social" and was "especially pleased with his lady, who is a remarkably fine woman." Merry's successor, David Montague Erskine, was censured by his government for not being sharper in his diplomatic dealings, but he and his American-born wife, a Cadwalader of Philadelphia, got on well with Jefferson and Madison.

Francis James ("Copenhagen") Jackson and his Prussian-born wife would not have been popular anywhere, but they were surrounded by an especially hostile atmosphere in Washington when relations between the United States and Great Britain were near the breaking point. A smoother and

185

more competent envoy might have stopped the trend, but Jackson, whose nickname harked to the time when he ordered bombardment of the Danish city, was blunt, unpleasant and critical. He made no effort to mask his dislike of Madison and described the President as a "plain and rather mean-looking little man" and Dolley Madison as "fat and forty, but not fair." Madison soon found that he could not deal with Jackson and declared him *persona non grata*.

Lord Lyons, who was the British ambassador during the Lincoln administration, made his imprint on Washington as the envoy who kept Britain from supporting the Confederacy, but he was known at the time as a strange bachelor who was wary of women. At forty-two, he wrote, "I am afraid marriage is better never than too late. American women are undoubtedly pretty, but my heart is too callous to be wounded by their charms"; and in later life he took pride in recalling that during his American tour of duty he "never took a drink or made a speech."

The most peculiar of all the early emissaries, however, was another bachelor, Henry Stephen Fox, who was minister from 1836 to 1844. He not only avoided society but also contact with people generally, and his meetings with colleagues were always by candlelight. He disliked paying bills and amassed debts all over town. His absorbing interest was entomology, and he collected insects from various parts of the world. Few Americans ever knew him, but he must have liked Washington; for after his retirement, he continued to live at Kuhn House on K Street, which had been the British legation. He died there in 1846 and was buried in the congressional cemetery.

Edward (later Sir Edward) Thornton long was to be remembered as the envoy who promoted the purchase of the British mission's first permanent home in Washington. The son of Edward Thornton, who was chargé d'affaires from 1800 to 1808, the envoy who arrived in the Lincoln administration first lived in Riggs House on I Street until he persuaded his government to buy the property on Connecticut Avenue where the first British legation was built. He was hotly criticized for choosing such a remote locale, although it was only ten blocks from the White House, but within five years after the legation was opened in 1874, it was the center of a select residential section. Meanwhile, Thornton was knighted; and Lady Thornton, presiding over the finest diplomatic establishment in the city, was the social leader in the foreign corps, vying with Kate Chase (Mrs. William) Sprague, wife of the senator from New Jersey, and Mrs. Hamilton Fish, wife of Grant's secretary of state, for acclaim as the leading hostess in Washington.

The Connecticut Avenue establishment continued to be a social center for many years. Then, James Bryce was appointed British ambassador from 1907 to 1913. He was a student of America at large. The routine partygoing scene of Washington did not interest him, and he and Mrs. Bryce lived as simply as their position would allow. They gave two receptions and two official dinners a year and gathered around them at informal affairs scholars, historians and naturalists. They were fascinated with the natural wonders of America and traveled as much as possible to enjoy them. The author of *The American Commonwealth*, written years before he became envoy, Bryce made many significant observations on American life during his tour of duty in Washington. He deplored the uniformity of customs and standards in our country and its preoccupation with the attainment of wealth, but he admired its energy and verve. He was fortunate that his diplomatic assignment coincided with a pleasant and undemanding period in Anglo-American relations.

His successor, Sir Cecil Spring-Rice, was not so lucky. Every inch His Britannic Majesty's ambassador in appearance and demeanor, he arrived in 1913, when World War I was in the making and the fear that America would be involved was strong. Arriving promptly to present his credentials to Secretary of State William Jennings Bryan, Spring-Rice was trimly turned out in morning coat and striped trousers. Bryan, talking with a trio of minor politicians in his inner office, kept the envoy waiting outside for two hours and then appeared in a cheap, wrinkled suit.

Within a short time, Spring-Rice had more frustrating problems. As war clouds continued to darken, anti-British sentiment focused on him, and he was censured in the press and on platforms throughout the country. The active German Embassy figured in his unpopularity in Washington. Wily Franz von Papen, the German military attaché, and Captain Karl Boy-Ed, the naval attaché, moved in the city's most exclusive circles right up to the moment when both were declared *personae non gratae* for involvement in the German espionage apparatus. German Ambassador Count von Bernstorff and his American-born wife regularly entertained the most prominent people in social and official Washington and frequently scheduled dinners on the same evenings as those given at the British Embassy. Washington gossiped that almost anyone in the city, given a choice, accepted invitations from the Germans.

Lady Spring-Rice, a charming hostess and the daughter of Lord Lascelles, who had been British ambassador to Germany, managed more gracefully than her berated husband. With the help of her good friend Mme. Jusserand, she gathered around her a solid phalanx of loyal friends; but as the anti-British furor grew more intense, the Spring-Rices virtually withdrew from society until public opinion swung to the British.

German Ambassador and Countess von Bernstorff were hospitable, but discriminating. Before war broke out in Europe, Washington's residential aristocracy and ranking diplomats made up the guest lists for their lavish dinners and exclusive musicales. The red brick German Embassy, dominating the block-long Massachusetts Avenue terrace, had been Germany's official home in Washington since 1894, but it began to take on added interest when the Bernstorffs refurbished it shortly after their arrival in 1908. It was a flourishing social center for years.

In the light of later developments, Washingtonians were to remember that after war broke out in Europe, the German Embassy dinners included more and more United States senators and representatives; members of the press were frequently invited to receptions and stag luncheons; and Germans of noble and military title, ostensibly on brief visits to the United States, were regularly feted by the Bernstorffs.

By early 1914, the German ambassador and one or two members of his staff could be glimpsed two or three times a week on Capitol Hill, where they listened attentively to speeches and later called on senators and representatives in their offices. The Germans were well aware that several members of Congress had constituents of German and Irish heritage and others who were openly sympathetic to the Central Powers or were determined to keep America neutral on any account.

When Britain and France, with the British fleet in full control of the seas, began shipping war material in volume from America in 1915, a thoroughly organized pro-German lobby went into action throughout the United States. At the same time, a sabotage network was set up to disrupt American factories with British and French contracts and to blow up harbors from which munitions were being shipped.

Years later a number of Washingtonians recalled the puzzling attitude of Von Bernstorff after the departure of his naval and military aides. He seemed relieved—even delighted—that they had been ordered home. Repeatedly professing that he knew nothing about their illegal acts—indeed, that he was completely unaware that there was a German espionage network in the United States—he continued his busy social calendar and ignored the general antagonism that was growing around him. His once-close associations with French Ambassador Jules Jusserand and British Ambassador Sir Cecil Spring-Rice had ceased, but he still had a coterie of American friends who noticed that he seemed less perturbed, on the whole, than the British and French envoys. They were under tremendous pressure to counteract German propaganda vigorously; but soon no organized countercampaign was needed. American sympathy was swinging to the Allies.

By the winter of 1916 alignments in the diplomatic corps were so sharply drawn and the atmosphere was so tense that the White House canceled its annual diplomatic reception and gave two diplomatic dinners. On January 21, representatives of the Allied nations, including Sir Cecil Spring-Rice, were honored, along with the neutrals favorable to them among the South Americans and Europeans. On January 25, Von Bernstorff headed the guest list for the White House dinner for envoys of the Central Powers and those from countries sympathetic to them.

There were no White House fetes for diplomats the next winter. The United States was on the verge of war.

It came quickly. On January 8, 1917, the German High Command voted to wage unrestricted warfare on the high seas, beginning February 1; and on January 30 Von Bernstorff appeared at the White House and handed Wilson a note announcing that, henceforth, "all sea traffic will be stopped with every available weapon without further notice."

Von Bernstorff stayed in Washington until the United States declared war on Germany in April 1917. Although he had spent almost ten years in our country, his first book, published in 1920, was entitled *My Three Years in America* and covered only his tenure during the war period. In it, he stressed that if Germany had followed less flagrant policies, she could have kept the United States out of the conflict, that he could get no support from Berlin for his opposition to submarine warfare and that he had no connection with the espionage apparatus.

British prestige, which had risen steadily since the beginning of the twentieth century, approached its zenith when Sir Esmé Howard, the popular British ambassador from 1924 to 1930 and dean of the diplomatic corps for four years, laid the cornerstone for the new million-dollar embassy on Massachusetts Avenue in 1928 and dispersed the location of Embassy Row.

Sir Edwin Lutyens was the architect for the Queen Anne–style red-brick and stone structure with a pillared portico and terrace leading to a rolling greensward on the south side of the residence and the chancery built around a courtyard facing Massachusetts Avenue. Opened in 1931, it was the most magnificent diplomatic complex in Washington, and the mansion was a stately setting for the dinners and garden parties that established Lady Lindsay, wife of the new British ambassador, as the leading hostess on Embassy Row.

A teapot tempest shook that status in 1939. Sir Ronald Lindsay had been dean of the diplomatic corps for five years and Lady Lindsay had enjoyed unimpeachable social prominence for eight when the planned June 1939 visit of King George and Queen Elizabeth was announced in April. By neither inclination nor past performance were the Lindsays prepared to handle the touchy task that confronted them.

A paragon of the traditional British diplomat in the Kitchener era, sent out to carry on among a bunch of colonials, Sir Ronald was a towering hulk of a man with a walrus mustache and an aloof air. He had no conception that the sun was setting on the British Empire; but in his ceremonial uniform, heavily weighted with decorations including the Order of the Garter, he was monumental, as he led the foreign corps at diplomatic receptions at the White House. He was impressive on all official occasions; also, august. Actually, his forbidding dignity hid a shyness that dissolved on closer acquaintance. The comparatively few persons who got to know him found him genial and often amusing.

Although an American by birth (she was the former Elizabeth Colgate of Long Island), Lady Lindsay through many years as the wife of a career British diplomat had become more English than Yorkshire pudding. An aristocrat dowager in the Queen Mary tradition, she could be imperious. She reigned supreme in the most rarefied social strata but had less success with the average Americans she happened to meet. Yet, when she occasionally unbent, she could be charming. And she was talented. A one-time landscape gardener and architect, she transformed the grounds of the embassy into a miracle of manicured lawns, with neatly clipped hedges and flowerbeds abounding in roses and tulips. Her well-organized social calendar included two typically English garden parties to mark the British sovereign's birthday each spring. While an orchestra played, hundreds of guests wandered over the greensward, gathered under the luxuriant magnolia, red oak, and ginko trees, and enjoyed the sandwiches and tea, giant strawberries and Devonshire cream, beneath striped marquees. Standing on the portico with the ambassador to greet the company, the hostess, in a semitailored frock and a small hat, was a notable contrast to many of the women who arrived in flowing gowns, picture hats and long white gloves.

She had been a girlhood friend of Eleanor Roosevelt, and, at the latter's annual parties for wives of Gridiron Club members on the night of the club's stag dinner, Lady Lindsay was a frequent guest and featured speaker. Her comments made good copy for the women reporters present. Typical of her remarks on such occasions was a suggestion for her own epitaph: "Served by all; of service to none; died of the tea hour," and a self-description paraphrasing a seed catalog's note on a rose that had been named in her honor: "Thorny; inclined to ramble; sturdy, but in need of cultivation."

She could have been popular with the press, but she did not appreciate the value of manipulating it properly. All her press relations were handled by her Canadian-born social secretary, Miss Irene Boyle, who irritated reporters. Lady Lindsay professed to disapprove of what she called "social puffs in the columns," but she was delighted with the glowing accounts of her garden parties, and, through Miss Boyle, she regularly released names of her dinner guests to the local newspapers. There, confusion generally set in, for Miss Boyle consistently refused to give first names of male guests. Typical was her tart reply to a reporter who once asked the first name of a "Mr. Thompson." "Lady Lindsay's guests are so well known, they need no special identification," snapped Miss Boyle.

The excitement with which Americans anticipated the first visit of ruling British sovereigns to the United States was understandable. Americans have an inherent curiosity about, and a secret devotion to, crowns and coronets. Newspaper readers all over the country were avid for every detail about plans for entertaining the royal visitors in Washington, and Mrs. Roosevelt was characteristically cooperative. At her first weekly press conference after the visit was announced, she said she would answer all questions as White House plans developed for entertaining Their Majesties. Embassy arrangements would have to be released from the British Embassy.

With Miss Boyle in charge, that posed a problem, but a distressed columnist tackled it courageously. She managed to get Lady Lindsay on the telephone and poured out her woes. "We're desperate!" she cried. "Everybody in the country wants to know what the embassy is planning, and we can get nothing from Miss Boyle—*as usual!*" Astounded, Lady Lindsay asked advice on what she should do. The columnist suggested a press conference as soon as possible.

Cards immediately went out to ten women reporters, inviting them to the embassy the following week.

In taking over, Lady Lindsay naturally assumed that everything would go off without a hitch. She began her initial meeting by apologizing for her social secretary's ineptness with the press and indicated that she herself would assist in every possible way. She was in for some sharp surprises then, and they were mere harbingers of what was to come. But she patiently answered a volume of questions, after saying that the British Embassy had planned an official dinner and a garden party for Their Majesties. Yes, she would curtsy to the royal pair ("I am a British subject"). Even if she were not a British subject, she said, she might bend a knee "as a matter of politeness; but it is not obligatory, of course." She avoided giving an opinion as to whether the First Lady should curtsy. "You'll have to put that one to the White House," she said. She also declined to divulge what she would wear to the garden party, but added that either floor-length or street-length frocks would be appropriate. She was a bit more explicit about the proper male attire. "Men should wear just what they would to any other formal garden party," she said. Informed that local men's shops were virtually divested of gray toppers, striped trousers and cutaways, she went on, "Well, anyway, that's what you would see at garden parties in London."

The conference filled countless newspaper columns from coast to coast, and the hullabaloo began. Wives of high officials were queried as to whether they would curtsy to Their Majesties and what they planned to wear to the garden party. The Gallup poll came up with the report that 78 percent of Americans opposed curtsies or even low bows to royalty. The question of proper dress became a burning issue in Washington, although Mrs. John Nance Garner, wife of the Vice President, promptly announced, "I'll 'go short.' I'm opposed to buying a long dress, for just one party." Mrs. Claude Swanson, wife of the Secretary of the

Navy, was among those holding out for sweeping garb. "I have a long dress; I bought it for my son's wedding—and I certainly don't plan to cut it off," she said.

The opening hubbub about proper dress and demeanor was a Pandora's box for Lady Lindsay. At her next conference she was quizzed about her garden party plans. Who would be invited? How many officials were on the list? How many from Congress? She said that fewer than a thousand guests would be high officials—the Vice President, Cabinet, most of the Supreme Court—members of the Senate foreign relations and the House foreign affairs committees, "personal friends of the embassy, of course, and some other nonofficial guests."

Then she was pressed about how she had selected the nonofficial guests. "Why, from the *Social Register*, of course," was her prompt answer. The remark immediately hit the headlines. Repercussions from influential Americans not in the exclusive register came from all parts of the country and developed into a concerted howl that resounded on Capitol Hill and echoed to Downing Street. The British foreign office dispatched a corps of public relationists to New York and Washington to soothe ruffled vanities. Their chores multiplied after the British ambassador, trying to be helpful, broke a lifetime rule to hold a press conference.

"I can't pretend I enjoy this," he drawled, as he unfolded the prepared 500-word statement on embassy plans for the royal visit. When he finished reading, he invited questions, and the barrage began. Why would the King and Queen not have a chance to meet more "average Americans" at the garden party? he was asked. "There's such an awful lot of them," he replied slowly, his mustache curving into a smile. He sidestepped the curtsy queries, but when asked whether men "should bow from the waist" when meeting Their Majesties, he opined, with a twinkle, "I think they might do what I do when I meet your President—I bow. Whether it comes from the waist, I don't know."

The subject reverted to the garden party, and the conference dissolved in guffaws after a reporter wanted to know
how the guest list was compiled. "Oh, that," he said lightly.
"That's just like Heaven; some are chosen, some are not."

Following nationwide headlines that His Britannic Majesty's ambassador in Washington had tabbed the vaunted
garden party, "like Heaven," embattled Lady Lindsay held
her final press conference. "My head is bloody, but un-
bowed," she observed, wistfully, as it began. The garden
party would, of course, be "nothing like Heaven," she went
on. She had merely hoped to give a pleasant teatime party
for the King and Queen, with "representative guests." She
had wanted to invite 900 at most, but the original number
had been enlarged—"slightly" she said—and added, "We
cannot ask everyone who wants to come. The 13,000 enemies that may result from omissions are mine, and mine
alone—not England's."

The list had actually been enlarged by several hundred
because Mrs. Garner, besieged by disappointed Senate
wives, urged the Vice President to "do something." He
came through by inviting the British ambassador to lunch
on Capitol Hill. Within a week, all the senators and wives
had been bidden to "Heaven." Meanwhile, others in the
British Embassy were beset and berated by acquaintances
who were not that lucky. The diplomats tried to dismiss
complaints as lightly as possible. For example, at a dinner a
few days before the garden party, a disgruntled dowager
teased the witty British secretary, Angus McDonnell. "We
Americans are not impressed with you Red Coats," she
said haughtily. "After all, we can't forget that you British
once burned our White House and Capitol."

He chuckled and replied, "But you should thank us for
torching them. As a result you have a much finer White
House . . . and your Capitol *has wings!*"

The controversial garden party went off pleasantly
enough. But even there, the 1,300 guests were not in agree-

ment on the curtsy question. As the King and Queen, accompanied by Ambassador and Lady Lindsay, made their separate tours around the greensward, some women bobbed with self-conscious speed, and some virtually prostrated themselves. Most Americans bowed slightly. A few shook the royal hands. One ebullient Texas congressman bid for headlines in the cow country by boldly stepping into the Queen's path and caroling, "Hi-ya, Cousin Elizabeth!" as he extended a plump palm. Lady Lindsay froze. But Her Majesty, momentarily startled, quickly regained her composure, smiled warmly and returned the handshake. The ecstatic congressman reenacted his role by approaching the King with a "Hi-ya, Cousin George!" and had a similar response. "I got the idea," the representative said later, "when I saw the Vice President shake the King's hand and give him a hearty slap on the back. I could see His Majesty liked it a lot better'n all that bowing and scraping. That's not the American way!"

Their Majesties chatted with a couple of hundred prominent guests, apprised in advance that they were to be personally presented by the host and hostess, and conducted themselves with expected regal fortitude and grace, apparently unaware of the storm that the party had precipitated.

Lady Lindsay was a subdued chatelaine during her few remaining months in Washington. She had taken the brunt for a situation that thoughtless remarks promoted but certainly did not cause. She and her husband would have been more guarded in their comments had either realized the tenor of a country in which powerful isolationists were ready to pounce on any mistakes the British might make. The disappointments of many in Washington who tried to wangle garden-party invitations were fanned by the German Embassy. Hans Thomsen, the chargé d'affaires, and Frau Thomsen pointed up the commotion at a steady series of small dinners planned around chagrined members of Congress and their wives and others who were hotly annoyed at

"The British"—and particularly Lady Lindsay. There were significant comments all over the city that she had done more to keep America out of the European war for a time than all the isolationists put together. There were also rumors that the "garden party" had liquidated Britain's hopes for the loan then pending in the Senate. But the loan passed on schedule; the berated Lindsays retired; and Washington awaited the next British ambassador.

He was an attractive bachelor, the Marquess of Lothian. Arriving late in 1939, he was patently aware of anti-British seethings in circles that could mean much to British welfare and began at once to make amends. Skipping purely social functions, paying little attention to *Social Register* celebrities—and none at all to ambitious hostesses—he turned his attention to members of the Senate and House, and, within less than two years, he managed to meet and entertain more of them than had any of his predecessors. His program was proceeding successfully when he died in 1941, and the Viscount Halifax took over and continued it, with an even greater concentration on key members of Congress.

Lord Halifax's determination to waste no time in getting acquainted on Capitol Hill, in fact, prompted him to defy what had been an unwritten rule since the German ambassador haunted the corridors of Congress before World War I: namely, that no foreign envoy calls on a United States senator or representative in his office without invitation. This does not include the vice president and the speaker, on whom many new emissaries call after asking for appointments.

Shortly after Halifax arrived in Washington, he went to Capitol Hill and, without advance notice, appeared in the office of Speaker Sam Rayburn. "What is your name, please?" a secretary asked the craggy stranger, as he diffidently approached her desk. "Halifax" was the answer. The speaker, informed that a "Mr. Flalifax" was in his outer office, was puzzled. "Must be a joke—nobody's named that," he mused. Then the light dawned. "Oh, it's *Halifax*, the new British ambassador!" he cried, as he jumped from his chair and rushed out to welcome the envoy. The towering, lank ambassador and stocky "Mr. Sam" had gotten along famously at a dinner a few evenings previously, and the speaker had invited Halifax to "drop in any time." The ambassador stayed thirty minutes, during which time no more significant subject was broached than a mutual interest in baseball and fishing.

At the height of the Lend-Lease debate in Congress, however, Halifax, flanked by his diplomatic officers, appeared in the office of Representative Sol Bloom, chairman of the House foreign affairs committee, and spent an hour with the congressman. A crowd of reporters and photographers gathered around the visitors as they were leaving. "Just a friendly conversation—no international business," said Halifax as he disappeared down the hall. "No, I didn't invite him," said Bloom, "but I like him, and he's always welcome."

Photographs with reports of the uninvited visit appeared in the press, and Halifax made no more such calls on Capitol Hill. However, he persisted in his intent to cultivate congressional leaders. Through Rayburn and Bloom, he got to know many. He met several others at Sunday night dinners given by Evalyn Walsh McLean, whose famous Hope diamond sparkled at big fetes for big people from the days of the Harding administration through the World War II period. "I shall always be indebted to Mrs. McLean; in her house, I have met half the persons of influence who have became my friends in Washington," Halifax said at one of her parties in 1945. It was a typical Evalyn McLean "little" dinner for some 200 prominent guests.

Evalyn McLean's gatherings included persons of diverse political persuasions. "Interventionists" and "isolationists" sat side by side at many of her dinners before Pearl Harbor.

After one of her parties, a noted columnist noted the numerous Republicans that she regularly entertained and likened her coterie of antiadministration intimates to Lady Astor's "Cliveden set" in England. Three days later, President Roosevelt lashed out at "Washington's Cliveden set" at a press conference. Many capital residents had heard of Cliveden only vaguely, if at all and had no idea that it was the name of Lady Astor's estate in England. Several called a local newspaper to find out how "Cliveden" was pronounced.

At a diplomatic reception, an editor spotted the British ambassador and asked, "Tell me, Sir, whether you call Lady Astor's crowd the CLYVE-den, CLEEVE-den or CLIV-den set?" His Excellency feigned astonishment before he answered, "Why it's pronounced CLIV-den." Then, with a sly smile he added, "But we don't *call* it, at all."

Despite his steadily increasing popularity in Washington, Halifax came in for occasional sideswipes in the press. Much was made of his participating in the "upper-class sport," fox hunting in Virginia. He was guilty of the unforgivable error of leaving an all-star baseball game before the final inning, with the excuse that he had promised Lady Halifax that he would be back at the embassy in time for tea. He was amused at the comments and vowed to friends who mentioned his publicized shortcomings that he would "try to do better the next time." He appeared not to mind when Winston Churchill, on visits to Washington, did not include him in his several conferences with FDR.

Halifax pursued his business of learning about America and Americans with as much fervor as if he were running for public office. He visited every state in the Union and spoke at colleges, city halls, aircraft factories, trade-union meetings, shipyards and churches. His host of friends in Washington were horrified when they read that a man had hurled an egg and a tomato at him during one of his speeches in the Middle West and applauded the envoy's wry comment "The United States is very lucky to have eggs and tomatoes to throw around. In England, we are lucky to get one egg to eat a month."

His attention to his social chores as an envoy was never more poignantly illustrated in Washington than the day after the death of his son, Peter Wood. Halifax was among envoys going down the line at the Soviet Embassy's "Great October Socialist Revolution" reception. He greeted the host and hostess, then departed. He had discharged a diplomatic duty on one of the saddest days of his life.

Lady Halifax was an able aide in making friends for Britain in America. She entertained throngs of women at tea, lent her name and gave her support to innumerable benefits and was active in the work of the Mission Church of Saint Agnes, which she and the ambassador regularly attended. She was a nature lover, as was Halifax, and they enjoyed taking long walks, daily when possible, in the woodland stretches near the embassy. They made an enviable place for themselves in Washington; they are still remembered as a charming pair, deeply devoted to religion, to each other and to the job at hand.

Several postwar British ambassadors have been highly popular in Washington; all have been respected. Sir Oliver Franks, envoy from 1948 to 1952, was typical of the intelligent "new breed" of British diplomats. He was young, erudite, tough and hard-working. One of the busiest envoys in the city, he stayed close to his desk, took only brief weekend holidays and observed on the hottest day of his first summer in the sizzling city, "I've so much to do, so much to learn, that I haven't time to bother about the thermometer." Asked at one of his garden parties how he expected to make use of his "hill allowance" in the United States, he was puzzled. "Hill allowances—for our diplomatic officers to get to cooler climates in the summer? Well, I certainly don't have, and couldn't use, such a thing," he said. "Can't imagine it. If we ever had 'hill allowances' for here, it must have been a long time ago." A native Washingtonian pointed out that for many years British envoys assigned to the United States were provided with funds to underwrite vacations away from sizzling Washington from June until September. "Seems incredible!" said Sir Oliver. "Well, my worthy predecessors in those days probably hadn't much else to do."

Sir Roger and Lady Makins had a host of friends in Washington before his appointment as envoy in 1952. Years before, as a young attaché at the British Embassy, he had met and married Alice Davis, whose father, Dwight F. Davis, was Secretary of War in the Coolidge administration. Unassuming and attractive, the Makinses parlayed their capital associations of long standing into wide popularity in official and social circles and British prestige reached another peak during their tenure.

Sir Harold Caccia, who succeeded Makins, presented his credentials to President Eisenhower in 1956, when Anglo-American relations were strained by the Suez crisis. As envoy in Vienna just before assignment to the United States, he had been called by colleagues, "a tireless diplomat," and he made the most of his energy and intelligence in restoring Anglo-American amity. He enjoyed the social life in the capital, and he and Lady Caccia entertained constantly, but always with judicious attention to cultivating powerful contacts. Caccia was to be remembered by party-goers as one of the best dancers in the foreign corps and as a host who gave a special touch of elegance to the annual Queen's Birthday party by appearing in a trim gray cutaway; but he was known to government leaders as an able diplomatic tactician.

It was while he was ambassador that the largest single building ever erected outside Britain by the British Ministry of Works was opened as the new British chancery. Adjoining the complex designed in 1930 by Luytens, the $3-4 million structure planned by Eric Bedford has as its most striking feature a rotunda with a copper-covered dome and glass walls fitted with a seamless white satin curtain that

opens and closes at the touch of a button. Into one of the
Purbeck marble walls near the entrance of the building, the
foundation stone is set; and above it are carved names of all
the British envoys to he United States, beginning with
George Hammond, who presented his credentials to George
Washington in Philadelphia in 1791.

The illusion of youth that dominated the Kennedy administration extended to the diplomatic corps, and younger
and younger envoys were sent to Washington. The youngest British emissary in several decades was forty-three-
year-old Sir David Ormsby Gore (later, Lord Harlech). He
had a built-in advantage over his diplomatic colleagues
when he arrived in November 1961. His friendship with
President Kennedy had begun twenty-three years earlier
when Joseph Kennedy was ambassador at the Court of St.
James's. Lord Hartington, a cousin of Ormsby Gore (the
name, although unhyphenated, was under *O* and not *G* in
alphabetical listings) married Kathleen Kennedy, who first
knew Lady Ormsby Gore as Sylvia Thomas, daughter of the
British ambassador to France.

From the outset it was noticeable, however, that the new
British envoy expected no special privileges because of his
ties in the White House. With a decade of experience in
diplomacy, he conducted affairs of his country in the traditional way—through the State Department.

Lady Ormsby Gore, known to her intimates as "Cissie,"
was a beauty, with dark brown hair and hazel eyes. The tall,
slender mother of five could easily have passed for a college
girl. She dressed in the understated manner that is fashion
at its best, favoring short, simple frocks for all except the
most formal occasions and then appearing in classic creations
of Belinda Bellville, the noted London designer.

She had one of the most substantial housekeeping and
entertainment allowances in the foreign corps—$94,680—

and used it wisely. Her favorite type of party was the dinner for not more than twelve, but she gave many galas, in addition to the queen's birthday parties. Fashion shows promoting British designers, balls and after-theater parties distinguished her entertainment calendar. Among the more memorable affairs at which she was hostess was the champagne supper and dance after a performance of *Macbeth* by the Old Vic company. A similar event, after the Washington premiere of *Mr. President*, was a highly successful benefit for the Joseph F. Kennedy, Jr., Foundation. Ormsby Gore became Lord Harlech after the death of his father in 1964, and the departure of the charming couple the following year was widely regretted.

Just before Sir Patrick Dean, Lord Harlech's successor, was shifted from the United Nations to Washington, he said, "I shall now have only one client, instead of the 114 at the UN," which recalled a statement he had made some months earlier: "Delegates to the UN have a curious feeling of detached existence, of being on American soil but not really in America." In Washington, the tall, sandy-haired envoy appeared to be very much "in America," but it was soon apparent that he did not regard his job "with only one client" as an easy berth. He worked hard, and like his wiser predecessors, he got acquainted with congressional leaders and ingratiated himself with the White House circle. President Johnson's special regard for him was noticed at the White House diplomatic reception in 1967, when LBJ, greeting the envoys in the Blue Room, grasped Dean's hand with unusual warmth, then placed an arm around his shoulder and engaged him in a conference of several minutes, while some of the other ambassadors waited in the East Room to be received. A few moments later, in the State Dining Room, Vice President Humphrey disengaged himself from three other envoys to talk with Sir Patrick for almost fifteen minutes.

Reporters invited to meet Lady Dean shortly after she

arrived in Washington noted that she was, as one put it, "petite, pretty and poised" and that she had a nice sense of humor. Her delicate features and size-10 figure belied her background, which included a girlhood in Argentina, a period of plowing fields, milking cows and feeding pigs as a member of the Women's Land Army during part of World War II and, later, work with a British group in the resistance movement in occupied countries. More in keeping with her appearance was her expressed fondness for heirloom jewelry and antique English silver and the collection of Royal Worcester, Meissen and Crown Derby porcelain displayed in the embassy drawing room.

The Deans, not so outgoing, not so intent on getting acquainted in all circles as the Harlechs had been, entertained frequently (with little publicity) at luncheons and dinners ("eighteen is the happy maximum of guests," Lady Dean said); and they invited throngs to their queen's birthday parties although the 1968 reception was canceled because of Senator Kennedy's death.

The British government does not delay in appointing ambassadorial successors. In March 1968, shortly after Washington learned that Sir Patrick Dean would retire in 1969, when he reached sixty, the mandatory retirement age for British envoys, the foreign office announced that his successor would be John Freeman, former editor of *New Statesman* magazine and later high commissioner to India, his first diplomatic post.

11

The French Now and Then

BEFORE LEAVING FOR THE
1814–1815 Congress of Vienna as envoy of the restored
House of Bourbon, Talleyrand told Louis XVIII, "I have
more need of casseroles than written instructions." There
was precedence for the remark. Years before, Napoleon had
dispatched an emissary to London with the instruction *Tenez
bonne table et soignez les femmes* ("Have a good table and
flatter the women"). In any case, Louis agreed with Talleyrand about the "casseroles," and Talleyrand took with him
his excellent chef, Carême, whose cuisine pleased the
palates of delegates from England and Austria and perhaps
played a role in framing the secret alliance of France, England and Austria.

In Washington, foundations for working friendships have
long been laid in embassy salons and cultivated over dinner
tables, with hard-core negotiations following in chanceries
or at the State Department. Since diplomacy is not a science
but rather the art of sensing, understanding and manipulating, its nuances must be delicately assessed in order to be
smoothly handled. The dinner table lends itself to that purpose much more gracefully than the cold conference room.
Even a mass embassy reception offers possibilities. No diplomats have been more conscious of this than the French.

Mme. Henri Bonnet, wife of France's first ambassador in
Washington after World War II, was one of the most suc-

cessful diplomatic hostesses in the history of the city. She privately described her mammoth receptions as "a pleasant enough way, I hope, to entertain a mob and keep everybody happy." After she and her husband retired to Paris, she advised an embassy hostess never to worry about inviting too many persons to a soiree. "Cram them in," she said. "Stand them up as in the Métro. Push them, shove them in. That's what I did in Washington. People say they hate it. They love it."

Hellé Bonnet's social supremacy was not achieved by her practice of giving mammoth receptions, however. It derived from her rare understanding of Americans and her gift for establishing contact with the productive bees as well as the social butterflies of Washington. She regularly presided over some of the most exclusive dinners on Embassy Row, but she was anything but a snob; she knew how to make friends for La Belle France at all levels. "And why not?" she once asked, by way of a reminder that she and her husband had known and worked with people in all walks of life. The former Hellé Zervoudak Aghnaides, daughter of a wealthy Greek merchant, she and Henri Bonnet escaped from Paris to London just before the Nazi occupation of France and became active in the Free French movement. When the Vichy government confiscated their possessions in France, they managed to get to New York, where they struggled for survival—he, as a teacher and she, as a milliner—until his appointment as the first French ambassador to the United States after his country was liberated.

Henri and Hellé Bonnet worked superbly as a team. The envoy's grasp of United States politics surprised and delighted Cabinet officers, Supreme Court justices and senators who regularly dined at the embassy. Hellé Bonnet's chic and her forthright manner figured perceptibly in her wide popularity; so did her cleverness in compiling guest lists. While receptions drew vast numbers of acquaintances who may or may not have been important to her, her dinners were planned around those who could be helpful to France.

She was unfailingly cooperative and friendly with the press and frequently included reporters in her dinner parties. And she set a precedent that is still widely followed on Embassy Row. Before her time, diplomatic wives often sponsored and gave fund-raisers for the needy in their own countries. Hellé Bonnet opened the doors of the French Embassy for a tremendous bazaar to bring in money for the American Red Cross. Since then, many American institutions have benefited by embassy fetes.

Before the Bonnets left Washington in 1954, the city broke out in a rash of farewell parties for them. No diplomatic couple ever departed with a greater display on the part of so many friends. And there was wide speculation that the French Embassy never again would achieve the preeminence it had attained under that popular pair.

The next ambassador, Maurice Couve de Murville, and his wife made no attempt to follow the pattern of their immediate predecessors. They entertained with less fanfare; they were seldom seen on the cocktail circuit. But in their brief stay in Washington, they made powerful friends whose interests were similar to their own. For relaxation, the ambassador enjoyed golf, bridge, the theater and reading. Jacqueline Couve de Murville had been reared in the European tradition that the home comes first for a wife and mother. Her three daughters were married. She devoted much of her attention to redecorating the embassy and in the process discovered that paint on the library walls concealed beautiful paneling, which she had restored. She was fond of music and was an avid reader, but in her Dior and Givenchy creations she was also an excellent advertisement for the *haute couture*. A petite, pretty woman, and gracious in a quiet way that gushy Washingtonians sometimes take for mere politeness, she once gently remarked at a tea,

"Women who rush around doing things are terrifying." Neither she nor her husband "rushed around" socially in Washington, but they made an impact in the city's intellectual and cultural circles, and their departure after nine months was deplored by those who had been privileged to know them.

Hervé Alphand, the next French envoy, was already known in Washington, when he was appointed in 1956. He had been an economics expert for the French Embassy in 1940, but he was completely out of sympathy with the Vichy government. He managed to liquidate French war contracts in the United States and to transfer all he could to the British before he resigned in June 1941. The enraged Vichy government then revoked his citizenship and condemned him to death; but he made his way to London and joined General de Gaulle in September. Alphand was serving as French ambassador at the United Nations when he was sent to Washington.

His wife at the time, the former Claude Rober-Reynaud, had been a supper-club singer in Paris and New York. Washington's demanding and sometimes starchy social calendar was not to her taste, but she entertained often and sometimes played the guitar and sang for her guests. She had a fling at redecorating a part of the embassy. When the conservatory was finished, she invited a group of newspaper women to see it, and in showing the new room, done in combinations of gray, blacks and whites, she proudly pointed out that "French thrift, aided by American bargains, did the trick." The ceiling-high draperies, she said, were old and from France, but she had bolstered them with American chintz in a steel-gray shade. The chubby black flower vases were brandy glasses purchased at a local variety store and painted black. Square coffee tables, with tops of highly polished slate, gray slip-covered chairs and sofas and a black and white woven rug were other furnishings she had added. Her massive bouquets there and in other

rooms were exceptionally beautiful. Artfully combining arti-
ficial blossoms ("from France, of course," she said) with
fresh flowers ("American, naturally") they were to become
a signature of the French Embassy and to be copied by
many capital hostesses.

In 1957, almost a year after Hervé and Claude Alphand
arrived in Washington, they gave a big garden party before
leaving for France, ostensibly on a vacation. Few, if any, of
the 400 guests realized that the pleasant affair was the hostess' last appearance as embassy chatelaine. A month later,
many were shocked to read that the Alphands were divorced, by mutual consent. "One of the reasons is that I
cannot stand official life," Claude announced. "I loved
Washington, but not as an ambassadress."

The former Nicole Merenda Bunau-Varilla, a divorcee
with a grown son and daughter, arrived in Washington as
Hervé Alphand's bride in May 1958. Three evenings later,
she was hostess at a dinner in honor of Secretary of State
and Mrs. Dulles. In her first press interview, the new ambassadress was asked if she planned to be as socially active
as Hellé Bonnet had been. Unhesitatingly, she replied, "I
would like very much to do like Mme. Bonnet because I
have such admiration for her. And I am very much interested in the social part of life."

She was superbly equipped for her role. Even those capitalites who were not prepared to like her could not help
admiring her burnished blond hair, blue-green eyes, tall,
slim figure and stunning Paris wardrobe. In time, many of
them were enchanted with her wide smile, her cordial
manner and her gay parties. During her eight years in
Washington, the French Embassy became one of the most
widely publicized, the most avidly admired and the most
hotly envied social centers in the United States.

Her phenomenal energy found many outlets. She refurbished the embassy from basement to attic. Round tables
seating from six to sixteen guests replaced the big center

table in the dining room for many sizable parties. Other changes were forthcoming. Paintings that had once adorned Le Petit Trianon at Versailles paneled the dining-room walls. The embassy's supply of Porthault linens, Baccarat crystal, Lapar silver and blue and gold Sevres china was increased to take care of as many as eighty guests at a time.

"The life of diplomats in Washington is exceedingly crowded," said Mme. Alphand when she had been embassy hostess less than a year. "My husband and I attend two or three cocktail parties almost every day, as well as a luncheon and a dinner. And sometimes after dinner, we go on to a dance, concert or art exhibition."

When they were not going to parties, they were giving them. Fully aware that the facilities of entertaining, constantly and properly employed, can open many powerful doors in Washington, Mme. Alphand made the most of the embassy's sizable representation fund (the French Ambassador gets $100,000 a year in salary, housekeeping and entertainment allowances) at a steady series of receptions, dinners, luncheons, fashion shows and balls. Her occasional flirtatiousness delighted the men. It would have infuriated their wives had she not taken pains to be equally engaging to them. She was active in the International Neighbors Club, made up of fifty wives of high United States officials and diplomats. She either gave or attended a ladies' luncheon at least three times a week.

Ambassador Alphand's gift for mimicry, which convulsed many dinner parties, amused Senator and Mrs. John F. Kennedy on several occasions. By the time JFK became president, Nicole Alphand was one of the First Lady's closest friends on Embassy Row, and the French Embassy's prestige skyrocketed.

One of the liveliest parties of Mme. Alphand's Washington career was a fashion show, in November 1963, when Cabinet members, senators and social notables ogled mannequins who were flown from Paris to model Pierre Cardin's creations in the embassy salons. The evening ended with the year's gayest dance, lasting long after fifty-six-year-old Hervé Alphand disappeared at 1:30 A.M. The gala inspired a five-page spread on Washington society in *Time* magazine, with the hostess pictured on the cover.

"Giving good, and sometimes superb parties is the most important thing in Nicole Alphand's life," went the story. "It sounds like a frivolous occupation, but her husband often gets more done in ten minutes of quiet conversation at one of Nicole's dinners than in a day of shuffling papers."

Not long before she left Washington in 1965, Nicole Alphand was asked which of her parties she remembered with the happiest glow. She thoughtfully replied, "Why—all of them. But I suppose the best ones, really, were the kind I enjoy giving most, the smaller dinners. Anyway, Hervé liked them best." But however diplomatically fruitful or pleasant they may be, smaller dinners for even the most distinguished guests generally go their quiet way without the kind of publicity that made Nicole Alphand the most prominent hostess on Embassy Row. Her glittering chapter in the annals of Washington was based on her flair for making news with big parties—such as the dinner she gave for ninety guests before the showing of the "Mona Lisa" at the National Gallery in 1961, her spectacular fashion shows and her grand finale, the fabulous 1965 Opera Ball, which poured thousands of dollars into the coffers of the Washington Opera Society.

Washington heartily welcomed Charles Lucet as the next French envoy. He and his wife were already widely known in the city in which he began his career in 1935 as the youngest of six diplomatic officers of the French Embassy, then on 16th Street. When he resigned from the Vichy government in 1942, Mme. Lucet took a job with the International Red Cross. After the war, they were stationed in Beirut and then Cairo before transferring back to the United States in 1953. While her husband served as counselor of the

French delegation at the United Nations, Jacqueline Lucet served as a volunteer librarian at a hospital. Later he returned to the embassy in Washington, and they were in the city several years before his appointment as envoy.

He took over in a difficult period. French and American relations had bogged down, and many Americans were prone to forget that policy objectives of France are formulated in President de Gaulle's office at the Elysée Palace and activated from the Quai d'Orsay—and not from the French chancery on Washington's Belmont Road. Yet the solid friendships that the Lucets had made over the years were evident at even the toughest time.

With no desire to achieve the social supremacy that Nicole Alphand cherished, Jacqueline Lucet with characteristic modesty said, shortly after becoming ambassadress, "I can't do what brilliant and beautiful Nicole did. I haven't her energy or imagination, but I want to do everything I can." Her friends had no doubts that she would do well as embassy chatelaine in a city that was virtually her second home.

Every wise envoy tries to enlarge his circle of congressional acquaintances. As the Lucets' social calendar got under way, they invited some of the new members of the Senate and House to dinner from time to time, but that practice suffered a setback when one recipient's comments about his invitation made headlines around the country. In a newsletter to his constituents, a California congressman wrote of his surprise at having been bidden to the French Embassy, which formerly was "supremely exclusive among party givers, especially during the Kennedy era." He speculated that if even a freshman congressman and his wife could get invited, General de Gaulle's diplomatic establishment must be having tough sledding and wondered whether he should have accepted, "what with the icy attitude of Washington toward Paris these days." Carried away by his own whimsy, the House member continued, "If there were a black market in invitations, one Spanish would be worth one and a half Kuwait, and a Kuwait would be worth five French. It's been a tough year for the French." He and his wife went to the party, he wrote, and had an enjoyable time, as "the meal was a masterpiece and the wines were up to some of California's finest." In conclusion he observed that he and his wife "sat back and waited for the next invitation. None came from the Spanish; none from the Kuwait; and none from the State Department. We have not been invited to another embassy party since—not even one of those small-country embassy parties."

His missive may have evoked smiles in the representative's home district. Sophisticated Washington found it distasteful, and the Lucets' popularity soared. But their invitation lists were promptly revised.

Since Revolutionary days, when the young Marquis de Lafayette fought with General Washington, Americans have been sentimental about the French and have generally esteemed French emissaries. Until 1902, however, when Jules Jusserand was appointed ambassador to the United States, France, like many other major countries, considered America a backwoods nation and dispatched its top diplomats elsewhere. In the early part of the nineteenth century, when the new capital city was little more than a village, some odd French envoys appeared. Later in the century, two of them were to annoy American leaders by interfering in internal affairs. A few made the best of an unwelcome assignment and found it rewarding, after all.

Louis André Pichon, the chargé d'affaires in 1801, took one look at the scrubby federal city and found lodgings in "more civilized" Georgetown. Later, for convenience, he moved to a Washington boardinghouse, where he and his wife disturbed other tenants by their "loud quarrelings." The Pichons agreed on nothing, it seemed. Mme. Pichon doted on the little capital's social life; she loved Washington. Pichon termed it "hateful" and begged his government to recall him. But he was a saint in comparison with his successor, General Louis Marie Turreau de Garambouville, Baron de Linières, Napoleon's minister from 1804 to 1806.

Secretary of State Madison had advance notice from General John Armstrong, American minister in Paris, that Turreau was "very profligate" and that he was "an ex-Jacobin, notorious for cruelty in war," but nobody in Washington was prepared for Turreau's abominable conduct and his sensational wardrobe. After Turreau made his first call on Thomas Jefferson, John Quincy Adams wrote in his diary, "The President appears displeased by the profusion of gold lace on his clothes. He says they must get him down to a plain frock coat, or the boys on the streets will run after him as a sight."

"They" did not prevail. At the President's 1805 New Year's reception, Turreau was swathed in gold lace and gold braid and loaded with diamond-studded decorations. Later he acquired a gilded carriage, and he gave sumptuous dinners in his resplendently furnished legation at the corner of Pennsylvania Avenue and 19th Street. His wife had a difficult time. He avoided introducing her to society, beat her often, refused to support her and brought prostitutes to the legation. His diplomatic colleagues were horrified. British Minister Merry wrote home about Turreau's immoral conduct, and British Secretary Foster reported that he was "called upon to give charitable assistance to the wife of Napoleon's minister." Secretary Madison interceded, but Turreau insisted that his spouse was mentally deranged— and sent her back to France. He stayed on for a time, and at President Madison's Inaugural Ball in 1809, he escorted Mrs. Madison in to dinner and sat on her right. Dolley was equally courteous to him and to the new British minister, David Montagu Erskine, who was on her left.

The next French minister, Count Jeane Pierre de Sèrurier, was a dilettante, a dandy and an opportunist, but he was also a charmer and a superb host. He could talk about anything; he dressed with verve, wore the finest satins and velvet suits seen in Washington; and he had managed to stay in favor with both Napoleon and the House of Bourbon. He knew how to make the most of "casseroles." His table in Washington far surpassed those of others in the diplomatic corps, and no man was ever more adept at flattering the ladies. He devoted much of his attention to Dolley Madison, but he also cultivated her husband, and he achieved the goal of every envoy—he became a close friend of the President and First Lady. He dined regularly at the executive mansion, encouraged Dolley to do more reading and lent her books and advised her to purchase a splendid carriage, which he helped select. He lived in The Octagon, the finest private mansion in Washington. John Tayloe had built and furnished it handsomely, but with the outbreak of the War of 1812, Tayloe moved his family to his country estate and asked the French minister to occupy the house for its protection.

The envoy later had a chance to prove his friendship to the Madisons. When James Madison learned that the British were bent on burning the "President's Palace," he dispatched Dolley to friends in Georgetown and followed soon afterward. The French minister, meanwhile, had sent a letter to the British high command—Admiral Sir George Cockburn and General Robert Ross—pleading that they not destroy the executive mansion and asking them to post a guard before The Octagon. Ross granted the latter request but explained that he was under orders to burn the "President's Palace." De Sèrurier dispatched another plea but the mansion was in flames before the message reached Ross. The envoy then offered his residence to the Madisons, and they lived there a year while the President's House, thenceforth to be known as the White House, was being restored.

Jean Guillaume, Baron Hyde de Neuville, who became

French minister in 1816, was described by a colleague as "a most estimable man with a kind wife who enjoys making others happy." But he was hot tempered; and before the end of his stay in Washington, he was involved in a negotiation that temporarily disrupted his relations with Secretary of State John Quincy Adams. Furthermore, early in his tour of duty, Hyde de Neuville quarreled with the British minister, Sir Stratford Canning. The enmity exploded at a White House dinner and as the two envoys rose from the table with swords drawn, President Monroe drew his own sword and struck theirs from their hands.

Hyde de Neuville's close friendship with the Spanish minister, Luis de Onis, led him into trouble with Secretary of State Adams. One of his country's cleverest diplomats, Onis had been dispatched to Washington to keep the United States from acquiring Florida. He asked his French colleague to help, and Hyde de Neuville agreed to serve as mediator. He did his best, much to the annoyance of Adams, who at one point vowed he would give the French minister "a certificate as a faithful liege to the King of Spain." Hyde de Neuville retorted that Onis "would give a certificate that I am an honest American." But practical Frenchman that he was, he withdrew from the fray when the Spanish minister threatened that his country might go to war with the United States. Onis finally capitulated and signed the treaty to sell Florida for $5 million on February 12, 1819.

By that time, Hyde de Neuville was tending to the business of his own country and cultivating needed friendships over dinner tables in the handsome house he had leased from Mrs. Stephen Decatur on Lafayette Square. His social calendar absorbed him until he was transferred.

Henri Mercier, minister of Napoleon III in 1861, was reputed to "set the best table" in Washington. Guests were volubly impressed with his twelve-course dinners, superb wines and aptitude for flattering the ladies, which enhanced his popularity in exclusive, residential echelons. But he found little in common with officials. Lincoln was not his idea of a gentleman, Secretary of State William H. Seward was too blunt for his tastes, and Secretary of the Treasury Salmon P. Chase rarely accepted his dinner invitations. Privately Mercier observed that he and his diplomatic colleagues retained "the only real vestiges of civilization" in the capital. Polished Confederate leaders were more to his liking, and he traveled to Richmond to confer with them, while urging his government to organize the major European powers into unified recognition of the Confederacy. If that could be managed, he assured Napoleon III, the Confederacy might then support France's scheme to take over Mexico. He got encouragement in Richmond but no promises, nor were they forthcoming; and by the time Napoleon III put Maximilian on the Mexican throne in 1864, Mercier's usefulness as an envoy in Washington had ended. Northern leaders ignored him, and he was recalled when the Maximilian regime toppled.

The most celebrated envoy in the history of Washington was Jules Jusserand, the French ambassador from 1902 to 1925 and dean of the diplomatic corps for more than a decade. A slight, bearded, bright-eyed man, he was the author of eleven books in English, five in French and one in Latin and an authority on English and American history and literature. His tall and dignified but gracious wife, although born abroad, was the daughter of American expatriates. Invitations to their dinners, in the mansion that the French government leased from Mrs. John B. Henderson on upper 16th Street—the original Embassy Row—were avidly sought by high officials and the old social guard.

In his early days in Washington, Jusserand became an intimate of President Theodore Roosevelt, and the two often took long walks, played tennis and dined together. He was also a friend of Roosevelt's successor, William Howard Taft. He had, in fact, become accustomed to preferential

treatment from the White House on down by the time
Woodrow Wilson was elected president. With the Democrats in power, the envoy who had been a crony of Republican leaders realized that a new game had begun, and he
prepared to play it with all the finesse at his command. He
made an appointment to call on Secretary of State William
Jennings Bryan. Arriving promptly, the envoy was kept
waiting three hours in Bryan's outer office and then was
told that the Secretary would be tied up another hour. Jusserand left in a huff.

With no direct line to the White House and his contact
with Bryan stymied, Jusserand invited to lunch an old
friend, John Bassett Moore, the State Department counselor, and learned that he was on the verge of resigning.
Jusserand begged him to stay on the job and convinced him
that he was the only person in government with whom an
envoy could conduct legitimate business. Moore stayed a
year. When Bryan resigned in 1915, nobody in Washington
was happier than the French ambassador. He methodically
cultivated the next secretary of state, Robert Lansing, and
as World War I clouds gathered, he was of inestimable help
to Lansing in keeping tab on the Kaiser's ambassador, Von
Bernstorff. Through Lansing, Jusserand managed to get on
fair terms with Wilson, but by then the French ambassador
was so widely revered that he no longer needed the bolster of
intimacy with the White House.

A thousand persons, including the Cabinet, the Supreme
Court, eighty members of Congress and the foreign mission
chiefs attended the farewell dinner for Jusserand at the
Willard Hotel in December 1924, with Speaker Frederick
H. Gillette as toastmaster. All of them, and many others,
contributed to a memorial that stands today in Rock Creek
Park—a marble bench engraved: "JUSSERAND—A PERSONAL
TRIBUTE OF ESTEEM AND AFFECTION."

Two undistinguished diplomats successively served as
French envoys before Paul Claudel, the famed poet and

dramatist, who had been emissary to Tokyo, was appointed ambassador to the United States in 1927. He was brilliant and conscientiously attentive to his diplomatic duties, but he was not aware of the social uses of diplomacy. He side-stepped parties when possible and contributed little to those he had to attend. Dinner partners were appalled when he was unresponsive; casual acquaintances were annoyed when he failed to recognize them; colleagues were disappointed when he declined to lunch with them, unless diplomatic business was on the agenda. He would have been a total failure socially but for his lovely and understanding wife. She was an excellent hostess; she made friends easily; and her clothes by Worth established her as the best-dressed woman in Washington. She was also unfailingly considerate of her absent-minded husband and succeeded in convincing many that his social aberrations were due solely to his poetic genius and his preoccupation with affairs of state.

On one important occasion, however, Claudel's thoughtful wife was not on hand to look after him. She was in France when he attended a White House diplomatic reception and delayed the receiving line twenty minutes. En route, he took off his tight-fitting, gold-braided jacket and wrapped himself in a cloak to be more comfortable during his ride. At his destination, he stepped out of his limousine and it pulled away. He was not aware that he had left his jacket in the car until he took off his cloak and found himself in shirt sleeves with suspenders showing. While police cars scouted the town to find the limousine, President Hoover was informed that the French ambassador, who ranked second in line, had lost his coat. "I don't care what he has lost," growled the President, "we're going ahead!" The tardy queue proceeded into the Blue Room, and Claudel retrieved his coat barely in time to join his colleagues at the end of the line.

Yet Claudel made some solid friendships in Washington.

He got on amiably with Secretary of State Frank B. Kellogg and with intellectuals in residential society. The more intelligent members of the foreign corps admired him and often sought his advice on important matters.

Claudel's vision and alertness in judging at least one leader were evinced after he called on Franklin Roosevelt in Albany six days after the 1932 presidential election and reported to the Quai d'Orsay that the incoming president was a man of liberal mind with an intelligent grasp on both national and international problems. Claudel also predicted that FDR might bring about dramatic changes around the world. The message did not impress the foreign office. Claudel was transferred to Belgium, and an envoy reputed to have an "in" with the new president was sent to Washington.

He was André de Laboulaye, grandson of the man who presented the Statue of Liberty to the United States. He and his wife had known Franklin and Eleanor Roosevelt during the Wilson administration, when FDR was assistant secretary of the Navy and De Laboulaye was secretary of the French Embassy.

Mrs. Roosevelt was ready to resume the association at once. The morning after the De Laboulayes arrived, she called on the ambassadress and they spent an hour chatting about their earlier days in Washington. Any other diplomat's wife would have been ecstatic about an unexpected visit from America's First Lady, but Mme. de Laboulaye complained later because Mrs. Roosevelt had appeared without previous notice. "As the wife of the President, she should know better," the ambassadress was said to have said. The report got to the White House, and the First Lady never called at the embassy again, nor were the De Laboulayes ever invited to anything at the White House except the routine diplomatic dinners and receptions.

Whether or not Mme. de Laboulaye's faux pas seriously affected her husband's diplomatic duties in Washington is a matter of doubt, but it was noticeable that Mrs. Roosevelt's friendly overtures toward another old friend, Lady Lindsay, wife of the British ambassador, were very much appreciated and that Lady Lindsay was a frequent guest at the First Lady's intimate parties.

André de Laboulaye chalked up at least one sterling achievement before he was transferred. He negotiated the purchase of the gray stone and brick neo-Tudor mansion that has been called "the most embassylike of all embassies in the nation's capital." Several envoys had been interested in the home of John Hays Hammond, the multimillionaire gold and diamond mining engineer, and the Brazilian government had once offered $500,000 for it. A month before Hammond died, the French got it, along with the furnishings, for $450,000.

It is an imposing house. Set back from the street, it has spreading wings, which give it a wide front on Kalorama Road. The flagstone terrace and rolling gardens to the rear command one of the finest views in the city: the Taft Bridge above the towering trees of Rock Creek Park. With thirty-four rooms, the mansion dominates an estate of almost four acres. The interior at the time of purchase was an elegant museum piece of its era, with heavily carved woodwork and imported furnishings that might well have been selected for an embassy.

Mme. de Laboulaye, first chatelaine of France's first permanent home in Washington, made few major changes in the interior, but she called on the Garde-Meuble, the national storehouse of furnishings, for French china, glass and silver embossed with "R.F." (*Republique Française*). And she supervised extensive planting of shrubs, hedges and flowers.

Georges Bonnet, the next French envoy, was the former finance minister and was widely publicized as the financial wizard of France. He looked like a wizard of some sort, with his prominent nose and keen blue eyes; but he was a dynamic person who tackled his job with a directness one rarely notes on circuitous Embassy Row. He had little time for anyone who was not in the Cabinet or Congress, and he was especially eager to meet and entertain the isolationist senators and representatives. Stunning, dark-eyed Mme. Bonnet had a smashing wardrobe, a lively manner and an avid interest in getting acquainted with the gay group in which some of the young attachés moved. Since her husband was not a career diplomat, she could avoid much of the routine tedium that absorbed wives of other envoys, and she went her merry way as she chose. Bonnet gave one stag dinner and luncheon after another, with Capitol Hill figures and members of the press prominently present. In interims, he charmed the ladies at embassy receptions. After nine months of trying to gauge the mind and temper of the leaders he met in Washington, he left with the conviction that America would not join England and France in a war against Nazi Germany and returned home to serve as secretary of state.

Count René Doynel de Saint-Quentin, who was ambassador when France fell, was an able career diplomat who might have turned in a superb performance at any other time. A rich aristocrat and a bachelor with great charm and understanding, he could have been the darling of Washington's preponderance of socially mad widows and spinsters. Instead, he focused his attention on Capitol Hill, as Georges Bonnet had done, but with more subtlety and a better "table." But the die was cast. France was at war, and lines were sharply drawn in Washington, with many influential residents regarding the French Embassy as a propaganda apparatus to bring America into the conflict. On June 25, 1940, Saint-Quentin and his staff watched sadly as the Tricolor at the embassy entrance was placed at half mast. France officially had laid down her arms.

Gaston Henry-Haye, emissary of Nazi-occupied France, proclaimed his devotion to America at a steady series of gourmet dinners, but he made little impact on Washington.

He is remembered, if at all, as a fairly pleasant little man who spoke excellent English, professed regret that he was unmarried and at every opportunity expressed the hope that America would not allow itself to be drawn into the European war.

It was during his tour of duty, that the daughter of a late United States Marine Corps colonel extracted from the French chancery vital information for British intelligence. As Amy Elizabeth Thorpe (known to her friends as Betty), she had married Arthur Pack, Second Secretary of the British Embassy, in 1930. After years as a diplomat's wife in Spain, Poland and Chile, she separated from her husband and returned to the capital in 1941 as a secret agent for the British, with the code name of "Cynthia." She cultivated contacts at many parties on Embassy Row, and in the role of a news correspondent for a Latin American publication, she arranged to interview the French ambassador.

At that time, she met Captain Charles Broussé, the French press attaché, who was to aid her in her greatest coup and, also, to become her husband. He secretly despised the Vichy government, and he had supplied Betty with a volume of secret data from the chancery when, in March 1942, she was directed to get the most important material of all. Plans were under way for the Allied invasion of North Africa, and ciphers to the code by which the Vichy government communicated with its navy were in the chancery. They were kept in a constantly guarded room and Broussé did not have access to it.

Escorting a pretty woman into the chancery at night, however, was no problem for him. He simply bribed the guard and suggested that the chancery was an ideal place in which a French diplomat with a suspicious wife could rendezvous with his loved one. Evening after evening, Broussé and Betty spent hours in the hallway adjoining the code room. The guard seemed pleased with his role in promoting a clandestine romance and generally left them alone.

On the evening Betty planned to get into the code room, she took no chances. She gave the guard a glass of drugged champagne, and while he was insensible, she ushered in a professional safecracker.

He picked the lock easily, but opening the safe took hours. The job was not finished until 2 A.M., too late for the books to be removed, passed to the agent waiting outside to photograph them and returned to the safe before 4 A.M., when the day watchman took over. Betty reluctantly directed her expert to close the safe and to give her the combination.

The next evening, she picked the lock to the code room herself and tried unsuccessfully to open the safe. The expert would be needed again. He accompanied Betty and Broussé to the chancery the following night and again waited outside for her summons. As she began to pick the lock on the door, she heard the guard approaching. While Broussé stood dumbfounded, Betty began to strip off her clothes. She had just divested herself of all her garments when a powerful flashlight scanned the hallway. The watchman's light caught her full force at the code-room door, but she snatched up her slip and held it in front of her, with an embarrassed smile. The guard, gathering he had interrupted a torrid love scene, clicked off the light and muttered apologetically, "I didn't know . . . ," and fled.

Betty made the most of every moment of grace from then on. She admitted the safecracker. He opened the door to the code room and the safe and helped her to extract the books and to pass them to operatives posted outside the window. A long and agonizing wait ensued while the contents were being photographed; but the books were back in the safe, the door to the code room was locked and Betty was fully dressed before the trio departed from the chancery shortly before 4 A.M. Her "impossible" mission had been accomplished.

There was little resistance from the Vichy French fleet

when American and British troops landed in North Africa a
few months later. Colonel Ellery Huntington, an American
intelligence officer who met Betty as both were boarding a
train for New York on November 8, 1942, told her in the
course of the trip:

> We have reached the turning point in the war.
> American and British troops have landed in North
> Africa, and have met with practically no enemy re-
> sistance. The reason there has been no resistance is
> a military secret. But I think that *you* should know
> it is due to *your* ciphers. They have changed the
> whole course of the war.

As to official Franco-American relations, after the United
States broke relations with the Vichy government in November 1942, the French Embassy was placed under guard-
ianship of the Swiss legation, and the handsome residence
was unoccupied for almost two years until Henri Bonnet
arrived as ambassador.

12

Global Kaleidoscope

$\mathbf{S}$INCE WASHINGTON BECAME
the capital, the United States has engaged in eight declared wars and has been involved in several others. Each
affected Embassy Row to some extent, but none disrupted it
so significantly as World War II. Portents of that conflict
began to embroil diplomats and other Washingtonians as
long as a decade before December 1941.

Forerunner of the turbulence was the comparatively
peaceful era from 1920 to the latter part of the Hoover administration, when envoys had little to worry about except
polishing their decorations, dusting off their high silk hats
and deciding where they would spend their lengthy summer vacations.

In 1929, the Japanese ambassador, Katsuji Debuchi, selected a three-acre site for his country's new headquarters.
However, the new Japanese residence and chancery, inaugurated in 1932, began to draw an uneasy spotlight before
they were finished.

Emissaries of the Rising Sun had been well received since
1871, when the first minister, Jugoi Amoni Muru, presented
his credentials to President Grant. The legation was raised to
an embassy in 1906 at Theodore Roosevelt's suggestion, and
since the Taft administration, Japan's friendship with the
United States had been symbolized by the Tidal Basin's
annually blossoming cherry trees, which the city of Tokyo
gave to the city of Washington.

Many Washington residents followed with interest the construction of the new embassy, but no one had the remotest conception of the attention it would attract in the coming years.

The establishment was almost finished when rumblings from Asia presaged the decade in which militancy abroad rocked Washington, split the diplomatic corps and finally brought the United States into war against the Axis. When Japan took over Manchuria in October 1931, Debuchi became the first of a succession of envoys summoned to the State Department to explain aggressive acts. Debuchi made use of his considerable charm and intelligence to convince Secretary Henry L. Stimson—and the press—that although his embassy had no advance notice of the Manchurian annexation, it would bring law and order to the chaotic area and posed no threat to United States interests in the Far East.

As excitement subsided, Debuchi devoted himself to supervising completion of his residence and its adjoining chancery. Perceptive guests among the hundreds at the opening reception in the spring of 1932 observed that although the restrained neoclassic lines of the buildings in no way suggested the national architecture of Japan, the formal interior of the residence, with a general color scheme of gold and deep porcelain blue, displayed the artistry of the Far East in silk paintings, delicately ornamented screens and low, pearl-inlaid tables. Particularly noteworthy was the uncluttered spaciousness of the broad transverse corridor, the state dining room and a central salon opening on a terrace overlooking Rock Creek Park.

Hiroshi Saito, Debuchi's successor in 1934, used the dining and reception rooms to good advantage for almost three years. He and likable Mme. Saito had a guest list that included not only the socially elite and officials but also civic leaders and members of the press. At his pleasant parties, Saito convinced many that the sword-rattling clique in Tokyo did not represent the general tenor of Japan. He beat a path to the State Department to expound the same thesis. An avowed pacifist, he was intent on keeping American-Japanese relations on an even keel, "until," as he repeatedly said, "my country can work out her own problems." When war broke out in earnest between Japan and China, the Saitos canceled their social calendar for a month.

Concurrently, Dr. C. T. Wang, the Chinese ambassador, disappeared from the party scene. A widower with two pretty daughters, Wang had been in Washington a comparatively short time, but he was highly regarded. A distinguished succession of Chinese envoys, in fact, had been favorites in the capital since 1878, when the first Chinese minister, Chan Lau Pin, appeared in a rich satin robe and with a long queue dropping from beneath his small round hat to present his credentials to President Rutherford B. Hayes. Wang's immediate predecessor was the beloved Dr. Sao-Ke Alfred Sze, who served twice as minister to the United States and became China's first ambassador in Washington when the legation was raised to an embassy in 1935.

Headquarters of the mission was a vast, red-brick house at 19th and Vernon Streets, described when it was acquired in 1903 as a forty-three-room "mansion and the finest and most costly diplomatic residence and chancery in Washington." The surroundings had long since deteriorated when Wang selected one of the finest estates in the city, and his government leased it, with an option to buy, early in 1937. (China did not purchase the property until 1946, when Dr. Wellington Koo was ambassador.) Called Twin Oaks, the hilltop Victorian house, surrounded by nineteen acres on Woodley Road, was the former home of Gardiner Greene Hubbard, father-in-law of Alexander Graham Bell. Furnished with exquisite Chinese treasures, it was an imposing setting for Wang, the munificent host. Invitations to his receptions and his dinners of bird's nest soup, shark fins and eight-jewel rice were prized.

Even though the Sino-Japanese war temporarily halted Wang's entertaining, the Chinese Embassy's prestige soared. Countless friends called on the ambassador and inundated him with invitations. When he and his daughters resumed their social calendar, they were more popular than ever; the attention revolving around them accentuated the coolness shown to the Japanese.

Ambassador Saito's conferences at the State Department had become unsatisfactory and embarrassing. A retinue of reporters waited outside to question the nervous ambassador each time he emerged, so he sometimes sought secret meetings with Secretary Cordell Hull in the latter's apartment. The visibly perturbed little envoy was already breaking under the strain when, in December, Japanese planes bombed and sank the American gunboat *Panay* and three Standard Oil tankers on the Yangtze River. Saito hurried to the State Department to apologize for "the very grave error" and to promise that his government would scrupulously refrain from any such misconduct in the future. He was a shattered man when he repeated his statement to the press.

A week earlier he and Mme. Saito had issued invitations to a musicale in mid-December. The function was canceled when "regrets" poured in after the *Panay* incident. At the annual White House reception, six days later, Saito and his delegation responded with fixed smiles and nervous bows to the few frigid greetings they received. Several in the company openly snubbed them. Exactly half an hour after the event began, the Japanese left.

The embassy continued to be a target of resentment until Saito took to his bed, gravely ill, early in 1938. Later that year, he resigned, and he and his wife and their two small children moved to a hotel.

By the end of 1938, the *Panay* disaster was largely forgotten. Aggressions in other areas were alarming America, and Japan's war machine seemed far less menacing than

Nazi Germany's. The new Japanese ambassador, Kensuke Horinouchi, exuded serenity and was clever at reminding acquaintances that envoys had to justify government policies with which they sometimes did not agree. He saw Saito often and engendered sympathy for the ailing man by reporting that he was dying of a broken heart. Hundreds attended Saito's Buddhist funeral rites at the embassy in February 1939, and his ashes were sent to Japan on an American warship—an unprecedented gesture of personal regard for a private citizen who had done all he could to preserve amity between his country and the United States.

Within six months, the Japanese embassy was back to normal. With the help of a clever social secretary who had also served German and Italian ambassadors, Horinouchi and his wife entertained with notable frequency and distinction, and their names appeared on many exclusive guest lists. Their standing, however, never approximated that of Horinouchi's opposite number in the Chinese Embassy, Dr. Hu Shih, who had replaced Wang in 1938. A slim, graying man with bright eyes behind horn-rimmed spectacles, Hu had exceptional charm and understanding. His fame as the "Father of the Chinese Literary Renaissance," the author of numerous books and a superb lecturer across the United States in 1937 preceded him to Washington. He had influential friends in the city from his college days at Cornell and Columbia universities; and one of his intimates was Dr. Stanley K. Hornbeck, head of the State Department's Far Eastern division, who had known him in China.

Hu never turned down an invitation unless he had a previous engagement. His sumptuous dinners and luncheons, generally small and unpublicized, drew a succession of Supreme Court justices, Cabinet members and Capitol Hill leaders; also, influential Protestant and Catholic clergymen; economists, authors and educators. No envoy was more socially active.

China's calendar in Washington was flourishing in 1940,

but the time for Japanese dinner-table diplomacy ceased when the United States failed to renew its trade agreement with Japan that year. Horinouchi was recalled, and a chargé d'affaires headed the embassy until the former foreign minister Admiral Kichisaburo Nomura arrived as ambassador in February 1941. Nomura, who had been naval attaché during the Wilson administration, had no time for parties on his second tour of duty in Washington. His business revolved between his chancery and the State Department. Secretary Hull recalled in his *Memoirs* that Nomura's "outstanding characteristic was solemnity, but he was given to a mirthless chuckle and to bowing." Hull added, however, "I credit Nomura with having been honestly sincere in trying to avoid war between his country and mine."

In November, Saburo Kurusu, who as Japanese ambassador in Berlin had signed the Tripartite Pact with Germany and Italy, joined Nomura as a special emissary. Few persons outside the White House and the State Department ever saw him. Hull wrote, "Kurusu seemed to me the antithesis of Nomura. Neither his appearance nor his attitude commanded confidence or respect. I felt from the start that he was deceitful."

Less than a month after Kurusu arrived, Japan and the United States were at war. Three days after war broke out, the Chinese ambassador relayed to the State Department the rumor that Nomura was under orders to commit hara-kiri so his government could claim that he had been murdered. Hull asked the Swiss minister, Karl Bruggmann, to talk to Nomura. After a lengthy visit with the discomfited envoy, Bruggmann reported that Nomura did not deny the possibility of suicide; he had said, merely, that his fate depended on "the decision of a higher authority." Shortly afterward, along with the other Japanese diplomats, he was sent to internment at Hot Springs, Virginia. Washington was not to have another Japanese ambassador until 1952.

The experiences of the prewar German emissaries paralleled those of the Japanese in many ways, but Hitler's diplomats on the whole were more effective than Hirohito's. When armed fleets began churning European waters in July 1934, the German diplomats were in for precarious sailing in Washington, but up to nine months before the United States entered the war, they behaved with remarkable self-confidence. To the last, and to a man, every Nazi emissary insisted that he was not a member of the Nazi party and implied that he was merely carrying out orders with which he might not personally agree.

Many German diplomats came and went after Hitler's first envoy arrived in 1933. Rotund, genial Dr. Hans Luther was a widower with two teen-age daughters. He managed to get acquainted with everybody who had even the remotest interest in Germany, and he presided over his lively *bierabends* like a benevolent burgomaster. Many who quaffed regularly from his sturdy beer mugs hailed him as the most delightful host on Embassy Row. Since he had been chancellor of a pre-Nazi cabinet and was president of the Reichsbank when Hitler's troops took it over, his friends naturally assumed that he was not heart and soul with the New Order.

Some 150 key members of Congress and newspaper correspondents clicked steins at Luther's 1936 *bierabend*, which featured a German band, embassy staff members in Bavarian costumes and Bavarian waiters who replenished drinks until 3 A.M. On the pretext of feting one fellow ambassador after another, Luther had given a series of elaborate dinners and filled out his table with influential Americans. One evening his distinguished company drank toasts to his honor guests, French Ambassador and Mme. de Laboulaye. The next day, the German Army marched into the Rhineland, and Luther hastily called a press conference. "This is a memorable day for all of us," he announced. "The last cause of friction between us and former enemies is being removed. The peace of Europe is assured."

From that day on, Luther, the once expansive host and engaging guest, was a solemn Nazi partisan, extolling Hitler at the slightest opportunity. Meanwhile, the German first secretary, Herbert Scholz, who joined the embassy in 1935, was attracting even more attention than his chief. Scholz was tall, streamlined and dashing, and he had a beautiful blond wife, the former Lilo von Schnitzler, daughter of the director of the powerful I. G. Farben dye trust. The two entertained constantly, were favorites in the smartest social set and yet took great care to cultivate anyone who was even slightly responsive to their discourses on *Der Führer* and their warm personal friendship with him.

Suspicions arose that Scholz might be more than an engaging and able first secretary, and there were whispers that he was in reality a Gestapo agent posted in Washington to shadow the ambassador and to set up a propaganda program. Then, Luther was abruptly recalled in 1937. Scholz was suspected of having advised the Wilhelmstrasse that a younger envoy more representative of the New Order was needed in Washington.

Hans Heinrich Dieckhoff arrived in May. He had been counselor of the German Embassy in 1926, when his pleasant smile and winning manner were helpful in soothing rancors left by World War I.

The embassy headquarters, still a symbol of the old Germany, did not appeal to Dieckhoff as a proper social setting for the new envoy of the Third Reich. Besides, his rapidly expanding staff needed more working space. The antiquated dwelling was turned into offices, and the new ambassador leased the home of Countess Széchényí, the former Gladys Vanderbilt, on Massachusetts Avenue. The roomy mansion admirably suited his purposes, and soon the German Embassy's social schedule was full.

Dieckhoff was a stimulating host, always articulate and

often amusing. With his curly hair flowing back from a high forehead and his ruddy face beaming, he dispersed his propaganda with coatings of wit and light innuendo, but few persons ever left his presence without having been reminded in some way that Germany would brook no outside interference to its program for "justifiable expansion." Quiet, self-contained Frau Dieckhoff, who refrained from entering into any political discussion, was an effective aide to her outspoken husband.

Early in 1938, while chandeliers sparkled on German Embassy dinners, lights began to burn all night at the chancery. The propaganda apparatus was in action.

On March 11, 1938, a few hours after news of the *Anschluss* broke, Dieckhoff called at the Austrian legation. Edgar Prochnik, the Austrian minister, and his family had spent so many years in the capital that neither of his grown daughters spoke German. His wife was American-born; the many friends of the Prochniks regarded them as permanent residents of Washington.

Prochnik was unhappily aware of the purpose of Dieckhoff's call, and he was also resigned to fate. Without protest, he turned over the keys to the legation, although Dieckhoff invited him to stay on as a minister of Germany, at least until the situation was clarified. Prochnik said he would vacate the premises as soon as possible. He and his family moved to a private residence the next week, and he later joined the faculty of Georgetown University.

Immediately after the Anschluss, the Germans redoubled their efforts. Quelling fears that this was only the beginning of Nazi expansion was difficult, but they met the challenge with diplomatic aplomb—and entertainment. The Dieckhoffs had two or three big dinners a week and a reception drawing hundreds every other week; and, although leading journalists appeared on every German guest list, Dieckhoff gave a cocktail party "for the press" twice a month. Other members of the embassy wined and dined smaller groups in their homes. All the Germans were under orders to entertain anybody and everybody who was socially acceptable, remotely influential and receptive to Nazi propaganda.

Meanwhile, Dieckhoff proceeded with plans for a new embassy residence on S Street, just off Massachusetts Avenue. Talking about it to guests at a dinner in the early autumn of 1938, Dieckhoff observed, "It's a splendid location, near the home of Mrs. Woodrow Wilson." He added, chuckling, "That should ensure our social standing, shouldn't it?"

That same evening, he mentioned that German diplomats had a new ceremonial uniform. The ornate, heavily braided attire that had distinguished the German corps at official functions since the mid-nineteenth century had been discarded; diplomats of the Third Reich henceforth would appear at such events as the annual White House affairs in white tie, with eighteen-caret gold buttons on the tail coat accenting the narrow gold stripe down the side of the trousers. "Just enough gold to dazzle," the ambassador said with a broad smile, "but not enough to blind."

Dieckhoff never had a chance thus to dazzle Washington. A month before the 1938 White House diplomatic reception, Hitler's first massive attack against the Jews had so deeply shocked America that Hugh Wilson, our ambassador to Germany, was called to Washington for consultation. In turn, Dieckhoff was summoned to Berlin. Before he left Washington there were many conferences with Secretary Hull; when the envoy emerged from the last of these conferences his cheery smile was missing and he declined to answer questions. He was no more talkative the next day as he left Washington. "I have nothing to say," he quietly told reporters who clustered around him at Union Station. "I'm just like your Mr. Wilson, who doesn't say anything either."

Frau Dieckhoff stayed on in Washington for six months, but a week before invitations to the White House reception were issued, she requested that her name be omitted. ("My husband is absent," she said, "and I am not officially here.")

Hans Thomsen, who was promoted to minister early in 1938, led the German diplomats as the new chargé d'affaires at the reception. All were resplendent in their new diplomatic attire except the military and naval attachés who wore the formal dress of their services, and Herbert Scholz —who appeared in the full uniform of the SS.

A slim, handsome man of Norwegian descent, Thomsen was a linguist and an intellectual of highly cultivated tastes and sensitivity. He had a nice sense of humor. He was given to understatement. He was silk-smooth in his dealings with the State Department and so consistently courteous to critics of Germany that some of them wondered if he privately agreed with their views.

The ample representation fund (budget for entertainment and housekeeping expenses) provided for Dieckhoff was withdrawn when he left. Plans for the new embassy were abandoned, and the lease on the Széchényí mansion was not renewed. The frequent big receptions of the Germans were over; their parties generally were smaller, more select and even more purposeful in the next year.

When Czechoslovakia fell, March 1939, Karl Resenberg of the embassy staff had the chore of informing the respected Czech minister, Vladimir Hurban, that his legation was German property. Hurban flatly refused to move from his house and office and declared that he would "take no orders from Berlin." Dumbfounded, Resenberg retired and scurried to the chancery for further instructions. They were not forthcoming. The United States government refused to recognize the conquest, and Hurban stayed on at the legation and continued to be received at the State Department as the heroic Czech minister.

Envoys of countries attacked or threatened were the center of capital attention in rapid succession. The Polish ambassador, Count Jerzy Potocki, said at one of his elegant dinners early in 1939, "We envoys of countries about to be invaded ought to organize a bridge club. We now have precisely enough for three tables, and the fates are dusting off chairs for a fourth."

Less than three months before, at the British Embassy garden party given by King George and Queen Elizabeth, Potocki spotted Hans Thomsen in the crowd and observed, "I wonder how long he will be coming to British parties. For that matter, I wonder how long any of us will even be speaking to the Germans." By September, he was speaking to neither the Germans nor the Russians.

Potocki had been sharply criticized by the Communist press for months. By background and inclination, he symbolized a privileged way of life that the Communists deplored. A titled aristocrat with enormous wealth, he was a devotee of big-game hunting and horse racing. His embassy on 16th Street was furnished with many of his own priceless possessions, and his lavish dinners were second to none on Embassy Row.

A month after his country fell to Germany and the Soviet Union, Potocki resigned and left Washington to join his Peruvian-born wife in her native land.

A number of diplomats resigned as their countries submitted to Germany. John Pelenyi, the Hungarian minister, gave up the Albemarle Street estate that had been the Hungarian legation and the scene of many beautiful parties for several years and left Washington. Explaining his reason for choosing to live elsewhere in the United States, he said, "I don't want to be anywhere near the German Embassy and its pack of insidious agents."

As the government of Carol II began to align itself with Germany, several members of the Rumanian legation resigned. Georges Boucesco, counselor, was the first to go. He and his monocle-wearing wife (known all over social Washington as "Nippy") were personable and popular; but they were increasingly unhappy about the changing policies in Rumania. Fully aware that his break with the government might mean the sacrifice of all his worldly possessions at home—and they were sizable—Boucesco resigned and remained in Washington as a private citizen. His wife immediately took a job as a clerk in a department store.

Rumania's minister, Radu Irimescu, turned in his credentials when Germany's control over his country became imminent. A few months earlier, however, he had some difficulties with Hans Thomsen's wife, who had become the biggest question mark in the diplomatic corps. Frau Thomsen was pretty and appealing, but she was strange. She was inordinately fond of animals, spent two or three afternoons a week at the zoo and talked incessantly about her pet squirrel. She was devoted to fortune tellers and consulted one regularly. She did not look "German." Her vivid brown eyes and auburn hair suggested southern European ancestry; and she so frequently referred to her days in Budapest that many acquaintances assumed she had Hungarian parents (until an enterprising news reporter verified that she was the daughter of a German general and a mother who was half German, half French). But the most puzzling thing about her were her astounding remarks about the Nazi regime. At a tea in her own house, guests were deeply touched as she hinted that she had relatives in a concentration camp and declared that she hoped "never to have to go back to Germany while those inhumane Nazis are in power!"

Her American friends assumed a protective attitude about her. They called her Bébé and pitied her plight. Others had conflicting views. Some thought her unbalanced; some suspected her outbursts to be shrewdly calculated to uncover fertile fields for Nazi propaganda. A secretary of the Rumanian legation exploded at a dinner at the Chevy Chase Club one evening when his hostess expressed grave concern about "poor Bébé Thomsen." "*Poor nothing!*" he cried. "Hitler has a Bébé Thomsen in every capital of the Western Hemisphere! She's using the oldest device in intrigue; she lambasts the Nazis to get a rise—to find out how *you* stand!

You can depend on it that every response she gets, pro and con, goes straight to the German foreign office!"

The Rumanian minister had a telephone call from Frau Thomsen the next day. She insisted that she must see him at once on an urgent matter—that afternoon, if possible; at his legation—privately, of course. Irimescu suggested that she communicate her problem in writing. Within three hours, a messenger delivered a letter from Frau Thomsen. It stated that a bachelor on his staff had said she was a Nazi spy. She insisted that he be reprimanded, told not to repeat such slander and ordered to apologize before her husband heard about it.

There were two bachelors in the legation. Irimescu summoned both and showed them the letter. One promptly confirmed that he was responsible, but declared that he would not correct an accusation he knew to be valid. Irimescu filed the letter and he never heard from Frau Thomsen again.

A ticklish situation within the German Embassy also involved Frau Thomsen. She and Frau Scholz were natural rivals, and open enmity between the two was a topic of tea-table talk before the discord between their husbands became noticeable. Thomsen as senior officer in the embassy refused to knuckle under to the SS officer, and Scholz used the friction between "Bébé and Lilo" as an excuse for informing the Wilhelmstrasse that further dissension in the embassy could be avoided only if Thomsen were replaced. Thomsen was called to Berlin, but not because of his first secretary's advice. Scholz had no idea how high his superior rated. Thomsen accompanied Hitler as chief interpreter on his historic first meeting with Mussolini; and when Thomsen returned to Washington, his position was more secure than ever. Scholz was promptly shifted to the German consulate in Boston. There, his troubles really began. An exclusive club blackballed him; the Boston City Council demanded an inquiry into his fifth-column activities; he was investigated by the Dies congressional committee.

Resentment and suspicions of the Germans were deflected to a certain extent in November 1939, when the forces of 180 million Russians assaulted the Mannerheim Line of 6 million Finns. The good-looking, six-foot-tall minister of Finland, Hjalmar Procope, was one of the most popular figures on Embassy Row. He had been a supersalesman for his threatened country for more than a year, and Washington sympathies welled around him.

Procope came to the United States in May 1938 on a high tide of American goodwill for his debt-paying little democracy. He leased a house on fashionable Tracy Place and promptly opened his doors to hordes of guests. Not for him the formal dinners at which no more than forty could be entertained at a time. The Finnish minister gave receptions and buffet suppers for hundreds. Divorced shortly before assignment to Washington, he was the most sought-after "extra man" in the city; and, keenly aware that influential contacts may be made at almost any capital party, he went everywhere. He charmed every American he met; and Washingtonians, who before 1938 could hardly place his country on the map, by 1939 were well aware of Finland's location, size, history and precarious plight as a tasty morsel for the hungry Russian bear on its border.

Procope worked tirelessly to translate his devoted following and the evident regard for Finland into a United States loan for guns and planes for defense. He was warmly received at the State Department. He had support in the press and help on Capitol Hill. Congress seriously considered his plea for an armaments loan but could find no way to float it without risking Russian wrath. When the Soviet Union finally invaded Finland, Procope got $10 million for food for Finland—but not for planes and guns. There were many nationwide benefits for Finnish civilian relief, endless eulogies for valiant Finland and more personal publicity and sympathy.

After the Mannerheim Line fell, Procope's social schedule sharply declined. His representation fund was cut; he stopped giving parties. He declined many invitations, and then he ceased even to be the darling of distaff Washington when he married an Englishwoman shortly after she appeared on the scene. By the time Germany armed Finland and the two countries joined forces against Russia in June 1941, Washington attention had shifted to other troubled envoys of countries invaded, occupied or at war.

The German Embassy had given no big parties since the departure of Dieckhoff. Herr and Frau Thomsen scheduled what was to be their first, and last, mass reception in March 1940, in honor of His Royal Highness, the Duke of Saxe-Coburg Gotha, president of the German Red Cross. The Duke had an inherited title and a merciful connection, and he was a grandson of Queen Victoria. Scores of Washingtonians who had been looking askance at the German diplomates were willing, for the moment, to forget the errors of the Nazi government. Calling cards showered the Thomsens' residence and those of several other members of the staff. In response, invitations went out by the dozens.

It was the biggest party of the season. It drew many of the socially prominent, some important figures in the administration and all the envoys who were still on speaking terms with the Germans. His Royal Highness, a pleasant little man, tired of shaking hands and complained that his "feet hurt" long before the last of the long line had been received. Guests hovered around the elaborate buffet and the bars for more than two hours. Many left in a glow of admiration for the royal guest of honor and his noble cause. Several hostesses planned to return the Germans' hospitality as soon as possible.

Two weeks later Hitler's forces invaded Norway and Denmark. Before the end of June, the Netherlands, Belgium, Luxembourg and France were also casualties of a war in which America was not yet officially involved.

Hans Thomsen for some time, and with varying degrees of success, had assidously courted the Norwegian minister, Wilhelm Munthe de Morgenstierne, and the Danish minister, Henrik Louis Hans de Kauffmann, as well as other diplomats of the neutral countries. Morgenstierne spent many years in consular and legation service in the United States before he became minister in 1934. He and his attractive Canadian-born wife had an extensive circle of friends before Hans Thomsen arrived on the scene. They accepted the social overtures of the German chargé d'affaires and his wife, went to their parties and repaid them in kind; but the soft-spoken, forthright Morgenstierne found little in common with the equally soft-spoken but artful Thomsen.

Thomsen had better luck with De Kauffmann of Denmark, who arrived in Washington in 1939. They had many mutual interests and acquaintances. De Kauffmann was born in Frankfurt and had served in the Danish legation in Berlin before assignment to Italy, China, Japan and Norway. Both men were linguists and devotees of music and art. De Kauffmann was a fabulous person. He was a connoisseur of Chinese art. He had scaled mountains in the Himalayas, explored the Gobi desert and dug for dinosaur remains with Roy Chapman Andrews. His wife, the daughter of a United States naval officer, was a lovely, unassuming person whose devotion to her stunning husband and their two daughters was notable. Quiet in manner and poised, she was the antithesis of emotive Bébé Thomsen. They were not close friends, although their husbands lunched together two or three times a week at Hans Thomsen's regular table at the Mayflower Hotel.

De Kauffmann was out of the city when Povl Bang-Jensen, the Danish attaché, received news that Germany had invaded

Denmark at 3:30 A.M., on April 9, 1940. The minister was back in Washington by nightfall. The German Embassy did not contact the Danish legation in any way. But at the State Department, De Kauffmann declared that "as a representative of the King of Denmark and nobody else" he would take no orders "from any German." Hull assured him that the United States would continue to recognize him as the minister of Denmark; and in that capacity, without asking approval from Copenhagen, De Kauffmann was to be of significant service in protecting the security of the Western Hemisphere.

He signed an agreement giving the United States permission "to construct and maintain" naval bases, landing fields, seaplane facilities and meteorological stations in Greenland, which was under the sovereignty of Denmark but was covered by the Monroe Doctrine. Thus, the Nazis were prevented from using Greenland as a base for operations in the Western Hemisphere.

The Nazi-controlled Danish government denounced the agreement, branded De Kauffmann a traitor and announced his recall. When Hull, on April 14, 1941, reassured Kauffmann that he was still the duly authorized minister of Denmark in the United States, he was dismissed from the Danish foreign service and indicted for treason. He stayed on in America. Congress passed a special bill enabling him to use frozen Danish assets, and he worked with a shipping concern in New York until after the war.

King Christian then formally authorized him to continue as Danish minister, and he led his country's delegation to the United Nations conference in 1945. He became ambassador when the Danish mission was raised to an embassy two years later; and in 1955, Americans of Danish descent raised $200,000 for a foundation, named in his honor, to promote cultural relations between Denmark and the United States. De Kauffmann remained in the United States as envoy until his retirement in 1958, but his life story had the saddest of endings. Washington friends were shocked at a dispatch from Copenhagen on June 5, 1963, stating that Mme. de Kauffmann, to rescue her husband from the agonies of incurable cancer, had killed him and then committed suicide.

Ten days before the Nazis invaded his country, Norway's Ambassador Munthe de Morgenstierne told Cordell Hull that Norwegian neutrality was threatened and that the Germans might move into both Norway and Denmark at any moment; when the invasion took place, the doughty minister was prepared to stand his ground. Three days after the occupation, the puppet management in Oslo notified him that, henceforth, he would obey orders from it or be held accountable. He replied that he would await instructions from his regular government and would be loyal only to it. With assurances from Hull that the United States had no intention of recognizing the new command in Oslo, Morgenstierne continued as the duly recognized minister of Norway.

On behalf of the President, Hull suggested that any or all members of the Norwegian royal family who had taken refuge in Stockholm would be welcome in the United States, and the White House followed through with an official invitation. In June, Crown Princess Martha and her children arrived on an American ship and took up residence at Pook's Hill, a Maryland estate, where she remained through the war. After King Haakon established Norway's government-in-exile in London, his mission in Washington became an embassy and Morgenstierne, the first Norwegian ambassador to the United States. He was to serve as dean of the diplomatic corps from 1947 until his retirement ten years later.

German-American relations, severely strained by the Nazi invasion of Norway and Denmark in April and of the Netherlands, Belgium and Luxembourg the following month, reached the near-breaking point when France collapsed in June 1940. Thomsen and his staff, in a city now seething with anti-Nazi sentiment, feared for their lives, and the chargé d'affaires asked the State Department for extra guards at his chancery and residence. They were provided.

Roosevelt's reelection, the subsequent passage of the Lend-Lease Act and the convoying of arms-loaded British and American ships shortly afterward signaled the end of diplomatic relations between Germany and the United States. German diplomats ceased to entertain and declined the few social invitations that came their way; but postwar disclosures were to prove that their apparent quiescence from May 1941 until Germany declared war on the United States masked accelerated undercover industry.

The embassy had been suspected of engaging in periodic subversive activity for some time. One of the reasons Dieckhoff went "on leave" in the autumn of 1938 was that Undersecretary of State Sumner Welles had warned he would be declared *persona non grata* if reports that his chancery housed a fifth-column apparatus could be proved. Later, Thomsen's troubles multiplied when rumor spread that the German press attaché, Herbert von Strempel, was under orders to finance any American magazine agreeing to promote Nazi propaganda.

On the surface, however, the Germans, during their final seven months in Washington, appeared to be diplomatically inactive. Thomsen and Karl Resenberg spent endless hours at auction sales and invested heavily in French paintings and American furniture. To anyone who asked, both emphasized they were buying for themselves and not for the German Embassy. (Almost seven years later, many of their purchases were again up for auction, along with all the embassy effects. For the first time in history, the furnishings of a conquered country's official residence in Washington were offered to the highest bidder. Many wondered at the time why the exquisite housewares of the Japanese Embassy were not similarly available. The answer lay in the Potsdam agreement that the German Embassy furnishings in all the United Nations were to be sold as war loot, the implication being that Germany never again was to have full diplomatic representation abroad. Japan was not so mentioned.)

Frau Thomsen was on an extended trip to the western United States while her husband was haunting auction sales. By the time she returned in the autumn of 1941, Thomsen and his staff were infrequently seen in public. They declined to see political reporters or to answer any question by telephone. On rare appearances at official functions they had to attend, they were morose and uncommunicative. But Bébé Thomsen was as talkative and as appealing as ever when she telephoned acquaintances and regaled them with reports of her trip. To the few loyal friends who went to see her, she poured out her fears as to her fate if she ever had to go back to "Hitler's Germany." She implied that her husband was similarly apprehensive. The "poor Bébé" wail was revived over countless capital teacups and was still echoing around Washington on December 11, 1941, when Thomsen delivered Germany's declaration of war at the State Department and returned to his chancery to burn confidential papers. "Nothing very important," he solemnly declared to reporters as they watched the smoke curling from the ancient chimneys. "Just routine office memoranda," he continued. "And I have nothing of interest to tell you. You already know that I am soon to be a diplomatic prisoner of your government."

In a flurry of unspoken farewells and muted contrition, the Germans were soon off to internment at the swank Greenbrier Hotel in White Sulphur Springs, West Virginia. Less than five months later, they boarded the diplomatic exchange ship *Drottningholm*, where they all appeared as elated as children just let out of school. A ship reporter noted that "Frau Thomsen looked particularly happy."

Two members of the group were to be seen again in Washington. After Von Strempel admitted at Nuremberg that the German Embassy in Washington financed at least one prewar publication for propaganda purposes, he and Thomsen were flown to Washington in November 1946 to testify at the sedition trial of the publisher of Scribner's *Commentator*. Thomsen's testimony revealed much of the story: The Berlin foreign office had ordered the embassy to speed up propaganda, and when Thomsen learned that Scribner's *Commentator* was sympathetic to the German cause, he instructed Von Strempel to advance money to the editor and publisher. He said he did not know how the negotiations were handled but believed that shortly afterward more than $10,000 was paid to the publication. Thomsen was no cringing, apologetic figure as he testified. Still a handsome man, with silver tinging his blond hair, he was as suave and composed as ever. Winding up his testimony, he offered his one personal line of defense: "I was merely following orders from my government. A career diplomat, even in wartime, has no other choice."

Less articulate and obviously nervous, Von Strempel was also hazy on details and could not recall how payments were made or how much they were. He appeared puzzled at a résumé of testimonies from the magazine's editor and publisher that a bundle of twenty-dollar bills, $15,000 in all, had been tossed through a window of their office at Lake Geneva, Wisconsin; that a subsequent payment had been made by "a man" in the street; that another $15,000 had turned up on a hall table at Lake Geneva. He did not confirm or deny testimony that the recipients did not know the source of the financial assistance.

A military prisoner, Thomsen was quartered under guard at Fort Meade, Maryland. Von Strempel, with a $70-a-week expense account from the Justice Department, stayed at a downtown hotel. Neither tried to contact Washington acquaintances.

Mussolini's diplomats and their predecessors had escaped much of the on-again, off-again attention that focused on the Germans in prewar Washington. But the Italians had troubles enough, beginning in 1936, when Italy invaded Ethiopia. The image of Italy's imperialistic boot crushing the ancient African kingdom arosed the righteous indignation of many Americans and the Italian Embassy was under attack. Agusto Rosso, the resourceful Italian ambassador, had served as a young attaché in Washington and had traveled widely in the United States; he understood the fluctuating temperament of the American public, and he handled the crisis admirably. Since becoming envoy in 1933, he had been in the business of cultivating reporters; they admired his keenly analytical mind and his wit. Many deeply resented the invasion; but Rosso treated everyone as his friend and quietly explained Italy's side of the case. He became a one-man propaganda machine, with soft-sell emphasis on "the necessity of the aggression," and news dispatches out of Washington soon began to reflect his views. Meanwhile, his cause was bolstered by a succession of lecturers sent over by Mussolini to plead for continued Italian-American goodwill. Within three months, United States antagonism had moderated considerably.

Rosso was a bachelor. After he married charming Mrs. Frances Bunker, of Denver, Colorado, he was shifted as envoy to the Soviet Union. His replacement in June 1936 was Mussolini's former undersecretary of foreign affairs, who had two strikes against him before he ever got started in Washington. As Fulvio Suvich, he presented his letters of credence as "Ambassador of the King of Italy and the Emperor of Ethiopia." The President accepted his credentials with reference only to "the King of Italy." Then, under the illusion that a "de" in his name would be more impressive in America, Fulvio Suvich became Fulvio *de* Suvich and was so designated in the *Diplomatic List*, but he continued to be called "Suvich" at the State Department. He had several handicaps. His English was faulty. He was on the defensive at any mention of Mussolini, no matter how innocent. When Signor and Signora de Suvich left, a year and a half later, there was no round of farewell fetes. They never found a way to fit into the Washington picture.

Il Duce sent as his last ambassador to the United States Don Ascanio dei Principe Colonna, scion of an illustrious Roman family dating back eleven centuries. Courtly, in the tradition of the story-book prince, conversant on art and music, as every Italian envoy is expected to be, and well informed on world affairs, he appeared an ideal choice for the post. The beautiful Grecian-born Princess Colonna was gracious and one of the best-dressed women on Embassy Row. At almost any other time, the Colonnas would have been outstanding in Washington, but they were just beginning to get acquainted when anti-Axis sentiment permeated the city, and the preponderance of Germans, Japanese, Spaniards and Argentinians at their dinners gave rise to gossip that the German Embassy was compiling their guest lists. Concurrently, the Italian Embassy was implicated in sabotage. The United States had taken into protective custody all the German, Italian and Danish ships in United States ports, when the Treasury Department obtained documentary evidence that the Italian naval attaché, Admiral Alberto Lais, had directed that all the Italian ships be put out of commission. Twenty-five vessels were badly damaged in the spring of 1941. The State Department notified Colonna that Lais was *persona non grata*, and the admiral was promptly recalled; but strict surveillance on the embassy continued.

The Colonnas withdrew completely from the party circuit, and so did all members of the embassy staff. Colonna's last official duty as envoy was discharged at the State Department on December 11, when he presented Italy's formal declaration of war on America. He and his wife were also interned at White Sulphur Springs.

13

Uneasy Fellowship

SOMETIMES IT TAKES ONLY A decade after peace is declared to forget the reasons for an armed conflict; but even before World War II ended, many on Embassy Row were apprehensive that the defeat of Germany would bring to the fore an equally formidable enemy. The "Herrs" and "Fraus" had long since disappeared from the *Diplomatic List*, but several new entries with the title of plain "Mr." and "Mrs." represented governments under Kremlin domination.

At the end of December 1941, the United States and two-thirds of the governments with missions in Washington were at war with the Axis. Diplomats from countries already occupied or besieged were heartened that America at last was officially with them, but many other residents were stunned at the unexpected way war had come. For two gloomy weeks after the almost crushing blow of Pearl Harbor, the city's social structure was shattered. Parties were called off in a spirit of sacrifice, and leading hostesses vowed they would not entertain again until the war was over.

This lugubrious tone was followed by a hectic reaction, as some 250,000 strangers began pouring in from all over the country and abroad to negotiate contracts or to take jobs toward winning the war. Some 10,000 persons from England, Australia, New Zealand and Canada had come to assist in the war program, which was already under way. All at once it was urgent for members of the War Production

Board, the Office of Strategic Services and countless other emergency operations to get acquainted with each other, to meet newcomers and to cultivate partners on Embassy Row in surroundings as relaxed as possible. The traditional social routine was revived and accelerated. Early in January 1942, Mrs. Evalyn Walsh McLean resumed her Sunday evening dinners, drawing a weekly average of some 200 government leaders, heads of new agencies, big brass of the military, foreign envoys and wives. "It's one of my contributions toward winning the war," she said. Other capital hostesses followed her lead, and soon party going and giving with global impact was an accepted part of the war effort.

The first diplomatic reception in 1942 was given by the Turkish ambassador, Mehmet Munir Ertegun. The envoy of a neutral country, Ertegun had been in Washington since 1934 and was widely known and respected. He had been courted by the British, the French, the Germans and the American State Department in the prewar period. Germany's Ambassador Dieckhoff and later, Chargé d'Affaires Thomsen had been particularly attentive, in hopes of augmenting the efforts of Hitler's shrewd envoy in Ankara, Franz von Papen, to make Turkey a Nazi ally. American friends of Ertegun had urged him to warn his foreign office about Papen, who as German military attaché in Washington before World War I had been implicated in sabotage and ordered out of the country. Ertegun duly dispatched the warnings, along with prolific reports of rising anti-Nazi sentiments in the United States. Meanwhile, he was consistently unreceptive to German blandishments. Everyone knew where he stood.

To their January 1942 reception Ambassador and Mme. Ertegun invited a representative cross section of official and residential society, diplomatic colleagues and newcomers already moving into high position on the capital scene. The company of well over 500 clustered around the bars and the laden buffet in a camaraderie that had not been seen since

Pearl Harbor. The pleasant, even exhilarating, atmosphere and the exotic setting were heartening indications that social intercourse in the cosmopolitan capital would continue, with inestimable help from Embassy Row.

The Turkish Embassy, housed in what had been one of the finest private homes in Washington, lent itself to huge gatherings. The government of Turkey had leased the house for several years before buying it, along with many rich Oriental carpets, masterpieces of painting and sculpture, Louis XVI sofas, chairs and consoles, as well as art items imported from Europe and the East. Unmistakably Turkish accents were added, such as the heroic bronze head of Mustafa Kemal Atatürk in the alcove on the stairway landing, an enormous brass brazier in the paneled reception room and Byzantine tiles in the solarium. But the basic structure of the house and many of its opulent effects were to remain as originally planned. The mansion took on added interest and Turkey's prestige reached a peak in May 1944, when Ertegun became dean of the diplomatic corps.

Rivaling the Turkish Embassy in magnificence was the residence of the Brazilian ambassador, Carlos Martins. The house was a popular gathering place throughout the war. Ambassador Martins, who had arrived in 1939, was a polished diplomat, and his wife, María, was fascinating and gifted. A sculptress, she turned out heroic, prize-winning works in her embassy studio, but she also found plenty of time to give gay parties, often accented with marimbas and lively dancers from Brazil, and always with notable guests.

The Brazilian staff, with twenty-six officers of diplomatic rank, was considered enormous in 1942. The Mexican and Argentinian staffs were almost as large. All the Latin American missions expanded as the war got under way, and all except Argentina's (and Chile's, until 1943) rallied early to help defeat the Axis. Nineteen Good Neighbor republics entered the war and six broke diplomatic relations with our enemies shortly after Pearl Harbor. The general status of the Latin American corps rose. It had taken an upturn in the early days of the New Deal when all the missions were raised to embassies, but diplomats from the smaller republics had continued to be ignored by European and Asian colleagues and either patronized or overlooked by capitalites. However, envoys of the major Latin American countries enjoyed prestige equal, and in some cases superior, to that of any of the other emissaries.

For example, Argentina's Felipe A. Espil and his wife had figured prominently in smarter circles just prior to the war. Handsome and personable, Espil was second in seniority in the corps. American-born Mme. Espil—as she preferred to be addressed—was constantly publicized for her chic and acclaimed in the smarter sets as a hostess of rare taste and discrimination.

The social rating of the Espils, high though it was, never quite approached that of Peru's Ambassador Manuel Freyre y Santander, an aging aristocrat with sophisticated tastes and charm, who moved in the city's more rarefied spheres and gave the most exclusive parties on Embassy Row.

It was noticed, however, that Freyre changed his method of operation after he succeeded Sir Ronald Lindsay as dean of the diplomatic corps in 1939. Peruvian Embassy guest lists suddenly expanded, and Freyre began to gather in his Latin American colleagues and to get acquainted with the city's civic leaders. Then, in May 1942, Peru's President Manuel Prado visited Washington amid great fanfare. Prado was the first chief of state to be received in the wartime capital. (He was to be followed by King George of Greece, King Peter of Yugoslavia and Queen Wilhelmina of the Netherlands, who arrived successively in the summer of 1942. The steady sequence of royal figures, presidents, prime ministers and other foreign dignitaries in turn, drew attention to their countries and their representatives in Washington throughout the war.)

Freyre retired in 1944, and Ertegun of Turkey became the diplomatic dean. He died seven months later, and the Belgian ambassador, Count Robert van der Straten-Ponthoz, held the exalted post for the briefest term in its history—December 1944 to the end of January 1945. The Latin Americans were particularly delighted when the honor then went to Mexico's Fernando Francisco Castilla Najera, a great favorite with his fellow *Latinos* and an outstanding figure on Embassy Row. He had been a noted surgeon and author before he became an ambassador; his interests were diversified, and he made friends in groups other than those constantly revolving around diplomats. He and his wife gave huge affairs for Washington partygoers in general, and the Mexican Embassy replaced the Pan American Union as the social center for the Latin Americans. His departure from Washington was widely regretted.

Distressing changes on Embassy Row, particularly toward the end of the war, marked the rapid expansion of communist power. The United States refused to recognize the Soviet absorption of Lithuania, Latvia and Estonia in 1944. Their legations in Washington remained open, with envoys and skeleton staffs as symbols of once-free nations. (The missions still operate. The latest *Diplomatic List* carries Dr. Arnolds Spekke as minister and chargé d'affaires of Latvia, Joseph Kajeckas as counselor and chargé d'affaires of Lithuania and Ernest Jaakson, acting consul general of Estonia in New York City.)

Two esteemed envoys, Constantin A. Fotitch, the Yugoslav ambassador, and Jan Ciechanowski, the Polish ambassador, resigned the same month—July 1944. Fotitch had worked tirelessly to solicit continued support in Washington for his London-based government; but there were sharp differences of opinion within the Washington staff when the youthful King Peter was persuaded to replace his cabinet with one approved by Marshal Tito. Vladimir Rybar, embassy counselor, argued that as long as King Peter was the recognized head of Yugoslavia, there was hope it could escape communist domination; and in April 1944, Rybar infuriated Fotitch by taking off to London to serve as assistant secretary of foreign affairs with the new cabinet. The ambassador stayed on until Tito established himself as dictator; then "the stubborn Serb," as Fotitch had come to be known in the pro-Tito clique, turned in his portfolio and took up private residence in Washington.

Ciechanowski of Poland moved out of his embassy shortly after Britain and the United States withdrew recognition of the Polish government-in-exile. His successor in September was Dr. Oscar Lange, a former professor at the University of Chicago, who had been taking orders from Moscow for some time. Dr. Lange was not welcomed with open arms in Washington; and, like emissaries of other Soviet satellites for the next several years, he was to be known by few outside his own mission, the State Department and the Soviet Embassy. (The only Polish envoy after Ciechanowski to become prominent in Washington was mild-mannered Edward Drozniak, who became ambassador in 1961. He wore himself out cultivating contacts, "as a human being," as he put it, and impressed many with his eagerness to know and understand the United States. He made innumerable trips over the country and was delighted at the reception he received. Rumors circulated that he was under surveillance by members of his own staff and that a door to his private office was left ajar when he received visitors. But, if that was true, he managed to slip the leash often enough to get about and make numerous friends. He died in Washington in 1966.)

Norway's Wilhelm Munthe de Morgenstierne, whose legation became an embassy when his government-in-exile established itself in London in 1942, took over as dean of the diplomatic corps in September 1947. He shepherded his distinguished flock with rare understanding, and new emissaries of the black-sheep Iron Curtain countries got the same courteous reception from him as others in the corps. He had an able aide in his protocol officer, Elovius Mangor, the Norwegian first secretary, who commandeered envoys of more than eighty missions into protocol line for official functions and served as Embassy Row's one-man supreme court on table seating, proper attire, the calling routine and the meshing of capital customs and international traditions.

Among the many new diplomats Morgenstierne welcomed in the early 1950s were the first postwar envoys of Germany and Japan. Heinz Krekeler arrived in 1950, with the title of chargé d'affaires of the German diplomatic mission. The stocky, genial man was a chemist, not a career officer, but he tackled the job of establishing his mission with the quiet self-confidence of a veteran diplomat. By 1954, he had the personal rank of ambassador, and a year later he was full ambassador of the Federal Republic of Germany with a fine residence owned by his government. The neoclassic, white-painted brick house on fashionable Foxhall Road, built in 1938 by Dr. James A. Cahill, was designed with a columned portico, unusually large rooms, a circular staircase rising from a wide entrance hall and a big wing for servants. Its grounds covered three and a half acres, extending to Reservoir Road. Within a few years, the complex would include the most spectacular chancery in Washington.

Japan's Ambassador Eikichi Araki settled into his country's twenty-one-year-old embassy in 1952. A slender, gray-haired man with a boyish smile, he made much of his "special ties with America." He spoke English fluently, having studied at Princeton and Cornell and having worked for several years in New York with the Bank of Japan. He was a widower; his twenty-one-year-old daughter, Tomika, was his secretary. Mme. Kamimura, wife of the minister, was hostess at his receptions and small dinners. Japanese parties, while frequent, were not to be elaborate for some time.

The man who had the advantage over all his fellow envoys was General Carlos P. Romulo, ambassador of the Philippines. Pint-size and peppy, an eloquent speaker, Romulo was a happy blend of the East and the West, with a master of arts degree from Columbia University. Most important, he had served in the U.S. Congress as resident commissioner of the Philippine Commonwealth from 1944 until his country gained independence in 1946. He was still considered a colleague by those with whom he had worked. Following announcement of his reappointment as ambassador after a shuffle in the Philippine Cabinet early in 1958, Representative John McCormack of Massachusetts, then majority leader, hailed the news as "welcome" in a speech before the House and paid tribute to Romulo as "our friend . . . who has fought uncompromisingly for his country in a way that has won respect and admiration of *his colleagues* in the United States Congress."

Romulo had also served his country as a newspaper reporter, editor, author, politician and aide-de-camp to General Douglas MacArthur on Bataan and Corregidor and in Australia. He was the new republic's first delegate to the United Nations, where he was president of the General Assembly. When he was appointed ambassador to the United States in 1952, he was already widely known throughout the country, having addressed mass audiences and accepted honorary degrees from coast to coast.

Romulo and his beautiful wife, Virginia, were regulars on the Washington party circuit. Their Queen Anne dining table accommodated its capacity—twenty-four guests—at weekly dinners and luncheons. Their receptions crowded the embassy's second-floor salons and the Philippine Room, which Mme. Romulo had planned. It is a tropical wonder, with walls of dao wood and hemp, a rattan parquet floor, a giant "Filipiniana" mural and every piece of furniture transported from the islands. Mme. Romulo and other ladies of the embassy donned the becoming *terno* dress, with graceful butterfly sleeves, for many parties, and menus invariably featured Philippine specialties.

Romulo's multiple contacts on Capital Hill and throughout the city proved a problem before the June 1958 state visit of Philippine President and Mme. Carlos P. Garcia. The embassy was too small for the enormous number of friends who expected to be invited to the reception, and available hotel facilities were also inadequate. Romulo selected the Pan American Union as the setting, and well over 1,500 turned out to the late-afternoon affair at which President and Mme. Garcia honored President and Mrs. Eisenhower.

Known to his intimates as "Rommy" and self-described as "a small man from a small country," Romulo continued as a prominent envoy and host in Washington for four more years. Asked at one of his big receptions toward the end of his tour if he ever tired of having so many people around, he said, "Never. Parties are important to diplomacy. Besides, people are my stock in trade."

An uneasy spotlight played on the Cuban Embassy in the 1950s. Six envoys served three governments in the decade before Cuba and the United States severed relations. Dr. Luis Machado, prominent in the World Bank, became President Carlos Prio Socarrás' ambassador in 1950. The Cuban Embassy on 16th Street, a vast sandstone house typical of many residences built by Mrs. John Henderson after World War I, was ideal for elaborate entertaining. The sweeping staircase divided at the landing and led on both sides to an enormous gallery opening into a series of salons. A ballroom almost as big as a tennis court overlooked a lawn at the rear. Machado cleared the lawn, strung bright electric bulbs on the surrounding trees and drew many prominent guests to fiestas in his new "moonlit garden." Cuba's status in Washington soared until the coup d'état of March

1952 brought Fulgencio Batista to the presidency. Batista asked Machado to continue as envoy. He refused. "Having been loyal to one president, I can't shift over and serve the man who ousted him," he said.

Cuba's most distinguished diplomat, Miguel A. de la Campa, arrived in Washington in the spring of 1955. He renewed acquaintance with fellow envoys whom he had known in other capitals, entertained often and elegantly and achieved high regard. Notables thronged the embassy at the reception to celebrate his golden anniversary as a diplomat in 1956. Two years later, Batista summoned Campa to Havana to take over as minister of defense and sent Nicolas Arroyo to Washington.

Young and dynamic, Arroyo had served as Cuba's minister of public works. He and his attractive wife, Gabriela, had also headed a successful architectural firm in Havana. In Washington, they redecorated the embassy and made it outstanding. They were delightful hosts. Despite repeated *Fidelista* threats that the mansion would be bombed, their parties went on with marked success.

They were out of the city when news of Batista's overthrow reached Washington on New Year's Day 1959. By the time they returned, many of their personal possessions had been confiscated, and the embassy safe had been rifled by Castro's minions on the staff. Our State Department could not intervene—the Cuban Embassy was foreign property—but faithful servants of the Arroyos managed to smuggle out some of their belongings, and Chief of Protocol Wiley T. Buchanan, Jr., on his own, assigned a bodyguard to the deposed ambassador. He and his wife and their young son, Lyn, stayed temporarily with friends, then moved to the Shoreham Hotel.

In time the Arroyos built a beautiful home for themselves in the city. Campa, who took refuge at the Chilean Embassy in Havana after Batista fled to Portugal, returned to

Washington and leased a house. Machado, by then a director of the World Bank, managed with great difficulty to get his wife and daughter out of Cuba and to establish them in a permanent home in Washington.

14

The Party-Go-Round

FROM ONLY FOUR ESTABLISH-
ments in the new federal city in 1801, the foreign corps had
grown to almost a hundred missions by the end of the Eisenhower administration. Embassy Row was to expand still
further—and then to decrease—within the next decade and
to change more dramatically in composition and character
than any period in its history.

The impact of African diplomats on Washington began
to be felt in March 1957, when Daniel Chapman, ambassador
of Ghana, the first of the emerging countries, opened a
chancery on 16th Street and began looking for a suitable
residence. When his government purchased the home of the
late Senator Joseph F. Guffey on exclusive Benton Place,
there were objections in the neighborhood; but Chapman
moved in quietly and began entertaining colleagues and
acquaintances in the State Department. Within a short time,
he was a familiar figure at diplomatic receptions, where his
toga of multicolored *kente* cloth easily identified him. He had
many friends when he left Washington in 1959 and Ghana's
place on Embassy Row was set.

A steady flow of young African diplomats poured into
Washington in the early 1960s. It was difficult and confusing for them to set up missions and find residence in a city
already beset with its own racial tensions. The State Department rallied to smooth out differences with prejudiced land-
lords, merchants and restaurant owners; and prominent

diplomats went out of their way to welcome the new emissaries. Sir Howard Beale, Australia's ambassador and senior
envoy of the Commonwealth nations, gave a reception in
honor of each African ambassador in the Commonwealth
group. France's Ambassador and Mme. Alphand included
French-speaking African emissaries in some of their most
select soirees. Belgium's Ambassador Baron Scheyven entertained the Congolese envoy. The United Arab Republic's
ambassador, Dr. Mostafa Kamel, senior emissary in the
African contingent, was consistently sympathetic and helpful
in easing the way for his young colleagues. Festivities for a
succession of visiting African chiefs of state further promoted the status of their diplomats in Washington and
pointed up the importance of holding their friendship with
the United States. Before the end of the Johnson administration, non-white Africans of thirty-one missions had become an accepted and interesting part of the city's diplomatic
life. They had proved to be eager to work in harmony with
foreign colleagues and with the United States. Their colorful
attire had become an impressive reminder of the variety of
cultures represented on Embassy Row, even though the vol-
uminous robes and ornate headgear worn by some individuals would not ordinarily be seen anywhere in Africa.
Several costumes that pass today as "natural" or "native"
bear labels of London or Paris designers, employed to turn
out attire symbolic of the spirit of the new countries.

The black Africans set great store by their national-day
celebrations. Most of them take place in hotels where the
buffet often includes one or two native dishes and, sometimes,
fabulous dancers and music. Such occasions provide the best
opportunity—after the White House diplomatic reception—
for showing off exotic costumes and publicizing background
and government of the new nations. At one such party in
1968, Burundi's Ambassador Terence Nsanze reminded
guests that his country had deposed its king and had become
a republic "without shedding a drop of blood." He added

proudly, "We are a young country, indeed. Our President is twenty-nine, I am thirty-one." Several listeners recalled the 1965 visit of the former king and the fanfare around his reception held in the same setting at the Shoreham Hotel.

Swaziland, newest of the African nations, marked its year of independence from Britain at a reception in September 1968 at the ballroom of the Washington Hilton. S. T. M. Sukati, the ambassador-designate, appeared in a leopard skin tunic with a matching thong around his head and a full cape of ox tails. Leopard anklets adorned his bare feet, and he carried a battleax, a spear and a Swazi shield. His wife and the embassy staff wore native togas. "To you who are not familiar with the Swazi custom, I wish to say you are not likely to see me often in this," His Excellency announced. He explained that Sobhuza II had asked all his emissaries to be thus attired on the gala day, and added, "Those of you who may be confused at the rapidity of change in Africa will be relieved to hear that Swaziland will still be Swaziland."

As they have settled into the capital picture, the Africans have moved up in diplomatic precedence. Respected S. Edward Peal, the ambassador of Liberia, was fourth; but his mission is not new in the United States. The oldest republic in Africa has had an envoy on a permanent basis in Washington since 1947.

From 1963 to mid-1967, the Kuwait Embassy, under the leadership of a new ambassador, Talat Al-Ghoussein, was prominent among the Arab missions. A series of what came to be called "Instant Arabian Nights" included some of the most exciting events on Embassy Row.

Equally delightful, and even more frequent, were parties given by Morocco's ambassador, Ali Bengelloun, and his wife, who wore exquisite caftans and made social headlines with luncheons and dinners at which guests settled on cushions at low tables laden with such delights as roast lamb, shad with dates, *couscous*, and *el majouin* (nut honey dessert). Fashion shows, highlighted by Oriental dancers writhing to Moroccan music, and a big reception every other month also accented the embassy calendar.

Just as active, though on a somewhat less lavish scale, was the Embassy of Jordan, with Ambassador Saad Juma and his wife attracting stimulating guests to their elaborate Middle-Eastern buffets. Bassima Al-Ghoussein of Kuwait, Jacqueline Bengelloun of Morocco, and Salwa Juma of Jordan—all beauties—became a triumvirate whose social supremacy was surpassed only by that of Mme. Alphand and Lady Harlech.

The Saudi Arabians gave their share of big parties under the aegis of their new ambassador, Ibrahim Al-Sowayel, in a ballroom added to their embassy in 1961. Ambassador of Lebanon and Mme. Ibrahim Al-Ahdab entertained with charm and distinction, as did Ambassador of Libya and Mme. Fathi Abidia, Iraq's ambassador, Nasir Hani, and his Dublin-born wife Eileen and Algeria's young ambassador, Cherif Guellal. Ambassador of Mauritania and Mme. Ahmed-Baba Miske gave one of the most unusual dinners in 1965, when they honored Secretary of State and Mrs. Dean Rusk and U.N. Ambassador and Mrs. Arthur Goldberg. On arrival, every guest was fitted out with an Arab abas, a square of white cloth slipped over the shoulders and falling below the knees. "Well, there's a first time for everything," said Goldberg, chuckling as he donned his garb for the evening and sat down at a low table to enjoy an all-Arab meal. There was no coverage in the daily press. The only photographer admitted was from *Diplomat* magazine, which carried a brief report and pictures two months later. "We didn't want to embarrass our guests," said Mme Miske. "We just wanted to give them an evening such as they might enjoy in our country. Friends who come to our embassy are really in Mauritania, you know."

When the Ambassador of Kuwait and Mme. Al-Ghoussein entertained Vice President and Mrs. Humphrey at dinner in March 1966, the new $4-million complex, housing the chancery and residence on Tilden Street, was on display for the first time. Guests could examine the interior, with its vast Middle-Eastern loggia and the Ommayad Room, with its centuries-old paneling, imported, piece by piece, from a palace in Damascus.

The image of the Arab embassies began to change early in 1967. Al-Ghoussein of Kuwait quietly hinted to friends in the press that he would prefer less emphasis on his social calendar. The spring 1966 ball to benefit the Washington Ballet Society had been a tremendously successful event at the exotic, new embassy, but Mme. Al-Ghoussein suggested that the 1967 ball be held elsewhere. The ambassador, who had rarely if ever worn Arab attire in Washington ("I don't wear it, even at home," he had said) appeared on a television program just before his country's national day fully turned out in a long dark *abaya* and *bisht*, with a *qatra* draped over his head, and his wife wore a flowing Arab costume. At their reception the next day, guests accustomed to an open bar grumbled that only soft drinks were served. This January party was the last large affair in the embassy in 1967.

As the 1967 Arab-Israeli crisis developed, the dent on Embassy Row's social scene deepened. Al-Ghoussein, who on behalf of his country had given $50,000 to the Kennedy Library in 1964, had planned his biggest party of the year to announce a donation of $100,000 to medical research in tropical diseases at Harvard. The reception was called off in May, although the gift was presented. Tunisia's foreign minister, Habib Bourguiba, Jr., former ambassador to the United States, was in Washington to inaugurate an exhibit of Tunisian mosaics at the Smithsonian Institution on June 7. He did not appear. Tunisian Ambassador and Mme. Rachid Driss were hosts at the large opening, but their Arab colleagues were noticeably missing. Plans for an addition to the Lebanese Embassy were abandoned. Syria's chargé d'affaires, Dr. Jawdat Mufti, ceased negotiating for a permanent residence.

Parties for two Arab envoys, who, some time previously, had been slated for transfer from Washington in June, were canceled. Iraq's Ambassador Hani was going to Beirut. The Lebanese Embassy scheduled a farewell dinner for him and invited a galaxy of State Department and other United States officials. Two days before the June date, Iraq severed ties with the United States and the party went off the calendar. Plans for Hani's own final reception, set for June 14, were discarded the following day. Scholarly Dr. Kamel, U.A.R. ambassador, was to be sent to Brussels, and Belgium's ambassador, Baron Scheyven, had arranged a stag dinner to honor him. It was canceled when the U.A.R. broke relations with the United States. Switzerland's ambassador, Alfred Zehnder, had invited Kamel to a dinner on June 5. Up until the morning of the dinner, the Swiss Embassy waited for the envoy's regret. When it did not arrive, the invitation was rescinded—there was no proper place to seat even a distinguished envoy at an embassy dinner in a country with which his own had ceased to have diplomatic relations.

Three days later, on June 8, 1967, the Office of Protocol announced that the *Diplomatic List* no longer included the names of ambassadors and staffs of the U.A.R., Algeria, Iraq, Sudan, Syria, Mauritania and Yemen. As emissaries of those countries left Washington, most of the other Arabs retired from the social scene. Meanwhile, the conflict focused special attention on the esteemed Ambassador of Israel and Mme. Avraham Harman. The first big party they attended after the June war was a reception given by the visiting President of Malawi, Hastings K. Banda. Surrounded by friends, the Harmans were grave and guarded in their comments. A few evenings later, by request of the ambassador, there was no dancing at the annual Israeli Independence Ball. Participants who had spent $1,000 each to buy Israel bonds, were entertained by Broadway and Hollywood stars, but the event was anything but a jubilant victory celebration. In January 1968, after a round of farewell parties, the Harmans departed from Washington, and General Yitzhak Rabin, who was chief of Israeli defense during the six-day war, took over as ambassador.

Six months after the war, the Embassy of Kuwait resumed its social calendar, but, by request, publicity was muted until they feted Secretary and Mrs. Rusk at dinner in the spring of 1968. Ambassador Al-Ghoussein returned to Kuwait to work out plans for the December visit to Washington of his Emir, who was scheduled at the time to be the last state guest in the Johnson administration.

At the end of the Arab-Israeli war, the foreign corps numbered 111 missions. Embassies of emerging countries—the Maldive Islands, Mauritius and Swaziland—were slated to be added later, but the all-time high of 118 establishments in early June 1967 was not to be reached again for some time.

The salon diplomacy of Embassy Row is no easy matter. The major problem is to determine those who must be entertained because they are legitimately involved with foreign relations and those who are interested only in going to parties. Negotiating this tightrope requires a delicate sense of balance, a gift for concentrating on the powerful without offending the sycophants. Huge receptions are meant to handle the latter. Smaller parties, where the host can talk at great length with each guest, zero in on the persons who really count. The diplomatic dinner invitation, therefore, is a distinct compliment, implying Status with a capital "S."

In several embassies, such affairs are splendid productions, with the finest viands and vintages provided in luxurious settings. Chandeliers and candelabra shine on exquisite china, crystal and silver. Ambassadors bolster distinguished honored guests with satin compliments and propose champagne toasts. From cocktails to after-dinner coffee and liqueurs, the event is a sumptuous reminder of the nation paying the bill, and the company departs in a glow of gratitude to host and hostess. Whatever the form or procedure, every embassy party is a propaganda facility, promoted with a certain pomp and as much charm and grace as host and hostess can command. Image building for the country is always there.

In 1962, Chile's Ambassador Sergio Gutierrez-Olivos brought this purpose into the open by initiating a two-year schedule of sixteen events—scientific exhibitions, art showings and concerts—under the title "Image of Chile." Each was preceded by a dinner, and eight were followed by receptions in the embassy. Radimiro Tomic, the next Chilean ambassador, pointed up his homeland's political advancement and economic goals at intimate dinners and small receptions rather than in these more direct displays, though the lovely Chilean Room, which Señora de Tomic planned as a mini-museum, displayed paintings of famed artists, hand-loom rugs, a collection of antique jewelry and ceramics. Ambassador Tomic, an articulate dynamo, returned to Santiago in 1968 to launch his campaign for the presidency. His successor, Domingo Santa Maria, initiated his own projection of Chile's image. In celebration of his country's independence day in September 1968, he sponsored a concert by Ena Bronstein, foremost young Chilean pianist, at the Pan American Union, and also an exhibition of modern Chilean paintings and drawings. In October, Santa Maria scheduled a film and a display of artifacts relating to Easter Island, a Chilean possession since 1887.

Ambassador Celso Pastor for almost five years—until he resigned after the October 1968 coup deposing his brother-in-law Fernando Belaunde Terry as president of Peru—called attention to his country's unique artistic background by bringing collections of ancient gold and silver effects from Peruvian museums to the United States. There were several showings at the Smithsonian Institution, and in

September 1968 Pastor opened an exhibition of works of the Mastercraftsmen of Peru at the Guggenheim Museum in New York. His personal collection of Colonial and Pre-Columbian Art, which adorned the embassy residence on Garrison Street, were also spectacular reminders of Peru's cultural heritage.

Denmark's genial Ambassador, Count Kield Gustav Knuth-Winterfeldt, and his refreshing Swiss-born countess also promoted their national image with flair and distinction. With a background of wealth, a husband whose title went back centuries and a household including two sons and a daughter, two Afghan hounds, ten birds, four maids and a housekeeper, Gertrud (Trudi) Knuth-Winterfeldt also had fabulous jewels and a wardrobe set off by creations of Holger Bloom, the noted Danish designer. However, she exuded democratic friendliness, and she was voluble about her enjoyment of Washington. "Some of our posts in the past have not been so pleasant," she once said. "I don't know which was worse—Germany with the bombings, Japan with the earthquakes, or Argentina with the Peróns."

The Knuth-Winterfeldts arrived in Washington the same month—October 1958—as Ambassador of Finland and Mme. Richard Seppala, and both couples left in 1965 for the same post—Paris. The Seppalas were also popular. Their lively parties attracted many government leaders. Smoked fish and cloudberries with whipped cream became favored fare in social Washington. The Seppalas also helped enforce their country's image by sharing their wonderful Finnish sauna with Washington friends.

Mme. Wilfried Platzer, wife of the Austrian ambassador (1958–1965) gave her parties in the residence she had made a symbol of romantic Vienna—with crystal chandeliers, silver Austrian curtains, Louis XVI furnishings and collections of centuries-old Viennese porcelain. No embassy hostess was ever more active than she in promoting and putting on benefits: her diplomatic event was a fashion show and dance to raise funds for the Kennedy Center for the Performing Arts in 1964.

Mexico's Ambassador Antonio Carillo Flores (1959–1965) presided over dinners and buffets with an exceptional cuisine. Señora de Carillo Flores planned her menus with tremendous care and personally supervised the preparation of every speciality. "Everything is as Mexican as I can possibly make it," she once said. At the first big party given by her husband's successor, Hugo Margaín, several guests were openly disappointed that the table presented a caterer's familiar menu—turkey, ham, chicken, salad and cakes. A senator's wife looked at the buffet and complained, "What? No *arroz con pollo!* No *tortillas!* No *tournedos el embajador!* And my cook's off tonight!" At subsequent receptions, the Mexican Embassy's cuisine again became notable.

A round of festivities in the spring of 1962 centered special attention on the popular Japanese Ambassador and Mme. Koichiro Asakai. The latter was the former Tamako Debuchi, daughter of the envoy who supervised the building of the Japanese Embassy in the early 1930s. The main event in 1962 was the opening of the ceremonial teahouse on the embassy grounds—a picturesque reminder of Japan that was to become a showplace of Washington.

The cast of Embassy Row has markedly changed in recent years, but the party drama goes on with the same basic plot, against a wide variety of backgrounds. At the end of the Johnson administration, several embassies were center stage with experienced performers, who have been stars in Washington for some time.

For example, the moment guests enter the Irish Georgian residence of Ireland's Ambassador and Mme. William P. Fay, they are "in" Ireland, with no mistake about it. The setting abounds in Donegal carpets, Waterford crystal chandeliers, eighteenth-century Irish silver and Sheraton sideboards from Dublin castle. A typical menu at the embassy includes Murphy dream cocktails, Dublin Bay prawns, roast Wicklow capon, baked Limerick ham and, of course, Irish coffee. Planned entertainment is rare. Mme. Fay, a pianist of concert status, may be persuaded to play Irish arias, but usually the chief diversion is lively talk, inspired by host and hostess with a seasoned background in diplomacy and a high quotient of warmth and Irish wit.

Infectious gaiety also marks parties at the Spanish Embassy. With a vivacity that hides great organizational skill, the Marquesa de Merry del Val is thought by many to be the unsurpassed hostess on Embassy Row. The embassy ballroom, which she redecorated into a "red salon," with chairs and divans upholstered in damask ranging from cerise to dark ruby and walls of crimson flocked silk, is the vivid focal setting for balls, dinners, fashion shows promoting designers and creations of Spain's *alta costura* and benefits for worthy causes. Entertainment may feature flamenco dancers, twirling and stamping to the music of a Spanish orchestra.

Across the street, in the Renaissance villa that is the Italian Embassy, a noted Italian artist may entertain, as might be expected in an official household of the most musical of countries; or Ambassador Egidio Ortona may take over at one of the pianos, while a talented guest is asked to accompany him at the other. (Norway's Ambassador Arne Gunneng is another accomplished pianist who often entertains his dinner guests with impromptu concerts.)

In their gem of embassy residences, a faithful reproduction of the Hotel Charolais outside Paris, Belgium's Ambassador Baron Scheyven, vice dean of the diplomatic corps, and the Baroness Scheyven preside over superb dinners. The baron, a gourmet, is fond of recalling that he "learned something about food" when he worked his way to China as a galley boy on a Pacific liner. (Years later, he returned to

China as envoy.) The dinner menu is the last word in excellence and attests to the adage "The French cuisine is good; the Belgian is divine."

Allurements of Turkey as the country bridging the East and the West enhance dinners given by the Turkish Ambassador and Mme. Melih Esenbel. Thirty guests are served in the mansion's mahogany paneled dining room. Companies of sixty sit at tables in the ballroom, elaborate with red velvet draperies, walls of mahogany wainscoting and crimson and gold brocade, and a coffered ceiling. Flower arrangements at the Turkish Embassy display Mme. Esenbel's proficiency in *ikebana*, an art she mastered while her husband was ambassador to Japan. The menu usually intersperses Turkish specialties with international dishes.

"Skal!" with aqua vitae warms dinner guests of Iceland's Ambassador and Mme. Petur Thorsteinsson. Fish from Icelandic waters and *hverabrand* (Icelandic bread) are sure to be on the menu, and the host observes a custom of his country when he proposes toasts while sitting.

And so it goes. Embassy after embassy pursues the most influential people in Washington with food and drink and a large helping of "native" atmosphere. The aim is always to impress on distinguished guests the unique character *and* special needs of the homeland.

Yet, no single contingent in Washington is more cooperative than the diplomatic corps in lending prestige and material help to worthy causes. Benefits on foreign premises or in hotels, with embassies helping to foot the bills, have aided innumerable cultural and charitable organizations in recent years. In return, goodwill—the aim of salon diplomacy—has redounded to the countries and the emissaries involved. Germany's Ambassador Karl Heinrich Knappstein had been in Washington since September 1962, but he expanded his circle of acquaintances considerably and made a host of new friends for Germany when he lent his six-tiered, steel chancery to the Washington Ballet Society for its spring 1967 ball. The December 1967 Symphony Ball sponsored by the Japanese Embassy favorably introduced the new Japanese Ambassador and Mme. Shimoda to Washington. Mexico went all out for the 1968 Symphony Ball. The popular Mexican Ambassador and Señora de Margaín arranged for a mariachi band and a chartered plane to bring prominent Mexicans to the event. The chancery of Iran, a Persian wonder styled after a fifteenth-century mosque in Isfahan, was the scene of the 1968 Care-Medico ball with Mme. Hushang Ansary, wife of the ambassador, as an acting and generous co-chairman. Mme. Khosro Khrosrovani, her immediate predecessor, was the only ambassadress in memory who was not annoyed by crashers at her parties. Informed by a fluttered secretary that six utter strangers had pushed through the door and were mingling with invited guests at one reception, she said gently, "Well, if they want to come to our parties *that much*, they are welcome. Of course, I hope they won't ever come uninvited to dinner."

The demanding social pace on Embassy Row has given rise to the fairly prevalent impression that ambassadors, if not their wives, are satiated with incessant, though elegant, wining and dining and that they secretly envy those who lead the simpler life. The notion is as farfetched as the idea that emissaries are essentially a light-headed lot, careening about in their "DPL" licensed limousines, flitting from party to party and living like kings without doing a lick of work. Both suppositions fail to take into account what diplomacy really is—a government assignment that is tackled in the traditional way; the hard work of the chancery follows the pleasant association in salons and dining rooms. The average envoy toils as hard, if not harder, than many of the individuals he entertains. His workday extends through the hours when most of his guests are relaxing. But he is no more bored with the high social life—and its trappings—than the scientist is bored with his latest experiments in a laboratory equipped with every instrument he can use. The diplomat, of all people, realizes that the social round is but a splendid sheath for the work of making friends and influencing powerful factors in a highly competitive world.

A capital grande dame who flutters around diplomats and sometimes gets a choice seat at their dinners surveyed the distinguished company and the beautifully set table at a recent embassy repast and whispered to her host, "Such a lovely affair. But tell me, don't you sometimes get bored with *all this social life?*" His brows elevated, and his eyes widened and twinkled. "No," he answered softly, "do you?"

With the speedup in communications and the growing practice of chiefs of state of discussing world problems face to face, the future of traditional diplomacy has become a topic of wide discussion. President Johnson's around-the-world flight—27,000 miles—in December 1967 dramatized his "new age of statecraft" as he talked to fifteen government leaders and called on Pope Paul VI. A strong advocate of what he called "personal diplomacy," LBJ received more chiefs of state at the White House than any of his predecessors and conferred with most of them at great length.

The idea prevails that such meetings will eventually eliminate the conventional ambassador's role—that the government leader wanting to get to the crux of any problem soon will dispense with traditional methods and will set up a conference with his foreign counterpart any time an emergency arises. On the surface, such an arrangement seem plausible. Certainly, exigencies are more pressing and warrant a faster procedure than they did in the late fifteenth-century, when Philippe de Comines, the famed French statesman and historian, observed, "Two great princes who wish to establish foolproof personal relations should never meet each other face to face but ought to communicate through good and wise ambassadors." However, recent encounters at the highest level seem to have yielded results that are more psychological than significant. They have stimulated tremendous publicity and have raised high hopes, but the results appear to be more amorphous as time goes on. In any case, professional diplomats still have the task of arbitrating differences of their superiors, translating agreements into workable action and tidying up. Though their chiefs may have the power, it is the diplomats who have the expertise.

Actually, the role of the ambassador is more important today than ever before. Although he does not decide or enunciate courses of government action, he has much to do with shaping them; his findings are the basis for policies, and it is his job to interpret, adjust and integrate them at the point of application.

Embassy Row would seem to be here to stay. Its purposeful social round will continue to flourish, and, chances are, the workings of its chanceries will become of wider interest to the general public. As Lord Strange, a former undersecretary in the British Foreign Office, put it, "In a world where war is everybody's tragedy, and everybody's nightmare, diplomacy is everybody's business."

Index

Abdi, Dr. Getachew, 81
Abell, George, 35
Abell, Tyler, 35
Abidia, Fathi, 266
Abidjo, Ahmadou, 74
Adams, Abigail, 1, 40
Adams, John, 1, 21, 40
Adams, John Quincy, 19–20, 21, 140, 142, 143, 215
Adams, Mrs. John Quincy, 21
Adenauer, Konrad, 71
Afghanistan, 5, 75–79, 165
Africa, 10, 66, 70, 89, 110, 119, 120, 121, 127–29, 130–31, 263–65; *see also* names of countries, e.g. Algeria
Al-Ahdab, Ibrahim, 266
Alexander I, Emperor of Russia, 140, 141
Alexander II, Emperor of Russia, 145
Alexis, Grand Duke of Russia, 145
Alfaro, Colón Eloy, 168
Algeria, 69, 119, 121, 266, 268
Al-Ghoussein, Bassima, 266–67
Al-Ghoussein, Talat, 265, 266–67, 269
Al-Kahyyal, Sheikh Mohammed, 63
Alphand, Claude Rober-Reynaud, 209–10
Alphand, Hervé, 11, 209–12, 264
Alphand, Nicole Merenda Bunau-Varilla, 12, 210–12, 213, 267
Al-Sowayel, Ibrahim, 266
Alvensleben, Friedrich von, 4
Andrews, Roy Chapman, 243
Anne, Queen of England, 103
Ansary, Hushang, 275
Araki, Eikichi, 258
Araki, Tomika, 258
Argentina, 250, 254, 255, 271
Armstrong, John, 215
Arroyo, Gabriela, 261
Arroyo, Nicolas, 261
Arthur, Chester A., 23
Asakai, Koichiro, 272
Asakai, Tamako Debuchi, 272
Aspiroz, Manuel, 32
Astor, Lady, 200
Australia, 7, 119, 252, 263
Austria, 21, 32, 54, 122, 147, 149, 206, 234, 271

Bagot, Sir Charles, 2–3, 21
Bakhmetev, Boris Aleksandrovich, 151–53

Bakhmetev, Georgi Petrovich, 149–51
Ball, George W., 52, 94, 131
Banda, Hastings K., 268
Bang-Jensen, Povl, 243
Barghoorn, Frederick C., 178
Baruch, Bernard, 14
Batista, Fulgencio, 261
Bayar, Clelal, 33
Beale, Edward Fitzgerald, 149
Beale, Sir Howard, 7, 263
Beale, Mary, 149
Bedford, Eric, 202
Belaunde Terry, Fernando, 270
Belgium, 31, 107–8, 131–32, 221, 243, 245, 256, 264, 268, 273
Bell, Alexander Graham, 229
Belville, Belinda, 203
Ben Bella, Ahmed, 69–70
Bengelloun, Ali, 84, 85, 265–66
Bengelloun, Jacqueline, 265–66
Bernstorff, Johann Heinrich von, Count, 188–91, 219
Betancourt, Rómulo, 88–89
Bhumibol Adulyadej, King of Thailand, 65, 135
Bianchi, Dr. João Antonio de, 37
Bingham, Theodore A., 26
Blaine, James G., 23
Blair House, 61–63, 64, 69, 70, 71, 72, 74, 79, 80, 88, 93, 100
Block, Leo de, 124
Blokhim, Nikolai, 179
Bloom, Holger, 271
Bloom, Sol, 199
Bodisco, Baron de, 144–45
Bolling, Barbara, 66
Bolshevik Revolution, 152, 154, 163, 167, 174, 180
Bonhomme, Arthur, 134
Bonnet, Georges, 222–23
Bonnet, Hellé Zervoudak Aghnaides, 206–8, 210
Bonnet, Henri, 206–8, 226
Boris, Grand Duke of Russia, 12
Boucesco, Georges, 238–39
Bourguiba, Habib, 60
Bourguiba, Habib, Jr., 267
Boy-Ed, Captain Karl, 188
Boyle, Irene, 193
Brazil, 9, 56, 84, 254
Bronstein, Ena, 270
Broussé, Betty, 224–26
Broussé, Charles, 224–25
Bruggmann, Karl, 232
Bryan, William Jennings, 188, 219

279